# Public Policy in the Eighties

# Public Policy in the Eighties

Charles S. Bullock III
*University of Georgia*

James E. Anderson
*University of Houston*

David W. Brady
*Rice University*

Brooks/Cole Publishing Company
*Monterey, California*

**The Brooks/Cole Series on Public Policy**

Charles O. Jones, *University of Virginia*
General Editor

Brooks/Cole Publishing Company
A Division of Wadsworth, Inc.

Printed in the United States of America

10  9  8  7  6  5  4  3  2  1

**Library of Congress Cataloging in Publication Data**

Bullock, Charles S., 1942–
  Public policy in the eighties.

  Bibliography: p.
  Includes index.
  1. Policy sciences.   2. United States—Economic
policy—1981-     .  3. United States—Social policy—
1980-     .  I. Anderson, James E.   II. Brady, David W.
III. Title.
H97.B837   1983        361.6'1'0973        82-22639
ISBN 0-534-01376-7

*Subject Editor:* Marquita Flemming
*Manuscript Editor:* Adrienne Mayor
*Production Editor:* Fiorella Ljunggren
*Interior and Cover Design:* Victoria Van Deventer
*Illustrations:* John Foster
*Typesetting:* Allservice Phototypesetting Co. of Arizona

# Foreword

At no time since the 1930s have domestic problems and policies been so centrally placed on the agenda of the national government. But now the situation is very different. In 1932 expenditures were less than $5 billion; in 1982 they exceeded $700 billion. President Ronald Reagan has vowed to gain control of budget growth.

> [Reagan] campaigned on a platform which emphasized that the major ills of the economy were caused by excessive federal government spending and budget deficits. Immediately upon inauguration, he set out to fulfill his campaign promises to cut the size and scope of the federal government sharply and to eliminate the deficit by the end of his term.*

Thus the stimulus for attending to domestic problems in 1982 was vastly different from that in 1932. Franklin D. Roosevelt sought to expand the scope of government; Ronald Reagan intends to contract it.

The budgetary struggle has been joined by others, and a major national debate is under way. The debate focuses on economic stability, growth of social welfare programs, costs and effects of federal regulations, and benefits available to the middle and upper classes. These are the major topics examined in *Public Policy in the Eighties*. Charles S. Bullock III, James E. Anderson, and David W. Brady have selected the significant domestic issues of our time. They have distilled literally mountains of information so as to provide succinct and readable analyses of the problems, programs, and prospects concerning each of the major issues. In their book, the authors provide a basis for understanding the present debate on the proper role for government in the social life of the nation. They inform us on what is being done now, how problems get to government in the first place, how programs develop support and momentum, and which alternatives are offered for resolving major domestic issues. The material includes recent policy struggles caused by the Reagan philosophy.

There was a time not too long ago when, in studying American government, political institutions and policy processes were stressed and public problems and

---

*Joseph A. Pechman, ed., *Setting National Priorities: The 1982 Budget* (Washington, D.C.: The Brookings Institution, 1981), p. 1.

government programs essentially ignored. That is no longer possible. What government *does* has come to be every bit as important as how it is organized to do it. Bullock, Anderson, and Brady tell us about the "what" in governing. *Public Policy in the Eighties* should be welcome as important text material in introductory American government and public policy courses.

*Charles O. Jones*
*University of Virginia*

# Preface

In this book we explore the major domestic policy areas of contemporary United States. Attempts to devise workable solutions to problems concerning the economy, energy, the environment, the needy, and consumer protection have absorbed vast amounts of attention from presidents, legislators, and governors over the last generation. As we go through the 1980s, none of these areas appears to be on the verge of resolution. Consequently, we anticipate that policymakers will continue to wrestle with demands from various quarters as they search for solutions to these issues on which there is no consensus.

In the course of this book, the reader will be introduced to the major policy statements in the five policy areas noted above. The requirements of important statutes and court decisions, the preferences of recent presidents, and the actions of the bureaucracies entrusted with carrying out the programs will be reviewed. The objectives of those who have been active in shaping policies—government officials as well as interest groups—will be explained. The degree to which program objectives have been achieved and the obstacles that have been encountered will be noted.

We think that this text is ideal as a supplement to American government courses and as a substantive core text for public policy courses.

The preparation of this book has benefited from the useful reactions of a number of people. Robert Barles, Jeff Howard, Larry Regens, James Sullivan, and Frank Thompson read parts of the manuscript and offered valuable comments. We'd like to express our appreciation to them and to the reviewers whom Brooks/Cole consulted. They are Irving Howards of the University of Massachusetts, Charles O. Jones of the University of Virginia, Robert Lawrence of Colorado State University, Michael Reagan of the University of California, Riverside, Walter A. Rosenbaum of the University of Florida, and Norman Thomas of the University of Cincinnati. All these readers provided substantial assistance in eliminating errors and tightening and clarifying the presentation, for which we are most appreciative. At times, however, we disagreed with our talented reviewers and, at our peril, ignored their advice.

Finally, we wish to express our gratitude to Jeannine Hall, who did a large part of the typing.

*Charles S. Bullock III*
*James E. Anderson*
*David W. Brady*

# Contents

# Public Policy in the Eighties

# Chapter 1

# Introduction to Policy Study

People often think of public policy as something that happens only in Washington, D.C., and only to someone other than themselves. However, as the following cases illustrate, all of us are deeply affected by public policies in our daily lives.

For example, during the last few decades American civil rights policy regarding racial integration has been dramatically reversed. As a consequence of this policy reversal, thousands of black Americans eat in restaurants, sleep in motels and hotels, and work in places where blacks had never been. Courts ordered busing plans to integrate schools, and neighborhoods previously all white became integrated because of laws prohibiting discrimination by realtors and owners. These changes in policy were accompanied by protests or demonstrations by both blacks and whites in the North and South. Riots in urban areas; busing and desegregation protests in several states; white backlash and black revolutionary action—all were claimed to be effects of America's "new" civil rights policies. It is almost impossible to estimate the impact that civil rights questions have had and will continue to have on the United States and its citizens.

Today most people would probably agree that the present rate of inflation in the United States is too high and that it should be reduced, perhaps through governmental action. No one likes to see the purchasing power of one's paycheck or pension eroded by rapidly rising prices; all but the richest or luckiest among us feel the pinch. There is, however, a lack of agreement on what policies, if any, should be used to reduce inflation. Is the present inflation caused by excess demand, administered wages and prices, or inflationary expectations? To what extent is it caused by public policies such as deficit spending or excessive regulation? Will the movement to pass a constitutional amendment for a balanced budget gain momentum? Should the Reagan administration use traditional fiscal and monetary policies or should it follow the precepts of supply-side economics? What part does balance of trade and gross national product play? Would a return to the gold standard help in controlling inflation? Will Reagan's administration be more successful than Carter's in combating inflation? The answer will be reflected in the consumer price index and our pocketbooks.

These are two fairly spectacular illustrations of the individual impact of policy-making. However, public policies also determine more mundane events, such as whether our garbage is picked up and our mail delivered. These things do not just happen; rather, they are the results of the actions of public officials taken in response to demands upon them.

Our purpose in this book is to systematically examine some American public policies and the political processes that produce them. To facilitate effective communication of our analysis, we need to develop a precise concept, or definition, of public policy.

## CONCEPT OF PUBLIC POLICY

The term *public policy* may be used quite broadly, as in "American economic policy," "Saudi Arabia's petroleum policy," or "Western Europe's agricultural policy"; or it may be used much more specifically, as in "the nuclear regulatory commission's policy toward nuclear energy as a power source," "the policy of the city of Chicago on pollution in Lake Michigan from Milwaukee, Wisconsin," or "the policy of the state of Texas on advertising on highway rights of way." Sections of textbooks devoted to defining *public policy* traditionally give three or four definitions, which are then shown to be inadequate. After showing the inadequacy of other definitions, the author's own definition is then put forward. Rather than use this approach, we will discuss the ideas or elements that an adequate definition of public policy should have and then present the definition of public policy to be used in this book.

If a definition of public policy is to indicate the essential characteristics of public policy, it must distinguish between what governments intend to do and what in fact they actually do. We cannot be content to say, for example, that the government's decision in 1964 to eliminate poverty in America fully represented public policy on the topic. Along these same lines, a useful definition must embody the idea that public policy is a course or pattern of activity and not simply a decision to act in some particular way; that is, public policy is a process and not merely a single decision in one place at a particular moment. Public policy may be viewed as a set of decisions directed toward the accomplishment of some goal. Although the goal of governmental actions is not always easy to discern, the assumption that public policy involves purposive governmental action is essential to the study of public policy. In sum, a useful definition of public policy will indicate that policy is a pattern of governmental activity on some topic or matter which has a purpose or goal.[1] Further, it will not equate decision making with policy or confuse the *stated* goal of action with what is *actually* done.

For example, concerning policy on educational facilities for black and white students, if one looks only at what the laws said prior to 1954, the policy would appear to be one of providing separate but equal facilities. However, if one inquires whether the separate facilities were really equal, one would find that the policy was in fact one of separate but unequal facilities, because neither the federal government nor the state governments enforced the requirement of equalness. Following the Supreme Court's 1954 and 1955 decisions in *Brown* v. *Board of Education,* if one views policy as a single decision (or a pair of decisions), one would have to conclude that the goal of integrated and thus equal facilities had actually been achieved. Moreover, with the enactment of the Civil Rights Act of 1964 the Congress joined the Supreme Court in deciding that public school integration should be public policy. Nevertheless, it was not until after 1969, when the federal government really began to exert pressure in support of integration, that public schools in the South were integrated in a meaningful way. Thus, it is important to note that public policy involves what is actually done to accomplish a goal. It is a purposive pattern of activity, not a single decision made at a given time by some person or group. Any definition of policy that neglects these matters will lead the reader astray in the search for policy. Obviously, policy involves more than such formal statements as statutes, administrative rules, and judicial opinions.

In view of the above discussion, we offer the following basic definition of policy: "A purposive course of action followed by an actor or a set of actors in dealing with a problem or matter of concern."[2] This definition focuses on what is done, as distinct from what is intended, and it distinguishes policy from decisions. Public policies are developed by *governmental institutions* and officials through the political process (or politics). They are distinct from other kinds of policies because they result from the actions of the *legitimate* authorities in a political system. David Easton designates the authorities in a political system as the "elders, paramount chiefs, executives, legislators, judges, administrators, councilors, monarchs, and the like, [who] engage in the daily affairs of a political system."[3] Moreover, these people are "recognized by most members of the system as having responsibility for these matters, and take actions which are accepted as binding most of the time by most of the members so long as they act within the limits of their roles."[4]

A summary of the implications of this concept of public policy is in order. First of all, public policy is purposive, goal-oriented behavior rather than random or chance behavior. Public policies are not acts that just happen, even though not all of their consequences or effects are anticipated. Second, policy consists of *courses of action*—rather than separate, discrete decisions or actions—performed by government officials. Policy involves not only the decision to enact a law but also the subsequent acts regarding implementing, interpreting, and enforcing the law. Third, policy is what governments *do* in controlling inflation, cleaning up the environment, or redistributing income—not what they say they will do or what they intend to do. Food distribution policy, for instance, involves what is actually done to provide food to the hungry and needy. America's poor cannot eat the government's good intentions. It is nonsense to regard an intention as a policy without regard for what subsequently follows. Fourth, public policy may be either negative or positive. Positive policy is involved when the government takes action to affect a particular problem; negative policy occurs when the government decides not to act in an area where government action is sought. Governments, in other words, can decide not to act, thus following a hands-off, or laissez faire policy. Fifth, public policy is based on law and is authoritative. For example, those who evade taxes or disobey campaign finance laws do so at the risk of fines and jail sentences. Public policy thus has an implied threat of legitimate coercion, which is usually lacking in the policies of private organizations. Finally, public policies are often determined by the politics of public policy.

## AN APPROACH TO POLICY STUDY

The study of public policy, or the actions of governments, can be approached in a number of ways. The theoretical approaches developed by political scientists to explain what governments do were not, in general, developed for the analysis of policy formation and administration. However, they can be converted—and have been—to that purpose with little difficulty. Major theoretical approaches to the study of public policy include (1) institutionalism, (2) elite theory, (3) group theory, (4) input-output models, and (5) systems theory. Each of these approaches focuses attention on aspects of politics that are more or less relevant to the study of public policy, depending upon what policy or policies are under discussion. Thus, in the study of civil rights policy, elite theory seems to best fit the data, whereas group theory provides the best analysis for the study of government regulation of atomic energy.

Here our focus is on *the policy process*; that is, the various activities by which public policy is actually formed. Since there is no one single process by which policy is formed, variations in the content of public policy produce variations in the manner of policymaking. Welfare policy, natural resource regulation, economic stability policy, and civil rights policy are distinguished by different processes. Policy in these areas is associated with specific governmental institutions, patterns of behavior, and political situations. Social Security as a part of tax policy is closely associated with the Ways and Means Committee of the House of Representatives, while the protection of consumers is closely associated with administrative agencies such as the Federal Trade Commission.

This does not mean that the environment of each policy area is unique in such a way that precludes generalizations about public policy. Rather, it means that there is no one "grand unified theory of public policy." We can make a useful start toward understanding American public policy by considering such matters as these: Who is involved in policy formation, and on what kinds of issues, under what conditions, and to what effect? Just how do policy problems develop?

In our conceptual framework the policy process involves six distinct stages of activity.[5] These categories are summarized in table 1–1.

**TABLE 1-1   The policy process**

| Policy terminology | 1st stage problem formation | 2nd stage policy agenda | 3rd stage policy formulation | 4th stage policy adoption | 5th stage policy implementation | 6th stage policy evaluation |
|---|---|---|---|---|---|---|
| Formal definition | Relief is sought from a situation that produces a human need, deprivation, or dissatisfaction | Problems, among many, that receive the government's serious attention | Development of pertinent and acceptable proposed courses of action for dealing with public problems | Development of support for a specific proposal such that the policy is legitimized or authorized | Application of the policy by the government's bureaucratic machinery to the problem | Attempt by the government to determine whether or not the policy has been effective |
| Common sense | Getting the government to see the problem | Getting the government to begin to act on the problem | The government's proposed solution to the problem | Getting the government to accept a particular solution to the problem | Applying the government's policy to the problem | Did the policy work? |

### Stages of the Policy Process

**Problem formation.**   A problem is, for our purposes, a situation that produces "a human need, deprivation, or dissatisfaction, self-identified or identified by
others, for which relief is sought."[6] Pollution, inflation, crime, unemployment, and
OPEC oil policy have become problems because they produce sufficient anxiety
and dissatisfaction to cause people to seek relief. There are all kinds of needs and
wants; only those that move people to action, and are articulated, become problems
demanding policy solutions.

Since our concern is with public problems, we need to know what makes a
problem public. The most important thing that distinguishes public from private
problems is the number of people involved. Thus, public problems have broad-
ranging effects, including consequences for persons not directly involved (as in a
labor-management dispute). Not all problems dealt with in government are public,
since, for example, congressmen often give private assistance to individual constituents (for example, helping someone to secure a welfare benefit). Such assistance
may be important to the person involved, but it has little or no meaning for the
broader public. However, the number of people involved does serve to distinguish
most governmental or public problems from private problems. It is important to
point out that whether a problem becomes public depends upon the number of
people who perceive it as one that government should handle, which leads to the
question of why some matters gain the attention of the government while others
do not.

**Policy agenda.**   Of the thousands of needs and wants for which people seek
governmental action, only a small number receive serious attention. The problems
that receive serious attention from the policymakers compose the policy agenda.
Why do some problems achieve agenda status while others do not? One obvious
reason is that often the interests of an important group are affected adversely and
the group seeks redress from the government. Depending upon the power, status,
and number of people in the group, the government may be compelled to put the
matter on the agenda.

Political leadership is another important factor in agenda setting. For a variety of
reasons—its usefulness in winning votes for election, wide citizen interest in the
policy area, officials' concern for the public interest, and so on—leaders may take a
problem to heart, publicize it, and propose solutions. The president of the United
States is an important agenda setter: economic deregulation secured a place on the
national agenda in the mid-1970s because of the interest President Ford displayed in
it, for example.

Crisis events, such as wars and depressions, are automatically agenda items. Less
cataclysmic events, such as recessions and the Soviet satellite Sputnik, also may trig-
ger agenda status for matters such as inflation and science research. Massive public
protests, such as the 1968 Detroit race riots and peace demonstrations during the
Vietnam War, are another vehicle for achieving agenda status. But the important
point is that not every problem gets the attention of government—and it is crucial

to an understanding of the policy process to know how and why certain problems do achieve agenda status.

**Policy formulation and adoption.**    Policy formulation involves the development of pertinent and acceptable proposed courses of action for dealing with public problems. Policy formulation does not necessarily result in the adoption of a law, order, or rule of some sort. In short, the fact that a problem is on the policy agenda does not mean that the government will act effectively to resolve it. Income tax reform has been on the policy agenda for several decades but little has been achieved.

The president and his advisers are now major sources of policy proposals in the national political system. If we expand our focus to include the various departments and agencies, then clearly most policy originates in the executive branch. Career and appointed administration officials formulate policy ranging from standards of inspection for nuclear power plants to major changes in American foreign policy. Presidential commissions, committees, and advisory groups are also sources of executive policy formulation.

Legislators and interest groups are probably the next most frequent sources of policy formulation. Sen. Edward Kennedy's (D.–Mass.) national health care package is a case of legislative involvement in policy formulation. Interest groups often formulate policy proposals and then have favorably inclined officials, both elected and appointed, formally propose the policy.

Successful policy formulations must deal with the question of selecting courses of action that can actually be adopted. That is, a chief component of policy proposals is formulating a policy that will be acceptable to the people who make policy decisions. Those formulating the policy will be influenced in what they propose and do by the need to win adoption of the policy. Certain provisions will be included and other provisions dropped, depending upon what builds support for the proposed policy.

The question of policy adoption is generally thought of as building majority support for a policy proposal in Congress. Thus, tax policy adoption usually includes getting the House Ways and Means Committee chairman to support it, and then getting a majority vote in both the House and the Senate. However, policy adoption does not always entail the familiar pattern of executive proposals, congressional approval, and presidential signature. Certain of President Nixon's administrative rulings on tax policy benefited corporations, and these policies were not approved by Congress or reviewed by the courts; rather, in these cases adoption ended with the president. The point is that adoption strategies and thus policy formulation will differ depending on how many branches of government are involved in the adopting process.

**Policy implementation.**    Once the adoption stage of the policy process is over, the law, rule, or order that has been adopted can be called public policy. Nonetheless, the content and effect of public policy may be greatly changed during the implementation stage. Thus, the implementation or administrative stage of the policy process is quite important because without application the policy has no effect, and the application of policy proposals sometimes changes the nature of policy itself. Administrative agencies are the primary implementors of public policy; but other actors, such as Congress and the courts, may also be involved.

Congress affects implementation in a number of ways. In some cases Congress passes specific detailed legislation which severely limits the amount of discretion administrators have available to them. Congressional concern with the details of the food stamp program—who should receive benefits and how much—is a good example of how Congress influences implementation.

The courts' relationship to policy implementation is more direct than is the congressional relationship. In many instances the very meaning of a policy results from judicial interpretation of rules or statutes. Antitrust policy, for instance, has been substantially shaped by judicial interpretation and implementation of the Sherman Act. Bankruptcy, naturalization for aliens, and divorce proceedings are other examples of judicial administration of policy. However, the most important way in which courts affect implementation is through interpretation of statutes and administrative rules and regulations.

The major means of policy administration is, of course, the administrative agency. Agricultural policy is administered by various units in the Department of Agriculture while military policy is implemented by the Defense Department and its branches. Administrative agencies, which are numerous, often act in situations where they have a wide range of discretion in the elaboration of policy and its implementation. For a number of reasons, which will be covered in later chapters, Congress often delegates great authority to an agency, which in turn makes policy in the implementation process.

It is obvious that agencies, courts, and the Congress often can alter policy through its administration. A clear-cut distinction between policymaking and administration may be desirable, but it does not do justice to the realities of the American policy process. Throughout the book there will be examples of the administration of policy altering or changing policy. At this point it will suffice to say that implementation sometimes affects policy content.

**Policy evaluation.**    The last stage of the policy process is policy evaluation. At this stage those who have made and implemented policy, or those who are interested or affected, attempt to determine whether or not the policy has worked. Thus, evaluators are concerned with appraising the content of policy and its effects. Evaluation may in turn lead to additional policy formation, which starts the policy cycle over. In general there are two types of policy evaluation: (1) "seat-of-the-pants" or political evaluation and (2) systematic evaluation. Seat-of-the-pants evaluation is impressionistic in nature. Such judgments are based on fragmentary evidence and are often strongly ideological or biased. To the oil companies freezes on oil prices or windfall profit legislation are ineffective, nonproductive, and so on. In the same way, the former Office of Economic Opportunity could not have been expected to find that the war *it* waged on poverty was lost. In short, political evaluation cannot sort out personal desires and agency interests from what the policy really achieved.

On the other hand, systematic evaluation of policies and programs seeks to objectively measure the societal impact of policies and the extent to which stated objectives are met. Systematic evaluation focuses on the effects a policy has on the problem to which it is directed. Thus, it gives all concerned with the policy process some feeling for the impact of policy.

### Advantages of the Sequential Approach

In sum, our approach to the study of public policy is to take a policy area, such as energy, and trace the process from the point where it became a problem through the point where energy policy can be evaluated. Often the policy process is viewed from an institutional perspective, in which, for example, the relationship between the Congress and public policy is explained. Instead, we will follow certain policy areas across institutions wherever they may lead. The sequential approach avoids assigning to the president the formulation function and assigning the Congress the adoption function. Of course, the president often formulates and Congress often adopts, but not always. The point, however, is that our conceptual framework allows a needed flexibility in capturing the policy process.

This framework has a number of advantages in addition to its flexibility. First of all, policymaking often does chronologically follow the sequence of activities listed above, so that our approach generally coincides with the flow of action in the policy process. Furthermore, various forms of data (for example, legal, quantitative, and normative data) are compatible with the sequential approach. Again, the approach is dynamic rather than static. It emphasizes the relationships among political phenomena rather than simply listing factors or developing classification schemes. Finally, it lends itself to manageable comparisons between policy areas and across political boundaries.

## CONTEXT OF THE POLICY PROCESS

The context within which the policy process takes place is crucial to an understanding of how certain policies prevail over others. History, in the form of past policies, is one important part of that context. Other elements are environmental factors and the structural characteristics of the American political system.

### Historical Context

Policy changes always take place in a context provided by past policies in the area involved. Thus, for example, changes in consumer policy have taken place within the context of already established agencies, such as the Food and Drug Administration, and a general governmental attitude that regulation rather than market forces should be used to control certain products. Similarly, in most of the other policy areas covered in this book, the problem has been around for some time, and the agencies that deal with these problem areas are often well-established ones, such as the Environmental Protection Agency or the Department of Agriculture. Therefore, in each of the chapters that follow, we give some attention to the history of public policy in the area covered, since the history of public policy in a given situation is an important contextual limit on present policy.

### Environmental Factors

One of the lessons of political systems theory is that policymaking cannot be adequately understood apart from the environment in which it occurs. From the environment come demands for policy action, support for the political system, and limitations or constraints upon what can be done by policymakers. Among the components of the environment are such geographical variables as population size, age distribution, ethnic composition, and spatial location; political culture and opinion; social structure, such as the class system; and the economic system. When foreign policy is at issue, other nations become an important part of the policy environment. In this section we consider several environmental factors: political culture, public opinion, the social system, and the economic system. Our concern is not to describe them but rather to give some indication of how they may affect policy formation.

**Political culture.**    An important factor shaping the behavior of individuals and groups in government decision making, as in other aspects of social life, is the culture of the particular society within which decision making occurs. While all persons are unique, they also have much in common. Those who live in a particular society share in the various common values and beliefs that constitute part of its culture. Culture is transmitted from one generation to another by a socialization process in which, by "thousands of specific experiences with specific persons (parents, friends, school teachers, political leaders, etc.) in specific situations," the individual learns the values, norms, and beliefs of the society.[7] Culture, then, is acquired by the individual, becomes a part of one's psychological makeup, and is manifested in one's behavior.

One segment of the general culture of a society can be designated as political culture. It consists of widely shared values and beliefs relating to the nature and exercise of political power and the purposes for which it is employed. Obviously, because of different patterns of development, environmental conditions, and historical factors, political culture will differ from one national society to another. Variations in public policy and policymaking among countries can be at least partially explained by their political cultures. For example, public medical care programs are more numerous and extensive in Western Europe because there has been greater public expectation and acceptance of such programs as a proper governmental activity. Conversely, in the United States public attitudes have been much stronger in support of mass public education, and these attitudes are reflected in our extensive public educational system.

Values are criteria or standards by which people evaluate the goodness or bad-ness, the desirability or undesirability, of goals and actions. They serve as general motives and guides for behavior. Sociologist Robin Williams has described a num-ber of "major value orientations" in American society, including individual freedom, equality, progress, and efficiency and practicality.[8] These values—and others such as democracy, individualism, humanitarianism, and material achievement and suc-cess—clearly have significance for public policymaking. Democracy is held, at a minimum, to require public participation in and control of government along with governmental responsiveness to recognized needs of the population. There is an adage to the effect that people have a right to be heard, officials a duty to hear. Such conditions contribute to the existence in the United States of what has been called a *participant* political culture.[9] The general approach of Americans to public problems has been practical, or pragmatic, concerned with developing solutions to present problems rather than systematic long-range planning or doctrinal purity. Thus, housing programs were established in the 1930s to encourage home owner-ship and stimulate the economy without much thought as to the effect they might have on urban development in the future. The same was true for the interstate highway system.

Beliefs are statements about what actually exists (or what we believe to exist), which are used to describe our environment. They are "pictures of reality," which we carry in our minds and which help determine our actions. Widely shared beliefs about the actual nature and operation of the economic system, for example, help shape the interests that groups try to protect and promote through governmental action. In the nineteenth century the belief that economy was governed by natural economic laws, and that a policy of laissez faire was therefore both wise and benefi-cent, certainly slowed the movement toward regulation. Antitrust policy is still handicapped by the belief that big business is always more efficient than small busi-ness, while the belief that government is less efficient than private enterprise has contributed to the minimal role of government enterprise in American society. On the other hand, the beliefs that government is subject to popular control and that many social and economic problems can be remedied by governmental action have contributed to expansion of government activity.

Widely shared social values, of course, do not remain constant. As they change, matters once viewed as beyond the power or ability of governments to control may come to be thought of as amenable to governmental action. The nineteenth-century beliefs that the business cycle is beyond governmental control (which continued to influence many, including Herbert Hoover, even in the face of the Great De-pression of the 1930s) has given way to the belief that the government can act effectively to maintain economic stability. The latter belief greatly increases the likelihood of some kind of government regulation of economic forces. Indeed, an administration that does nothing to attempt to control inflation or rising unemploy-ment quickly will be in severe political difficulty. President Carter learned this in 1980.

Within the "consensus" of belief that may exist on a given matter, such as the need for public education, Social Security, or action to maintain economic competition, there remains much room for disagreement. Although the widespread belief in the necessity and desirability of social security programs makes their abandonment unlikely, there is continuing controversy on such matters as eligibility requirements and amounts of benefits. Again, the belief that citizen access to the policymaking process is a necessity for democratic government is not accompanied by agreement on the arrangements required to provide access.

In sum, common values and beliefs help determine the demands made upon policymakers and act to inform, guide, and limit their behavior. As Karl Deutsch notes, political culture "is related to the *frequency* and *probability* of various kinds of behavior and not their rigid determination."[10] Also, widely shared values and beliefs serve as the basis for verbal formulations by which the actions of public officials can be explained or rationalized—as being, say, "democratic," "practical," or "in support of individualized freedom"—so as to win greater public acceptance for them.[11]

**Public opinion.**    Public opinion, as the concept is used here, designates expressions of public attitudes or beliefs about current political issues, such as whether the national government should prohibit discrimination in housing, provide support for the development of a supersonic aircraft, send or withdraw American troops in trouble spots in the world, or enact health care legislation. Political culture, which is more basic and fundamental than public opinion, underlies political opinion and molds it on particular issues. Thus, the political cultural notion that "a public office is a public trust" directs public disapproval toward officials who engage in chicanery in their public positions. Obviously opinion would differ were the use of public office for private gain widely accepted as proper in our society.

In examining the effect of public opinion on policymaking, we should distinguish between decisions that indicate the general direction of policy and the day-to-day, often routine, decisions relating to specific aspects of policy. Public opinion is not likely to be a significant factor in the second category. As V. O. Key has observed: "Many, if not most, policy decisions by legislatures and by other authorities exercising broad discretion are made under circumstances in which extremely small proportions of the general public have any awareness of the particular issue, much less any understanding of the consequences of the decision."[12] The legislator deciding how to vote on an obscure amendment to a statute will probably be unaffected in any direct sense by public opinion. While he might try to anticipate public reaction, he or she will have considerable room for the exercise of imagination.

A second useful distinction involves the time dimension within which policymaking occurs. In a crisis situation in which policymakers feel the need to act quickly on some problem, there will be less opportunity for public opinion to come to bear than when action extends over a longer period of time. Public opinion appears to have been less influential in the development of atomic energy policy in 1945–1946 and the Cuban missile crisis in 1961 than in the enactment of social security legislation in 1935 and air pollution control legislation in 1970.[13]

Generally, public opinion plays a part in mapping the broad boundaries and direction of public policy rather than the specific content of policies. Existing public attitudes make such actions as the nationalization of the steel industry, repeal of the Social Security Act, or abandonment of environmental protection laws unlikely. Conversely, officials may come to believe that public opinion demands some kind of policy action, as was the case with labor reform legislation in 1959, tax reform legislation in 1969, and tax reduction legislation in 1981. These were generalized rather than specific "demands," which left much of the specific content of policy to the discretion of Congress. In other instances public opinion may be "permissive" in nature; that is, acquiescing to but not requiring some action.

**The social system.**    American society is divided into a wide variety and large number of societal groups—social, ethnic, economic, political, and religious. Many of these groups serve as the basis for voluntary associations, labor unions, civil rights organizations, church associations, business associations, and recreational organizations, which, in turn, seek to influence governmental action on an intermittent or continual basis. When they do this they may be called pressure groups or, a bit more clinically, political interest groups.

In a pluralist society such as the United States, the existence of a multitude of organized groups serves to diffuse and moderate political power. The power of some groups is checked or offset by that of competing groups. Individuals may belong to several groups, which must compete for their loyalty and support. Nonetheless, power is quite unevenly dispersed in American society. Some segments of the population are much better organized, more active, and more effective in politics than are others. Many individuals and many interests are represented imperfectly, if at all, by the system of pressure groups. Schattschneider has remarked, "The flaw in the pluralist heaven is that the heavenly chorus sings with a strong upper-class accent."[14] It is not our intent to argue here the merits and demerits of pluralist or elitist theories of American society; we are simply using the term *pluralist* to indicate the existence of a large number of separate groups in American society. This is a matter of fact.

In the American political system, private (that is, nongovernmental) pressure groups are a major source of demands for public policy, being clearly more important in this respect than the political parties. Private groups who are dissatisfied with their situation or relationships with other groups commonly seek governmental redress for their grievances. Public policy formation, at least on most major issues, can be viewed as involving conflict and struggle among competing groups or alliances thereof. The policy analyst's task then becomes one of explaining why some groups win and others lose in particular instances, or, in other words, how politics shapes policy decisions.

**The economic system.**    A society's economic system is concerned with the production, distribution, and exchange of goods and services. Some economic systems, such as that of the Republic of Chad, are relatively simple; others, like that of the United States, are highly complex. One of the prime sources of conflict in modern societies is economic activity. Conflicts may develop between the interests of employers and employees, big business and small business, consumers and sellers, creditors and debtors, oil importers and domestic producers, railroads and motor carriers, the various users of the national forests, and so on. Those who are dissatisfied with their existing relationships with other private groups often seek governmental assistance to protect or advance their own interests. Usually it is the weaker or disadvantaged party in a private conflict that seeks governmental involvement in the dispute. The dominant group, which is able to achieve its goals satisfactorily by private action, has no incentive to bring government into the fray. To do so will expand the conflict and thereby change the nature and outcome of the conflict. As an economy develops and becomes more complex, economic groups become more numerous and interdependent, and opportunities for conflict and government involvement multiply. In the United States, legislation on economic matters currently makes up the major portion of the congressional policy agenda.

It is a truism that the level of a society's economic development imposes limits on the provision of public goods and services by government to the community. However, this fact is sometimes overlooked by persons who assume that the failure of government to act on some matters is caused by backwardness or unresponsiveness rather than limited resources. For example, one factor that clearly restricts what governments can spend for welfare programs is available economic resources. Even in the United States, which now has a trillion-dollar economy, government does not have sufficient resources to do everything that everyone wants done, and thus choices among alternatives must be made. Moreover, both economic resources and public problems are unequally distributed among the states and localities.

Those who possess economic power through the control of economic resources often thereby possess political power as well. This is perhaps most starkly revealed in communities where a single company is the dominant source of employment. What the company favors in governmental action is usually what gets done. A threat by company officials to move their plant if some disapproved action is taken is often sufficient to cause local officials to back off. More broadly, there are some who argue that government in the United States is dominated by those who own or manage large corporate enterprises and that public policy generally reflects their interests. From this perspective, the Populist, Progressive, and New Deal reform movements, which occurred between 1890 and 1940, represent efforts "by leading members of the business community to bring order, stability, and predictability to the chaos of the emerging industrial order, to incorporate labor into the business system through conservative unionism, and to prevent social revolution through the distribution of minimal relief benefits to the poor."[15] Although there is obviously much interaction and interrelationship between the political and economic systems in American society, the validity of such sweeping contentions and arguments is open to strong question. Nonetheless, such statements represent an important viewpoint that cannot be ignored. A challenging question to consider is: What should be the relationship between government and the economic system?

### Institutional Context

The formal governmental institutions of the American political system significantly affect the formation, implementation, and substance of public policies. Institutions—patterns of regularized, habitual, or stable behavior which have developed with the passage of time—lend continuity and stability, and sometimes rigidity, to the processes of policymaking and administration. If one wants to comprehend these processes, one must pay attention to more than just the motives and interests of particular individuals and groups, movements in public opinion, or socioeconomic variables. One must also consider the institutional context within which such factors act, or are acted upon. Heinz Eulau has stated, "Current behavior is necessarily circumscribed and directed by the past patterns we call institutions."[16] Thus, congressional norms supporting committee consideration of legislation and deference to committee recommendations help explain the importance of committees in legislative decision making. Again, the actions of independent regulatory commissions, such as the Federal Trade Commission, are circumscribed by procedural and jurisdictional constraints set by law.

**Federalism.**   In the American federal system governmental power is constitutionally divided between the national government and several state governments. The basic division can be briefly sketched. The Constitution delegates to the national government (that is, the Congress) such powers as those to regulate interstate and foreign commerce; to tax and spend for the general welfare; to establish post offices and post roads; to coin money and regulate its value; and to raise and support armies and navies. The national government is also given the power "to make all laws which shall be necessary and proper for carrying into execution the foregoing powers." Then, in the words of the Tenth Amendment, "The powers not delegated to the United States by the Constitution, nor prohibited by it to the States, are reserved to the States respectively, or to the people." Although the governmental powers reserved to the states are not specified by the Constitution, they can be grouped into four categories: (1) police power, or power to protect and promote the public health, safety, welfare, and morals; (2) power to tax and spend; (3) eminent domain, or power to take private property for public use upon payment of just compensation; and (4) proprietary power, or power to own and operate economic enterprises. Under the doctrine of national supremacy, the Constitution and congressional enactments in pursuance thereof take precedence over state constitutional provisions and laws when they come into conflict.

The *formal* constitutional division of power between the national and state governments reads much the same today as it did in 1787. The only amendment conferring substantial *positive* policymaking authority is the Sixteenth, which authorizes the national government to levy income taxes. However, much change has occurred in the *real* allocation of power. Within the framework of the rather vague and general language of the Constitution, and in response to changing political pressures and social and economic conditions, the role of the national government in our society and economy has greatly expanded since the latter decades of the nineteenth century. Today, for example, national economic regulatory activity is more important, if not more pervasive, than that of the states.

A number of factors have contributed to the expanded policy role of the national government. In the first place, government is often called upon to deal with problems that are beyond the ability and legal power of the several states. Illustrative are problems in such areas as inflation, unemployment, agricultural prices and surpluses, collective bargaining, consumer protection, industrial monopoly, and environmental pollution control. Generally speaking, to be effective governmental action must be as broad in scope as the problems with which it is concerned. The individual states, for example, certainly cannot deal effectively with rising inflation or unemployment. In the second place, in some cases uniform national action is needed to make policy effective. Laws relating to the grading of commodities, the labeling of products, and standards of quality for drugs are some examples. Moreover, national action is sometimes in order to make state policies effective. For example, the Connally "Hot Oil" Act of 1935, which prohibited the shipment of oil in interstate commerce when produced in violation of state law, was intended to support state regulation of petroleum production. Again, many federal grant-in-aid programs are designed to supplement and strengthen state programs, as in the area of health care. Finally, the failure of the states to act, or to act adequately in the view of some groups, has led to national action in such matters as child labor, natural resources conservation, meat and poultry inspection, mining and industrial safety, and civil rights.

The primary constitutional bases for the expansion of national policy activity have been the powers to regulate interstate and foreign commerce and to tax and spend for the general welfare, which are delegated to the national government by Article I, Section 8, of the Constitution. In the nineteenth and early twentieth centuries, questions of whether the national government had constitutional power to act played an important, and sometimes determining, role in national policy-making. However, given the broad fashion in which these powers have been interpreted by the Supreme Court, Congress now essentially determines the extent of its own power under the Constitution. Nonetheless, despite the absence of formal constitutional limits, there are still some limitations on the exercise of national power. Political opposition, expedience, constitutional habit (for instance, the belief that some matters, such as professional licensing, still are properly dealt with by the states), or other factors may restrict its exercise.

Notwithstanding the vast expansion of national action in the economic and social welfare domains in the twentieth century, the states continue to have a substantial role. If, as some claim, all power is moving to Washington, then the march is being led by a rather slow drummer. The states continue to be the primary policy-makers with regard to the rights of property ownership, the regulation of trades and professions, the provision of educational and welfare facilities, the construction and maintenance of highways, law enforcement, and, in the age of the "energy crisis," the regulation of domestic petroleum production. Many areas of activity—pollution control, banking, transportation, welfare—are shared by the national and state governments. Typically, when the national government enters a field in which the states are already involved, national action supplements rather than replaces state action. Indeed, it is difficult to find many governmental activities which do not involve both the national and state governments.

The objective of the Reagan administration's "new federalism" was to change this situation by separating clearly the roles of the national, state, and local governments. In 1981, fifty-seven categorical grant-in-aid programs were consolidated into nine new block grant programs which gave state governments more discretion in the use of funds. In 1982 the administration proposed that the national government should assume full responsibility for Medicaid while turning full responsibility for the aid to families with dependent children (AFDC) and food stamp programs over to the states. The administration also recommended a "turnback" arrangement under which forty-four other grant programs eventually would be given to the states. These proposals, which provided for a major restructuring of the federal system, quickly encountered strong criticism from persons who feared that the programs involved would be diminished or eliminated if left to the states.

Let us look at some of the ways in which federalism may affect the formation and substance of public policy. First, federalism affects the access of groups to government and, consequently, their opportunities to exert influence on the policy process. Some groups may have more influence at the national level, others at the state level. Those opposing the enactment of civil rights legislation often have done so in the name of "states' rights," arguing that the states have the primary responsibility here. They obviously have been motivated by a belief that civil rights policy will be more to their liking if made (or not made) in Richmond, Virginia, or Jackson, Mississippi, rather than Washington, D.C. In contrast, those favoring positive action on civil rights generally have been strong advocates of national action. Labor groups have found the national government more responsive to their interests than the states and thus have tended to favor national action on labor problems, while business groups opposing labor interests generally prefer state action, which is often more likely to be amenable to their viewpoint. In short, the position of most groups on whether policy should be made at the national or state level will be affected more by considerations of relative advantage than by philosophical or theoretical concern for states' rights or national power.

Second, in formulating national policy Congress is often quite sensitive to state and local interests whether governmental or nongovernmental, and appears reluctant to infringe drastically upon state powers and functions. Writing on American federalism, an English scholar has remarked, "Congress is composed of a number of individuals who are, at one and the same time, national statesmen and local politicians, although perhaps some members rarely achieve the former status even temporarily."[17] When Congress established the unemployment compensation program in 1935, such factors as the nationwide consequences of unemployment, the poor financial and administrative condition of the states, and the powerful support from within the executive branch pointed toward a solely national program. Congress, however, was unwilling to bypass the states, and so a national-state cooperative program was established. In the mid-1960s the Johnson administration, with the support of organized labor, recommended "nationalization" of the program because of the low quality and benefits of many state programs. Such a move, however, was strongly opposed by state officials, and Congress refused to take action. The various state programs continue to vary considerably in eligibility requirements, and duration and amounts of payment.

Third, in the American federal system the states, acting in response to different interests or perceptions of problems, can adopt policies that contradict or are inconsistent with national policy. National efforts to maintain economic competition, for instance, have been hampered by state action in the form of highly permissive incorporation and tax laws, resale price maintenance legislation, and restrictive occupational licensing laws. (National policy in the antitrust area has not, of course, been a picture of consistency.) The efforts of the Federal Reserve Board to control the money supply for economic stabilization purposes have been impeded by the existence and actions of state-chartered banks beyond its control. Problems of this sort, which are unlikely to arise in a unitary system, complicate the policy process and reduce the effectiveness of some policies.

Fourth, the administration of national policies is often importantly affected by federalism. Certain programs, for example (most notably grant-in-aid programs in such fields as welfare, highway construction, agriculture extension, and public housing), are administered by state and local officials in accordance with national policy standards. Cooperation between the national and state agencies concerned with such programs is necessary if national policy is to be effective, and such cooperation may be forthcoming only at a "price." For instance, much latitude may be permitted the states or their local subdivisions in the administration of these programs. Moreover, national officials usually do not make rules, regulations, and program changes without consulting state or local officials. Also, political realities may permit the existence of practices that run counter to the purposes of a national program. Thus, the Elementary and Secondary Education Act provides funds to improve the educational facilities and opportunities for poor children. Local school districts, however, have sometimes used the funds available for more general purposes. Because state and local officials have traditionally dominated public education, and because they have strong political support in this regard, national officials in the Department of Education cannot readily impose directives that conflict with local priorities. They generally have refrained from so doing.

State and local officials and interests also attempt to influence national administrative structure, personnel selections, and policy in most if not all areas of national action. Thus, local livestock interests have a strong impact on the administration of national grazing control programs in the western states. City government officials continued to exert strong support for retention of the community action program initially set up under the Economic Opportunity Act of 1964. They were successful until 1981, when the Reagan administration acted to phase out the program. Much interaction has occurred among national and state officials concerning air and water pollution control. Although the impact of localism on national administration and policy cannot be attributed solely to the existence of "semi-independent" state and local governments, their existence certainly contributes to the political power and influence of local interests.

**Separation of powers.**   Besides the separation of state and national government powers and interests, a second basic structural feature of our governmental system is the allocation of governmental powers among separate legislative, executive, and judicial branches. Under the corollary principle of checks and balances, each branch is given some means to check, participate in, or interfere with the exercise of power by the other two branches. Thus, although primary power to legislate is vested in Congress, the president can veto legislation, and the Court can rule on its meaning and constitutionality. The system is well-described as one of "separated institutions sharing powers."

This institutional arrangement increases the points of access through which groups and individuals can seek to exert influence on policy. A group that fails to realize its goals through congressional action may seek favorable executive or judicial action. If the congressional enactment of a law cannot be prevented, a presidential veto may be sought. If this fails, the law may be challenged in the courts. Although the likelihood of its being declared unconstitutional is not great, it may be interpreted in a way favorable to a group's interests or its impact may be delayed or modified. Even if a group fails here, it can still attempt to influence the agency entrusted with the administration of a law to act in a congenial manner. Indeed, some agencies have been alleged to be the "captives" of particular groups, as in the case of the Interstate Commerce Commission and the railroads, or the Federal Maritime Commission and the shipping companies.

Within Congress, power is further dispersed. Not only is power shared by the House of Representatives and the Senate but within each house it is scattered among a number of points—leaders and influential members, standing committees, and, often, subcommittees thereof. In short, power in Congress is diffused, not concentrated. Some consequences of this fact can be noted. First, it works to the advantage of those seeking to prevent the enactment of legislation. To succeed in this, a group may need to gain the support of only one center of congressional power, such as a committee or subcommittee or perhaps just its chairman. On the other hand, this dispersion of power works to the disadvantage of those supporting the enactment of legislation, because it multiplies the points at which the legislation can be blocked. Even if eventually passed by Congress, a bill may be substantially changed or watered down as a condition of its passage. A classic case of this involves the Employment Act of 1946, discussed in chapter 2. Second, the congressional committee system often contributes to more rational and comprehensive policymaking in such areas as agriculture, taxation, and labor relations, in that bills on these topics are dealt with by committees that have long experience in handling such legislation. The committee system, as is frequently said, provides Congress with policy specialists. A third consequence of power dispersal is that in some instances the committee system may impede effective policy formation. With regard to urban matters, jurisdiction over legislation is shared by several committees in each house, which undoubtedly contributes to the unsettled and fragmented nature of national policy toward urban problems.

The legislative and executive branches frequently come into conflict or disagree on policymaking, even when both branches are controlled by the same political party. Generally, Congress is more responsive to local interests than is the executive branch. The possibility of conflict is further increased by institutional loyalties, which have developed over time. Congress especially is often quite concerned to protect its prerogatives against executive "encroachment." If the two branches are controlled by different parties, as they were during much of the Eisenhower administration and all of the Nixon and Ford administrations, partisanship becomes another basis for interbranch conflict. This set of conditions has significant implications for policymaking, since most important policy decisions require approval or support by both president and Congress. Consequently, in order to avoid stalemate or inaction, bargaining and compromise will be necessary. For example, in 1968 the Democratically-controlled House refused to act on a tax increase to combat inflation requested by the Johnson administration until the administration had agreed to a reduction in spending. Again, the Reagan administration in 1981 bargained with conservative Democrats in the House to pick up votes needed to enact its economic program. Major policies are established only after consideration of a broad range of affected interests and viewpoints. The separation of powers may also contribute to generality in policy content and slowness in policy adoption.

The development of large-scale, complex bureaucracy adds another dimension to the separation of powers at the national level. Whether one wishes to designate the bureaucracy as a "fourth branch of government," as some have done, is a matter of choice. What is important is to recognize that *agencies often act independently* of the chief executive. Moreover, they frequently have been delegated broad discretionary powers by Congress to make rules and implement programs. Agencies then may become the focal points for intense policymaking controversies, as in the instances of the Environmental Protection Agency and pollution control standards or the Federal Energy Regulatory Commission and interstate rates for natural gas. In short, power to make policy is further dispersed by the existence of semiautonomous administrative agencies, which may adopt or pursue contradictory policies or redirect the thrust of congressional and presidential decisions.

**The party system.**    Together, federalism and the separation of powers have helped discourage the development of political parties able to act with unity at the national level. Federalism has helped to produce a decentralized party system in which the primary bases of strength are in state and local party organizations. The separation of powers has helped prevent the development of party cohesion within Congress or between president and Congress, even when both are controlled by the same party. This situation has resulted from constitutional provisions whereby the president, the House, and the Senate have different powers, different election constituencies, and staggered terms of election. The absence of strong, cohesive, policy-oriented parties has strengthened the position of special interest groups in the making of policy; undoubtedly, these groups have greater impact here than in countries with strong, unified parties. As David Truman has noted, "Because the legislator's tenure in office depends on no overarching party organization, he is accessible to whatever influences are outstanding in his local constituency almost regardless of more inclusive claims."[18] National issues are often viewed and acted on in the context of their meaning for state and local interests. The party system only partially bridges the gap created between president and Congress by the separation of powers. Much room is left for the play of interest groups in policymaking; whether one finds this desirable or undesirable, it does help shape the policy process.

## LEVELS OF POLICYMAKING

Not all policymaking situations are cut from the same mold. Rather, they differ on the basis of such characteristics as the range of participants, the scope and urgency of the issue involved, the governmental location (Congress or a federal court, for example), and the visibility of the issue and situation. Thus, some instances of policymaking involve major issues that affect large numbers of people and attract a wide range of policymakers (an example is the 1978 energy legislation), whereas others involve relatively minor issues affecting only a few people and involving only a limited range of policymakers (such as the enactment of a special tax provision). In this section we will briefly sketch three levels of policymaking; namely, micropolitics, subsystem politics, and macropolitics.[19] Although it is not always easy to draw the line between macropolitics and subsystem politics—or, for that matter, subsystem politics and micropolitics—that does not lessen the utility of these concepts in the study of policy formation.

### Micropolitics

Micropolitics customarily involves attempts by particular individuals, companies, or communities to secure favorable government action for their own benefit. Individuals may want a favorable ruling by an administrative agency or the enactment of a private immigration bill; companies may want a favorable ruling by the Internal Revenue Service or authorization for a motor carrier route from the Interstate Commerce Commission; a community may want a public works grant from the Economic Development Administration, or it may oppose the location of a public housing project within its boundaries. Usually only a few persons and officials are involved in these situations. However important the government action may be to those seeking it, it is of limited impact and interest to the general populace. Most citizens will be neither interested in it nor affected by it, nor, indeed, aware of it in most cases.

The enactment of special tax provisions by Congress is a good illustration of micropolitics. Every year or two Congress enacts amendments to the Internal Revenue Code that relieve a few persons or companies of paying taxes otherwise due. Sponsored by individual members of Congress, and frequently opposed (usually unsuccessfully) by the Treasury Department, these bills are commonly advocated as necessary to correct "inequities" in existing tax laws. These special tax bills attract little attention on their way through the legislative process and are "invisible" as far as the general public is concerned. They are, however, of much interest and value to their beneficiaries.

### Subsystem Politics

Subsystem politics are usually focused on a particular policy or functional area, such as commercial air transportation, agricultural extension activity, river and harbor development, management of public grazing lands, or the granting of patents. Normally, a subsystem consists of a pattern of relationships among some congressional committees or subcommittees, an administrative agency or two, and the relevant pressure groups concerned with the policy area in question. For example, the subsystem focused on agricultural extension activity is composed of the Agricultural Extension Service, the House and Senate Agriculture Committees, and the American Farm Bureau Federation. Another subsystem, which is centered around the management of public grazing lands in the western states, is composed of the House and Senate Interior Committees and appropriations subcommittees, the Bureau of Land Management, and groups representing western livestock raisers. This subsystem has expanded in recent years to include some environmental groups.

Political subsystems develop and persist because not everyone is concerned with every area of public policy, nor could one be, given limitations of time, information, and interest. Thus, the official or citizen who is keenly interested in maritime shipping policy may have little or no interest in agricultural extension or public land policies, and consequently will leave them to persons with stronger interests. They, in turn, may largely ignore someone else's preferred policy area. Within the government particular congressional committees and administrative agencies are set up for each area of public policy. As the government's specialists in their field, they develop continuing relationships with one another and with the concerned pressure groups.

These subsystems have considerable independence from other policymakers in the development and implementation of public policy in their field. Within the bounds of existing legislation, they largely shape governmental action in their area. Thus, for forty years a subsystem involving the House Agricultural Committee, the Sugar Division of the Department of Agriculture, and representatives of the sugar industry (especially producers) was primarily responsible for the formation of policy on sugar prices. In 1974 the authorizing legislation for sugar price supports came up for renewal, in a time of sharp inflation. Consumer groups and industrial users, concerned about high prices, opposed the renewal of the legislation and caused its defeat. This illustrates a second point: When new legislation or the renewal of legislation is needed, approval from the larger political system is needed. Often that approval will be forthcoming, as it was for decades in the case of sugar, since there is a tendency to defer to the experts in an area; however, some sort of disruptive event may expand interest in an area and cause defeat for a subsystem or, alternatively, induce control of it by the larger political system. It should be noted that the sugar program was reinstated in 1977. This time, however, sugar interests were willing and able to bargain with other interests to secure the votes needed to pass their legislation.

## Macropolitics

Macropolitics involves the community as a whole and the leaders of government generally in the formation of public policy—whether to combat inflation, provide for an adequate supply of energy, or reform the welfare system. Participants in the macropolitical arena include the president, executive departments, congressional leaders, the communications media, group spokespersons, and others. Participation is thus quite wide. Our attention is often drawn to macropolitics because it tends to be quite visible, spectacular, and well reported. Broad public interests are likely to be considered most fully when policymaking occurs in the macropolitical arena.

Policy decisions made in the macropolitical arena may be considerably different from what they would be if made at the subsystem level. Energy policies in the era before the current energy crisis were usually made within subsystems and were especially reflective of producer interests. Now that energy and environmental policies have been moved into the macropolitical arena, the range of participants has expanded and producers no longer enjoy the dominance they once did.

Whereas limited modifications in existing policies will probably be handled by subsystems, proposals for major changes or developments in public policy will usually be dealt with at the macropolitical level. In 1981 such proposals included renewal of agricultural price support legislation, the Clean Air Act, Social Security reform, income tax reform, and the deregulation of natural gas prices. Positive action occurred only on price supports tax reform and reduction. Major changes in public policies are not easy to achieve in most instances.

## NOTES

1. For other definitions of public policy see Thomas R. Dye, *Understanding Public Policy*, 4th ed. (Englewood Cliffs, N.J.: Prentice-Hall, 1981); Charles O. Jones, *An Introduction to the Study of Public Policy*, 2nd ed. (North Scituate, Mass.: Duxbury, 1977); Richard Rose, ed., *Policy Making in Great Britain* (New York: Macmillan, 1969), p. x.
2. James E. Anderson, *Public Policy-Making: Decisions and Their Implementation*, 2nd ed. (New York: Holt, Rinehart and Winston, 1979), p. 3.
3. David Easton, *A Systems Analysis of Political Life* (New York: Wiley, 1965), p. 212.
4. Ibid.
5. Some parts of this framework draw substantially on Anderson, *Public Policy-Making.*
6. Jones, *Introduction to the Study of Public Policy*, 1st ed. (North Scituate, Mass.: 1970), p. 17.
7. Robin M. Williams, Jr., *American Society*, 2nd ed. (New York: Knopf, 1960), pp. 22–25.
8. Ibid., chap. 11.
9. Gabriel A. Almond and Sidney Verba, *The Civic Culture* (Boston: Little, Brown, 1965), pp. 11–26.

10. Karl W. Deutsch, *Politics and Government* (Boston: Houghton Mifflin, 1970), p. 207.
11. More extensive treatments of American political culture can be found in Donald J. Levine, *The Political Culture of the United States* (Boston: Little, Brown, 1972); and Daniel J. Elazar, *American Federalism: A View from the States*, 2nd ed. (New York: Crowell, 1974).
12. V. O. Key, Jr., *Public Opinion and American Democracy* (New York: Knopf, 1961), p. 14. See also James J. Best, *Public Opinion: Micro and Macro* (Homewood, Ill.: Dorsey Press, 1973), chap. 7.
13. Cf. Charles O. Jones, "Speculative Argumentation in Federal Air Pollution Policy-Making," *Journal of Politics* 36 (May 1974): 438–464.
14. E. E. Schattschneider, *The Semi-Sovereign People* (New York: Holt, Rinehart and Winston, 1960), p. 35.
15. Edward S. Greenberg, *Serving the Few: Corporate Capitalism and the Bias of Government Policy* (New York: Wiley, 1974), p. 88.
16. Heinz Eulau, *The Behavioral Persuasion* (New York: Random House, 1963), p. 18.
17. M.J.C. Vile, *The Structure of American Federalism* (London: Oxford University Press, 1961), p. 90.
18. David B. Truman, *The Governmental Process* (New York: Knopf, 1951), p. 325.
19. See Emmette S. Redford, *Democracy in the Administrative State* (New York: Oxford University Press, 1969), chaps. 4–5; Anderson, *Public Policy-Making*, pp. 48–52; and Randall B. Ripley and Grace A. Franklin, *Congress, the Bureaucracy, and Public Policy*, rev. ed. (Homewood, Ill.: Dorsey Press, 1980), chap. 1.

## SUGGESTED READINGS

Anderson, James E. *Public Policy-Making: Decisions and Their Implementation*. 2nd ed. New York: Holt, Rinehart and Winston, 1979.
Dye, Thomas R. *Understanding Public Policy*. 4th ed. Englewood Cliffs, N.J.: Prentice-Hall, 1981.
Jones, Charles O. *An Introduction to the Study of Public Policy*. 2nd ed. North Scituate, Mass.: Duxbury, 1977.
Lineberry, Robert L. *American Public Policy*. New York: Holt, Rinehart and Winston, 1977.
Ripley, Randall B., and Franklin, Grace A. *Congress, the Bureaucracy, and Public Policy*. Rev. ed. Homewood, Ill.: Dorsey Press, 1980.
Smith, T. Alexander. *The Comparative Policy Process*. Santa Barbara, Calif.: ABC-Clio, 1975.
Wade, Larry L. *The Elements of Public Policy*. Columbus, Ohio: Merrill, 1972.

# Chapter 2

# Economic Stability Policies

Government influence on economic activity takes two general forms: the promotion, regulation, and control of particular activities or industries through such means as antitrust policy, minimum wage laws, environmental pollution controls, and employment programs; and the control of overall levels of economic activity through macroeconomic policies. The second form of government control, which is the subject of this chapter, involves the use of fiscal policies (concerning taxation and expenditures) and monetary policies (concerning money supply, level of interest rates, and management of public debt) to promote economic stability.

What do we mean when we talk about economic stability? Some economists define it as the absence of fluctuations, of periods of "boom and bust," in the business cycle.[1] Other components that, singly or in combination, may be employed in defining economic stability include stability of prices, such as the government's consumer price index; stable growth in economic output; rising national income; full employment; and a favorable balance of payments (that is, a trade surplus) in the area of international trade. These possibilities, in turn, are subject to varying definitions (for instance, what conditions constitute "full employment"?) and emphases (some are more concerned about inflation, others about employment levels). Conflict over economic stability policy may arise in part because of disagreements about the meaning of economic stability and, consequently, the causes of instability which policy is intended to remedy. Although we recognize the shortcomings of general definitions, economic stability will be viewed here as involving a rising national income under conditions that provide full employment and general price stability.

Economic *instability* takes the forms primarily of inflation, recession, or depression. Inflation involves upward movement of the general price level for goods and services, with a consequent reduction in the purchasing power of the dollar (or some other unit of money). *Demand-pull inflation* occurs when aggregate demand increases more rapidly than the available supply of goods and services. This is the classic case of "too many dollars chasing too few goods," with the result that prices rise as buyers compete for the available supply. *Cost-push inflation*, in contrast, occurs when prices or wages rise faster than productivity or efficiency because large companies or unions have sufficient market power to "administer" the prices or wages they charge. That is, they are able to exercise discretion and push prices or wages above the levels that would be set by the interaction of supply and demand in the marketplace. Some of the inflation that occurred in the 1970s was attributed to cost-push factors. The rate of inflation in the American economy has varied from one period to another; however, the long-range trend in the twentieth century has been for prices to move upward. (See table 2–1.) As a consequence, "the belief is widely held that 'creeping inflation' (which sometimes breaks into a gallop) has become a permanent ingredient of American economic life."[2] A major task of government is to hold inflation within acceptable limits.

**TABLE 2-1   Performance of the American economy for selected years (1929–1981)**

| Year | Labor force (000's) | Unemployment (percent) | Consumer price index (1967 = 100) |
|------|---------------------|------------------------|-----------------------------------|
| 1929 | 49,440 | 3.2 | 51.3 |
| 1933 | 51,840 | 24.9 | 38.8 |
| 1939 | 55,600 | 17.2 | 41.6 |
| 1945 | 65,300 | 1.9 | 53.9 |
| 1950 | 63,858 | 5.3 | 72.1 |
| 1955 | 68,072 | 4.4 | 80.2 |
| 1960 | 72,142 | 5.5 | 88.7 |
| 1965 | 77,178 | 4.5 | 94.5 |
| 1966 | 78,893 | 3.8 | 97.2 |
| 1967 | 80,793 | 3.8 | 100.0 |
| 1968 | 82,272 | 3.6 | 104.2 |
| 1969 | 84,240 | 3.5 | 109.8 |
| 1970 | 85,903 | 4.9 | 116.3 |
| 1971 | 86,929 | 5.9 | 121.3 |
| 1972 | 88,991 | 5.6 | 125.3 |
| 1973 | 91,040 | 4.9 | 133.1 |
| 1974 | 93,240 | 5.6 | 147.7 |
| 1975 | 94,793 | 8.5 | 161.2 |
| 1976 | 96,917 | 7.7 | 170.5 |
| 1977 | 99,534 | 7.0 | 181.5 |
| 1978 | 102,537 | 6.0 | 195.4 |
| 1979 | 104,962 | 5.8 | 217.4 |
| 1980 | 106,940 | 7.1 | 246.8 |
| 1981 | 108,670 | 7.6 | 272.4 |

SOURCE: *Economic Report of the President, 1981* (Washington, D.C.: U.S. Government Printing Office, 1982).

NOTE: The labor-force figure includes the armed forces. The unemployment percentage is for the civilian labor force.

A *recession* occurs when aggregate demand for goods and services falls off, investment decreases, and unemployment increases. Prices may also decrease, although in recent decades prices, in the phraseology of economists, have tended to become "sticky," moving upward more readily than downward. Before the 1930s, incidentally, economic declines were usually referred to as "panics." This language was then softened to "depression." The experience of the 1930s gave "depression" a bad connotation, with the result that "recession" has become the favored term.

Until the 1970s, those concerned with maintaining economic stability customarily confronted a situation involving either inflation or recession. In the last several years, however, *stagflation* (a high rate of unemployment combined with substantial inflation), and the persistence of high interest rates have compounded the task of policymakers. Action to reduce unemployment may contribute to more inflation and vice versa. There appears to be no easy solution to this problem.

## DEVELOPMENT OF GOVERNMENT RESPONSIBILITY FOR ECONOMIC STABILITY

Only in recent decades, and especially since World War II, has the national government assumed explicit and active responsibility for the maintenance of economic stability. This is probably the most important development in public economic policy in the postwar period.

Traditionally it was thought that government could do little to control fluctuations in the business cycle (even though they appeared to be an intrinsic feature of a capitalistic, industrial economy). The operation of the business cycle was supposedly governed by "natural" economic laws which made governmental action unnecessary and undesirable. Depressions, for example, were thought to be self-correcting. Did not Say's Law, a main feature of classical economic theory, state that supply creates its own demand and that continued unemployment or underconsumption is thus impossible? The best thing government could do was to balance the budget, by cutting expenditures and increasing taxes, lest business conditions be worsened by a lack of public confidence in the government's financial condition.

The actions of public officials and public policy reflected such attitudes. In 1921 the national government sponsored a Conference on Unemployment to consider what could be done about the existing depressed economic conditions. President Harding expressed the position of the government in his welcoming remarks: "There has been vast unemployment before and there will be again. There will be depression and inflation just as surely as the tides ebb and flow. I would have little enthusiasm for any proposed remedy which seeks palliation or tonic from the Public Treasury."[3] No government action was forthcoming. In the early 1930s, the Hoover administration called for a large tax increase in order to balance the budget. Congressional opposition centered largely on the form the tax increase should take; its size and desirability were not really issues. The Revenue Act of 1932 took effect in June, near the bottom of the Great Depression.[4] According to what is now accepted theory, a tax increase is just the opposite of what the situation really called for.

## Changing Attitudes

Acceptance of governmental responsibility for economic stabilization, and the alteration of public policy, resulted from the combined influence of several factors. The Great Depression, which began in 1929 and was the most severe the nation had ever known, and the persistence of massive unemployment throughout the 1930s contributed to the notion that depressions are not necessarily "self-correcting." Second, new tools of economic measurement and analysis were developed, such as national income accounting. Next, the economic impact of World War II brought a tremendous increase in government spending and the return of high employment and prosperity. Also of great importance were the ideas of the famed English economist John Maynard Keynes. In his *General Theory of Employment, Interest, and Money* (1936) and other writings, Keynes attacked the classical theory that a free-market capitalistic economy is a self-correcting mechanism that tends automatically to produce full employment and prosperity. He argued that deficit spending by government could add to the total demand for goods and services, offsetting a decrease in private demand and investment, and thus help to maintain a high level of demand, output, and employment. His ideas came to be widely accepted and constituted a rationale as well as a set of guidelines for the use of fiscal policy by government to maintain economic stability.

In 1933 Franklin D. Roosevelt came into office committed to fiscal orthodoxy, but was slowly converted to the Keynesian viewpoint. Consequently, his program for improving the economy—the New Deal—used deficit spending in an effort to stimulate the economy and bring recovery. This technique was often referred to as "pump priming" and "compensatory spending." The deficit-spending activities of the New Deal, though at the time they were regarded by many as highly radical, were really quite moderate (at least in retrospect). Indeed, it has been argued that the reason for the persistence of high unemployment throughout the 1930s was that the budget deficits incurred by the Roosevelt administration were insufficient to compensate for the large drop in private spending.[5]

What the deficits of the 1930s had failed to do was accomplished by the huge deficits (over $45 billion annually during 1943–1945) that resulted from the government's spending for the war effort of the 1940s. Stimulated by these large deficits, the economy expanded, production rose, and unemployment almost disappeared. This experience led to a general feeling that if large-scale government activity could expand production and maintain high employment in wartime it could also do so in peacetime. Before moving on, we might note that a charge frequently leveled against Roosevelt was that "he got us into war to get us out of the Depression." What brought economic recovery was not World War II but the *spending* for the war effort. Large deficits could have been run for other purposes, such as public works or health and welfare programs, but such actions were not politically acceptable. Large deficits became acceptable only when they were linked to national defense. The reader may draw his or her own conclusions concerning the nation's priorities.

## Employment Act of 1946

The Employment Act of 1946 formally committed the national government to action to maintain economic stability. The act reflected the belief, based on late Depression and wartime experience, that government could act effectively, through the use of its fiscal, monetary, and other powers, to stabilize the economy. Also contributing to the passage of the act was the fear, supported by the predictions of many economists, that the changeover from a wartime to a peacetime economy would be accompanied by a depression.[6] This had happened following World War I.

Much conflict attended the movement of the Employment Act through Congress. Truman administration leaders, and labor and liberal groups wanted to commit the government to the full use of fiscal policy to create conditions that would ensure "full employment" (although the legislation's sponsors were not able to agree on a precise definition for the phrase). In opposition, business and conservative groups argued that extensive use of fiscal policy to maintain "full employment" would lead to high labor costs, budget deficits, inflation, and excessive government intervention in the economy. Whether out of maliciousness or naiveté, some opponents interpreted the phrase to mean that people would have to work whether or not they wanted to. Conservatives emphasized the capacity of the private economy to provide jobs. Also, they placed more faith in the ability of monetary policy to stabilize the economy. Monetary policy had not been adequate to deal with the Depression, in the view of many persons, and it had consequently lost favor, especially with liberals and fiscal policy proponents.

The Employment Act in its final form was passed by overwhelming majorities in Congress, largely because anyone who voted against it might seem to be opposed to low unemployment as an important national goal. Since this was not a viable political position, conflict focused, rather, on particular provisions or language in the bill. This was especially the case in the more conservative House, and the final act was much altered from the bill originally introduced by Sen. James Murray (D.–Mont.). For example, the Murray Bill had specifically provided for the use of public works and favorable loans to maintain employment. This provision was replaced by a commitment to use "all practicable means." The goal of "full employment" in the Murray Bill became "maximum employment" in the final version. Such compromises were part of the cost of policy adoption. The Employment Act did not create a new fiscal policy. It did, however, represent a high level of agreement and a general course for public policy to follow. Also, as Stein suggests, "It helped put an end to a futile, tiresome, and largely meaningless debate between extremists and cleared the way for practical work to evolve a program [for stabilizing the economy]."[7]

The declaration of policy, in Section 2 of the act, states:

> It is the continuing policy and responsibility of the federal government to use all practicable means consistent with its needs and obligations and other essential considerations of

national policy, with the assistance and cooperation of industry, agriculture, labor, and state and local governments, to coordinate and utilize all of its plans, functions, and resources for the purpose of creating and maintaining, in a manner calculated to foster and promote free competitive enterprise and the general welfare, conditions under which there will be afforded useful employment opportunities, including self-employment, for those able, willing, and seeking to work, and to promote maximum employment, production, and purchasing power.

The act established some governmental machinery to help carry out the declared policy. A Council of Economic Advisers, consisting of three professional economists (usually drawn from big business and the academic world) and a small supporting staff, was created. The council has the duties of collecting and analyzing data on current and future economic trends and preparing them for the president's use. It also advises on how existing and new programs can be used to effectuate the Employment Act's policy statement. The council has become a major actor in the development of economic stability policy proposals. For example, it played a large role in formulating, and persuading President Kennedy to present to Congress the tax-cut proposals which became the Revenue Act of 1964.

The Employment Act also provides that the president shall deliver an economic report to Congress at the beginning of each session. In it the president analyzes current economic trends and conditions and presents "a program for carrying out the policy declared in Section 2, together with such recommendations for legislation as he may deem necessary or advisable." Within Congress the act established a Joint Economic Committee (as it is now called) to consider the president's economic report and to advise the two Houses concerning the president's recommendations. The committee also holds hearings and commissions studies on economic policy matters. In general, the council and the joint committee have helped focus attention on economic problems and have contributed to understanding of the overall operation of the economy and the relation of public policy thereto.

The adoption of the Employment Act "did not mean that the federal government proceeded, deliberately and continuously, to use the monetary and fiscal instruments at its disposal to maintain employment and control inflation."[8] Differences of opinion as to *when* government should act, *what form* government action should take, and what the particular *goals* of action should be, have persisted both inside and outside the government. Within the scope of the act's policy statement, ample room remains for political conflict and struggle over the shape of policy in given situations. The struggle over "Reaganomics" is illustrative.

## POLICY INSTRUMENTS

A variety of policy instruments are available to government decision makers in their efforts to maintain economic stability. These include monetary policy, fiscal policy, automatic stabilizers, wage-price guidelines, and direct price and wage controls. In this section they are treated primarily as means for dealing with inflationary and recessionary movements in the economy (that is, as instruments of counter-cyclical policy).

### Monetary Policy

Most of the instruments of monetary policy are under the direction of the board of governors of the Federal Reserve System, or Federal Reserve Board (FRB), and involve control of the supply of money, credit, and interest rates. The FRB has primary responsibility for the implementation of monetary policy because of its authority over the credit-creating and lending activities of the nation's banks. Changes in the nation's money supply result largely from changes in the volume of commercial bank credit. The Federal Reserve System was established by Congress in 1913, primarily for the purpose of adjusting the money supply to the fluctuating needs of commerce and industry and reducing the vulnerability of the nation's banking system to financial panics. One analyst has pointed out, "Nothing in the [Federal Reserve] Act relates the monetary authority to the function of national economic stabilization; yet this is its prime task today."[9] Legislation passed in the 1930s did clarify somewhat the FRB's authority in this area.

The Federal Reserve System has been aptly described as "a pyramid having a private base, a mixed middle, and a public apex."[10] At the top is the board of governors, whose seven members are appointed by the president, with senatorial consent, for fourteen-year, overlapping terms. Members are removable by the president for cause, but none ever has been. In the middle of the pyramid is the Federal Open Market Committee, comprised of the seven Federal Reserve Board members and five of the twelve Federal Reserve Bank presidents. At the bottom of the pyramid are the twelve district Federal Reserve Banks. These are "bankers' banks," formally owned by the Federal Reserve System's member banks in each district. All national banks must belong to the system, and state banks may if they meet certain requirements. The banks belonging to the Federal Reserve System account for about 85 percent of the total commercial bank reserves of the country.

**Instruments of monetary policy.**   The primary instruments of monetary policy employed by the Federal Reserve System in maintaining economic stability are open-market operations, control of the discount rate, and the setting of reserve requirements for member banks. Formally, these three functions are allocated to the Federal Open Market Committee, the Federal Reserve Bank boards of directors, and the Federal Reserve Board, respectively. In actuality, the exercise of all three is controlled by the FRB, which, in turn, at least in recent years, has been dominated by its chairman. Thus, William M. Martin, Arthur F. Burns, and Paul Volcker, the current chairman, have been highly respected, influential policymakers. Since the real substance of monetary policy depends upon the manner in which the various policy instruments are used, the nature of monetary policy at a particular time will be affected by the economic philosophy and conception of the proper role of the FRB held by the board chairman. In recent years there has been considerable cooperation between the FRB and the administration in office. However, the chairman and the board have sometimes acted independently; in late 1965, for instance, the board's action to restrict the money supply was contrary to the wishes of the Johnson administration. When President Nixon in 1970 appointed Arthur F. Burns, then one of his counselors, to the chairmanship of the FRB, some people thought that the "problem" of board independence would be eliminated. Such did not prove to be the case. On the other hand, in 1981 the FRB acted in general accord with the Reagan administration's desire for restraint on the rate of growth of the money supply. A short examination of the FRB's monetary instruments (open-market operations, discount rates, and reserve requirements) follows.

Open-market operations are the principal instrument of monetary policy. The FRB can buy and sell government securities through the Federal Reserve Banks in the open market—that is, the place where securities are bought and sold (usually New York City). When the board buys securities, they are ultimately paid for through the creation of new deposits at the Federal Reserve Banks. These new deposits serve as bank reserves, which can be used by commercial banks as the basis for further loans, investments, and deposits (that is, an increase in the money supply). Conversely, if the FRB wants to reduce the supply of money, it sells government securities, collecting as payment an equivalent amount of banks' reserves and thus reducing the money supply.[11]

The discount rate is the rate of interest charged by the Federal Reserve Banks to member commercial banks desiring to borrow money to finance lending activities. Raising the discount rate is intended to discourage borrowing by banks for the purpose of making loans, and lowering the discount rate has the reverse effect. Changes in the discount rate are usually moderate and are seldom sufficient by themselves to encourage or discourage bank borrowing. But, whatever its other impact, changes in the discount rate are a means by which the FRB can signal its view of the economy to the banks. If they encounter higher discount rates, the banks know that the FRB believes credit is expanding too rapidly and that they can expect further action to contract credit if expansion continues.

The reserve requirement refers to the ratio of reserves to deposits (or loans) that must be maintained by member banks. If the reserve requirement is 20 percent, banks can make $5 in loans for each dollar of reserves they have. By raising or lowering reserve requirements, the FRB can decrease or increase the amount of money that banks have available for loans, thus contracting or expanding the supply of credit. Open-market operations, however, are regarded as a more flexible and effective means of influencing the money supply.

Two other instruments used by the FRB are moral suasion and selective credit controls. Moral suasion refers to the power of the board to influence bank actions by suggestion, exhortation, and informal agreements. Selective credit controls are exercised over particular groups of borrowers. The board now regulates margin requirements for stock purchases—the minimum down payment that must be made by purchasers of stock. If the margin requirement is 80 percent, only 20 percent of the purchase price of stock can be borrowed. During the Korean War the board was empowered to regulate down payments for real estate and consumers' durable goods, but this power ended in 1952.

Another monetary instrument which may be used for economic stabilization purposes is management of the national debt. The national debt was about one trillion dollars in 1981. The Department of the Treasury, which handles the debt, is constantly refinancing it, even in periods when there are neither budget surpluses nor deficits. Previously issued securities come due and are paid off; new securities are issued to replace them. The way in which the debt is financed will affect credit supply and interest rates. Long-term securities, for example, usually carry higher rates of interest than short-term securities. In either case, the rate of interest paid on government securities will affect private interest rates and, consequently, private borrowing and investment. Again, during periods of recession the supply of credit can be increased if debt financing takes the form of borrowing through sale of short-term securities to commercial banks. This will enlarge their reserves and thus increase their capacity to make loans.

**Easy-money versus tight-money policies.**    In periods of recession or high unemployment it is expected that the FRB may act to stimulate the economy by following an "easy-money" policy—expanding the supply of money and lowering interest rates to encourage investment and consumption and thereby adding to aggregate demand for goods and services. This policy was adopted by the board during the 1953–1954 and 1970–1971 recessions, when the decline in spending and employment became apparent. Conversely, during an inflationary period the FRB typically acts to contract the money supply and raise interest rates in order to reduce borrowing and, hence, aggregate demand. This is referred to as a tight-money policy and was followed in 1966 and 1969. Collectively, such short-term actions are characterized as "leaning against the wind."

**Disadvantages of monetary policy.**    Although the FRB occupies the central position in the area of monetary policy, its actions may not be well coordinated with those of agencies concerned with agricultural, housing, and veterans' loan programs, all of which affect the overall supply of credit. They were, after all, set up to serve particular interests and purposes other than economic stabilization. The FRB may also be limited in effectiveness by demands that it facilitate the Treasury Department's debt management task. During the late 1940s the board was prevented from following an anti-inflationary (tight-money) policy by its agreement to help maintain low interest rates on government securities. In 1951 an "accord" was negotiated between the FRB, which had considerable congressional support, and the Treasury, which had presidential support. The "accord" committed the board to maintain an "orderly" market for government securities but otherwise left it free to use monetary policy for countercyclical purposes. Differences of opinion still develop between the two agencies, however, on debt financing. Chairman Burns once stated that he would "go to war with the Treasury" if its desire for help in selling securities conflicted with the board's tighter-money policy.[12] All is not harmonious in the monetary arena.

**Advantages of monetary policy.**    The proponents of monetary policy argue that it is more useful than fiscal policy for stabilization purposes because it is more rapid and more flexible. Decisions on monetary policy are made by an administrative agency (the FRB), which can respond quickly to changes in level of economic activity. Fiscal policy, in contrast, is often slower in application because of the need for congressional action on taxation and expenditures.

The proponents of monetary policy also argue that it is a "good" policy because it is indirect and impersonal in its working. The government, in using monetary policy, does not directly control or prescribe individual actions and decisions but rather acts to change the environment in which individuals act and make economic decisions. Thus, the proponents conclude, monetary policy involves less government intervention in private economic activity than does fiscal policy.

### Fiscal Policy

Fiscal policy involves the deliberate use of the national government's taxing and spending powers to influence the level of income, employment, and growth in the economy—that is, to maintain economic stability. When national spending was at low levels, the opportunity of the national government to influence the economy through fiscal policy was slight. With the national government's greatly increased spending in recent decades, this situation has changed. Cash payments by the national government now amount to over 20 percent of the gross national product (GNP), as shown in table 2-2. This volume of spending gives the national government significant ability to affect the overall operation of the economy, depending upon how the money is obtained and expended. Indeed, national spending will have fiscal policy *effects* even if it is not used intentionally to promote economic stability.

Fiscal policy operates to affect the aggregate volume of spending (or demand) for goods and services in the economy. The basic assumption is that at some level of GNP the economy will operate at a "full"-employment level. Gross national product is the market value of final goods and services produced by the economy during a year. It is the sum of private consumption spending, private investment spending, and government spending—or, in equation form, $C + I + G = GNP$. According to fiscal theory, if private spending for investment and consumption, plus "normal" government spending, is inadequate to produce full employment, government can act to increase aggregate demand, and hence production and employment, by spending more than it receives in taxes. Conversely, if an excess of aggregate demand for the available supply of goods and services is the cause of inflationary pressures, government can act to reduce aggregate demand by spending less than its tax take. The powerful instruments of fiscal policy are thus budget deficits and surpluses.

TABLE 2-2   Federal finances and gross national product
for selected years, 1955–1981 (in billions of dollars)

| Fiscal year | GNP | Budget outlays | Percent of GNP | National debt | Percent of GNP |
|---|---|---|---|---|---|
| 1955 | $ 381.0 | $ 68.5 | 18.0% | $ 274.4 | 72.0% |
| 1965 | 658.0 | 118.4 | 18.0 | 323.2 | 49.1 |
| 1966 | 722.4 | 134.7 | 18.6 | 329.5 | 45.6 |
| 1967 | 773.5 | 158.3 | 20.5 | 341.3 | 44.1 |
| 1968 | 830.3 | 178.8 | 21.5 | 369.8 | 44.5 |
| 1969 | 904.2 | 184.5 | 20.4 | 367.1 | 40.6 |
| 1970 | 960.2 | 196.6 | 20.5 | 382.6 | 39.8 |
| 1971 | 1,009.8 | 211.4 | 20.7 | 409.5 | 40.2 |
| 1972 | 1,111.8 | 231.9 | 20.9 | 437.3 | 39.3 |
| 1973 | 1,238.4 | 246.5 | 19.9 | 468.4 | 37.8 |
| 1974 | 1,358.6 | 268.4 | 19.8 | 486.2 | 35.8 |
| 1975 | 1,440.0 | 324.6 | 22.5 | 554.1 | 37.8 . |
| 1976 | 1,642.7 | 366.4 | 22.3 | 631.9 | 29.2 |
| 1977 | 1,864.0 | 402.7 | 21.6 | 709.1 | 29.6 |
| 1978 | 2,085.3 | 450.8 | 21.6 | 780.4 | 29.3 |
| 1979 | 2,357.8 | 493.6 | 20.9 | 833.8 | 27.3 |
| 1980 | 2,561.5 | 579.6 | 22.6 | 914.3 | 27.9 |
| 1981 | 2,858.6 | 678.2 | 23.7 | 1,003.9 | 27.8 |
| 1982[a] | 3,082.4 | 745.0 | 24.2 | 1,134.2 | 29.6 |
| 1983[a] | 3,443.6 | 773.3 | 22.5 | 1,258.4 | 29.7 |

SOURCE: Office of Management and Budget, *Federal Budget in Brief* (Washington, D.C.: Government Printing Office, 1982, and earlier years).

[a]Estimated figures for 1982–1983.

Discretionary fiscal policy involves changes by political decision makers (the president and Congress) in taxing and spending policies to achieve budget surpluses or deficits. These changes can be made in a number of ways: (1) Tax rates can be held constant and the volume of spending varied. (2) The volume of spending can be held constant, and taxes may be increased or decreased. (3) Some combination of changes in both tax rates and volume of spending can be used. Which alternative to use, if any, is often a cause of considerable political conflict.

To counter a recession or stimulate the economy, the government could increase spending, reduce taxes, or both, to inject more money into the economy. If tax rates were cut and spending maintained, more money would be left in the hands of consumers. Assuming "normal" consumer behavior, most of this money would be spent, thereby adding to aggregate demand. If tax rates were left alone and government spending increased, aggregate demand again would be increased. One may now ask: What difference does it make whether a budget deficit (or, in the opposite case, a budget surplus) is achieved by changing tax rates or spending volume, as long as it is achieved? The answer is, quite a bit. If a tax cut is used, private individuals determine how the additional funds will be spent, whereas additional government spending would necessarily be for governmentally determined purposes. Viewed from a "free-enterprise" perspective, the tax cut is more conservative, since it involves less direct intervention by government in the economy. It will thus probably be more acceptable to economic conservatives, although some still may oppose it because the resulting deficit would violate their concept of "sound" public finance. Those who see a need for more government spending for public works and facilities will be inclined to favor the increased spending route. Ideological differences may therefore lead to conflict here.

Budget surpluses and deficits come in two major varieties: those in the actual budget and those in the full-employment budget. Some actual budget surpluses and deficits are reported in table 2–3. The reader will note that deficits tend to be the

**TABLE 2-3**  National budget receipts
and outlays for selected years, 1901–1981
(in millions of dollars)

| Fiscal year | Receipts | Outlays | Surplus or deficit |
|---|---|---|---|
| 1901 | 588 | 525 | +63 |
| 1905 | 544 | 567 | −23 |
| 1910 | 676 | 694 | −18 |
| 1915 | 683 | 746 | −63 |
| 1920 | 6,649 | 6,358 | +291 |
| 1925 | 3,641 | 2,924 | +717 |
| 1930 | 4,058 | 3,320 | +738 |
| 1935 | 3,706 | 6,497 | −2,791 |
| 1940 | 6,361 | 9,456 | −3,095 |
| 1945 | 45,216 | 92,690 | −47,474 |
| 1950 | 39,485 | 42,597 | −3,112 |
| 1955 | 65,469 | 68,509 | −3,041 |
| 1960 | 92,492 | 92,223 | +269 |
| 1965 | 116,833 | 111,430 | −1,596 |
| 1966 | 130,856 | 134,652 | −3,796 |
| 1967 | 149,552 | 158,254 | −8,702 |
| 1968 | 153,671 | 178,833 | −25,161 |
| 1969 | 187,784 | 184,548 | +3,236 |
| 1970 | 193,743 | 196,588 | −2,845 |
| 1971 | 188,392 | 211,425 | −23,033 |
| 1972 | 208,649 | 231,876 | −23,227 |
| 1973 | 232,225 | 246,526 | −14,301 |
| 1974 | 264,932 | 268,392 | −3,604 |
| 1975 | 280,997 | 324,601 | −43,604 |
| 1976 | 300,005 | 366,418 | −66,413 |
| 1977 | 357,762 | 402,710 | −44,948 |
| 1978 | 401,997 | 450,804 | −48,801 |
| 1979 | 465,940 | 493,635 | −27,694 |
| 1980 | 520,050 | 579,613 | −59,563 |
| 1981 | 599,272 | 657,204 | −57,932 |
| 1982[a] | 626,753 | 725,331 | −98,578 |
| 1983[a] | 666,118 | 757,638 | −91,520 |

SOURCE: Office of Management and Budget, *Federal Budget in Brief* (Washington, D.C.: Government Printing Office, 1982, and earlier years).

[a]Estimated figures for 1982–1983.

rule and that in recent years their size has been increasing. The concept of the full-employment budget has been used by economists to gauge the impact of fiscal policy on the economy. According to some, this "budget" calculates what the budget surplus or deficit would be, given existing taxing and spending programs, if the economy were operating at a full-employment level (e.g., with 4 percent unemployment). It controls for the effect of economic conditions—inflation or recession—on budget levels. Thus, a budget deficit would not indicate an expansionary fiscal policy if it resulted from low tax receipts caused by a depressed economy rather than a deliberate decision to cut taxes. During the early 1960s the national budget was persistently in deficit; however, had the economy been operating at a full-employment level, there would have been substantial surpluses. Thus, according to the full-employment budget concept, fiscal policy in the early 1960s was actually deflationary, notwithstanding the deficits in the actual budget. The Nixon administration argued in 1971 that the budget deficit of $23 billion was not inflationary because, had the economy been operating at a full-employment level, there would have been a budget surplus.

At the urging of the Kennedy-Johnson administration, Congress passed the Revenue Act of 1964 to stimulate aggregate demand by cutting taxes, thereby creating more jobs and economic growth. The act provided for a $14 billion cut in personal and corporate income taxes over a two-year period. It was designed to overcome the deflationary or restrictive impact of the federal budget on the economy, as measured by the full-employment budget concept; and it did in fact contribute to increased employment and economic expansion. This was the first time that a tax cut had been deliberately used to stimulate the economy. Tax reductions had helped to mitigate recessions in 1948–1949 and 1953–1954; however, these actions were not planned for fiscal policy purposes (but simply to reduce taxes) and their timing was essentially accidental. From this, one can conclude that luck is sometimes a factor that can contribute to economic stabilization.

Since 1964 tax cuts have been used in a few more instances—1965, 1971, 1977, and 1981—to stimulate the economy. In 1968 a tax increase was imposed to restrain inflationary pressures, while in 1982 taxes were increased to reduce prospective budget deficits. Thus, taxes have become basic instruments of national economic policy, designed to alter the course of economic activity or to keep it on a desired course from which it might otherwise depart.

### Automatic Stabilizers

The fiscal and monetary instruments discussed thus far are discretionary in nature; that is, public officials must make decisions to utilize them in chosen ways in particular situations. Given the political pressures and the conflicting policy viewpoints that help shape the actions of officials, decisions to take action may be difficult to secure. In such situations, some automatic stabilizing devices—which have been built, unintentionally or intentionally, into the economy—may help stabilize the economy without positive action by government decision makers. The federal personal and corporate income taxes and Social Security taxes have automatic stabilizing effects. Without any changes in their rates, they bring in more revenue when national income rises and less revenue when national income falls. Moreover, as is well known, personal income tax rates are graduated (ranging from 14 to 50 percent) and consequently rise faster in proportion than does income; conversely, they fall faster than income when the latter declines. With respect to government spending, Social Security, unemployment compensation, and agricultural price supports have tended to increase in times of recession and to decrease in prosperous times. Thus, with growing unemployment in the 1970s, unemployment compensation payments increased from $3.4 billion in 1970 to $19 billion in 1976. This occurred automatically as unemployed workers drew the benefits to which they were entitled under the law. In general, for every dollar the GNP declines in a business cycle, there is about a 30-cent increase in the budget deficit, which helps limit the decline.[13]

The automatic stabilizers played an especially important role in controlling the recession of 1957–1958. While some argued for a vigorous program of government deficit spending to counteract the recession (by adding to aggregate demand), the Eisenhower administration was reluctant to engage in deficit spending and, further, was afraid that such spending would contribute to inflation. A balanced budget for fiscal year 1959 was sent to Congress. However, there was an actual deficit of $12.8 billion in the 1959 budget. This deficit resulted mostly from the automatic drop in tax revenues and the increase in Social Security and unemployment compensation payments caused by declining income. (Stepped-up spending under authorized programs and an expansionary monetary policy also helped alleviate the recession.) The automatic stabilizers clearly contributed to keeping the recession milder than had been predicted by many economists.

Economists generally agree that the automatic stabilizers by themselves are not adequate to maintain full stability. They mitigate but do not eliminate upward and downward fluctuations in the economy. Unemployment compensation benefits, for example, do not fully compensate for the loss of consumer spending caused by unemployment. Thus, automatic stabilizers, although helpful, are not widely regarded as a substitute for effective discretionary action controlling economic fluctuations.

### Wage-Price Guidelines

In the early 1960s, to counteract inflation, the Kennedy administration developed a set of wage-price guidelines. These guidelines specified that wage increases should be held to the long-run growth in annual average labor productivity. The guideline for wage increases was eventually set at 3.2 percent. Under the guidelines prices could increase in industries where productivity did not increase as fast as wages; in industries where productivity increased faster than wages, prices should fall.

These guidelines were "informal" in that they had no explicit legal base or force. They were implemented through "jawboning" (verbal persuasion and exhortation) and informal pressures. Perhaps the most dramatic and successful use of jawboning occurred in 1962, when the Kennedy administration caused the major steel companies to rescind an announced price increase which the administration considered inflationary.[14] As inflationary pressures built up in the 1960s, the guideposts were increasingly challenged, and after 1967 the 3.2 percent wage increase guideline was abandoned. The Johnson administration, however, did continue jawboning—for instance, against price increases in the aluminum and copper industries. In 1969 the guidelines were officially jettisoned by the Nixon administration. President Nixon vigorously declared his opposition to such interference with the private economy. (He later instituted a system of direct controls.) President Jimmy Carter also initially indicated an intention to avoid such intervention; however, in 1978 he changed his mind and put into effect voluntary wage and price guidelines. They were quickly terminated by the Reagan administration when it took office.

Economists disagree about the role that the guidelines played in restraining inflation in the 1960s.[15] Gordon's conclusion, however, seems reasonable: "Perhaps it is not far from the truth to say that the guidelines helped create an environment favorable to wage restraint but that the chief factors at work were the absence of inflationary expectations and a continued high level of unemployment."[16] When these conditions changed, the guidelines began to falter.

### Direct Controls

Direct controls over prices and wages differ from guidelines in that they are mandatory in nature. Various kinds of direct controls were imposed on the economy during World War I, World War II, and the Korean War to restrain inflation. Controls were most extensive during World War II, extending to wages, rents, and wholesale and retail prices. For older Americans, the Office of Price Administration (OPA) symbolizes price controls and rationing. The World War II controls were quite effective in holding down prices; the consumer price index rose only 5 points between April 1943 and June 1946, when most of the controls were eliminated. Between June and November 1946, the cost of living rose 14 points before leveling off.

Direct controls usually lack popularity with many groups—for instance, those whose activities are being restrained, political conservatives who dislike the exercise of governmental power involved, and economists who prefer free (i.e., unregulated) markets. In its 1968 report the Council of Economic Advisers expressed opposition to controls in these terms: "Mandatory controls on prices and wages ... distort resource allocation; they require reliance either on necessarily clumsy and arbitrary rules or the inevitably imperfect decisions of Government officials; they offer countless temptations to evasions or violation; they require a vast administrative apparatus. All these reasons make them repugnant."[17]

The sweeping program of direct controls the Nixon administration imposed on the economy in August 1971 were unprecedented in peacetime. These controls, which were part of the administration's New Economic Policy, and which came as a surprise to most Americans, will be discussed in a later portion of this chapter.

## LIMITATIONS OF POLICY INSTRUMENTS

It is generally agreed that the fiscal, monetary, and other instruments discussed in the preceding section can go far in controlling fluctuations in the business cycle and in encouraging economic growth. Nonetheless, they are not without short-comings of an economic nature. These shortcomings must be taken into account by policymakers in devising solutions for instability problems, since they will affect the impact of policy actions.

A major problem in the formation and implementation of economic stability policy is the difficulty in accurately analyzing and predicting trends in the economy. If stability policy is to be most effective, it must be geared to what is going to happen rather than what has already happened. Although the tools of economic analysis have been greatly improved, economic analysis is still less than an exact science; precise indicators of the flow of national income are still lacking.[18] This is the result of such factors as the complexity of our economic system and shortcom-ings in statistical data. Some sectors or industries in the economy may be prosper-ing while others are in stagnation or decline. Relationships between elements in the economy (for instance, between the levels of consumer income and spending) may be changing. Some economic data may be available only at quarterly, yearly, or longer intervals. Several months may elapse before analysts can say with certainty that a boom has ended or that recovery is under way. While proper choice and timing of stability policies are necessary if they are to be most effective, such decisions must be made on less than full information, thereby leaving room for error. Too, in the absence of clear-cut indicators of future trends in the economy, there is a tendency on the part of officials to "wait and see," to let matters work themselves out. Uncertainty may encourage inaction here as it often does elsewhere.

A related problem is limited knowledge of the full impact of particular policies. No one knows, for example, how much stabilizing action results from the operation of the automatic stabilizers; therefore, it is difficult to know when to use discretion-ary stability policies and to what extent. Nor can anyone say with certainty what effect a given fiscal or monetary action will have on, say, consumer spending. Problems of this sort are most important when concern is with moderate economic fluctuations. In the event of severe recession or inflation, there is less immediate need to be precise in the timing and degree of stabilizing action. What is most needed is strong counteraction until a measure of stability has been achieved.

Both fiscal and monetary policies are inadequate for dealing with cost-push infla-tion. In such a situation prices and wages rise because powerful corporations and unions push them upward. Fiscal and monetary policies, as we have seen, work by producing changes in aggregate demand. However, administered prices and wages may move upward even when supply exceeds demand; or when demand is falling, as was the case with steel prices in the 1950s. To control inflation caused by admin-istered prices (called a price-wage spiral) might require fiscal and monetary actions so restrictive as to touch off a recessionary movement before they affected the groups pushing up prices or wages. In this case, fiscal and monetary policies are too blunt in their impact to be effective. Other courses of action are possible, such as the use of wage and price guidelines by the Kennedy and Johnson administrations in the 1960s. Moreover, the power of corporations to administer prices may reduce the effectiveness of fiscal policy in combating economic decline. During the Great Depression some of the impact of New Deal deficit spending, especially in the later 1930s, was siphoned off into price increases rather than additional employment.

Another dilemma confronted by policymakers is that of the inflation-unemployment trade-off (the Phillips Curve; see figure 2-1). Some economic studies have confirmed the existence of an inverse relationship between inflation and unemployment—so that, for instance, if fiscal and monetary policies are used to reduce unemployment to low levels, one of the costs is likely to be inflation. In Western European countries, where unemployment rates are lower than in the United States, rates of inflation have been higher. Conversely, policy can be used to hold down inflation, but with the consequence of more unemployment. This relationship between unemployment and inflation is shaped by such factors as the structure of the economy, the composition of the labor force, and public policies. It does not seem to be amenable to alteration by fiscal and monetary actions.[19] Policymakers, in their use of fiscal and monetary policy, have the task of trying to achieve an optimum (and politically acceptable) balance between inflation and unemployment. Although recent experience and research have cast doubt on whether the economy is bound to a single Phillips Curve, the concept is still useful as a statement of the basic unemployment-inflation dilemma.

It is useful to keep in mind that stability policy, like all economic policy, is concerned with influencing human behavior. Economic theory holds in effect that, other things being equal, people will be influenced in borrowing and investing by the rate of interest. Among the "other things," however, are the psychological

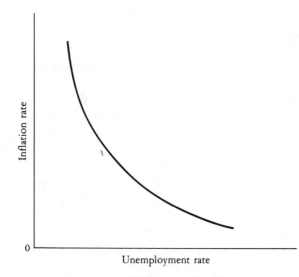

Figure 2-1    Phillips Curve (hypothetical).

attitudes and expectations of people (and these are not always "equal"). If these attitudes and expectations include a pessimistic evaluation of the economic future, they may well outweigh such material factors as lower interest rates in individual decision making. The restraining effect of the 1968 tax increase, sought by the Johnson administration to combat inflation, seems to have been limited by the fact that it was temporary in nature, while consumers geared their spending to long-range income expectations (which, of course, did not include higher taxes). The result was that consumers reduced savings and continued to spend almost as if taxes had not been increased. In economic activity, as elsewhere in social life, individuals do make a difference, and they do not always act in accordance with the precepts of economic theory.

The use of monetary policy to combat inflation may also have some undesired effects. Restrictions on credit may bear down more heavily on small businesses than on large businesses. When the FRB tightens credit, commercial banks are apt to restrict credit first to small businesses because of the larger amount of risk in such lending. Further, large corporations may meet their financial needs out of retained earnings and depreciation reserves; or they may have access to such sources of credit as insurance companies, pension trusts, and investment banks, which are beyond the reach of the FRB. Monetary policy, in its actual impact, is somewhat less impartial than its proponents sometimes contend. The housing construction industry seems to be especially sensitive to restrictions of the money supply.

The use of the budget for fiscal policy purposes is both restricted and made difficult because it is also used to finance the government's various foreign, military, and domestic policies and programs, and because the budgetary process is a highly political process. Nonetheless the budget is still a vital stabilization instrument. The process by which the national budget is formed and executed is sketched out in the following section.

## THE BUDGETARY PROCESS

The federal budget is several things at once: a financial statement; an expression of the policy preferences of an administration; a means for executive control of the departments and agencies; and an instrument of fiscal policy. It is the last aspect of the budget, and the budgetary process, that is of special interest to us here.

Submitted to Congress by the president in January of each year, the budget runs for a single fiscal year, extending from October 1 of the year in which it is submitted through September 30 of the following year. It takes its name (e.g., fiscal year 1982) from the calendar year in which it ends. Although the budget is for a twelve-month period, the total budgetary process, from the time work begins on the budget in the executive branch until the end of the fiscal year, covers a span of approximately thirty months.

The national budgetary process can be divided into four stages.

1. *Preparation of the budget.* This is handled by the executive branch under the direction of the president and the Office of Management and Budget.

2. *Authorization of the budget.* This is the responsibility of Congress. The Constitution provides that "no money shall be drawn from the Treasury, except in consequence of appropriations made by law."
3. *Execution of the budget.* This stage involves the actual expenditure by the departments and agencies of appropriated funds.
4. *The audit.* This activity is performed by General Accounting Office, which is an "arm" of Congress.

### Preparation of the Budget

Work on the budget in the executive branch begins in March of the year preceding the time it is submitted to Congress. At this time the agencies begin reviewing their operations and program objectives and make projections as to their budgetary needs. By May or June the president, with the aid of the Office of Management and Budget (OMB), makes decisions on general budget policy (including fiscal policy considerations), major program issues, and budgetary planning targets. By the end of June tentative budget ceilings are formulated and transmitted to the agencies by the OMB, along with a call for agency budget estimates and policy letter setting forth the president's decisions on governmentwide policies and assumptions. Guided by the tentative ceilings, the agencies develop their budget estimates, which are submitted to the OMB by the middle of September. From then until the end of November agency requests are reviewed by OMB examiners and hearings are held at which agency officials are called on to explain and justify their funding requests, which may exceed the tentative ceilings. On the basis of these reviews and hearings, recommendations are made to the director of the OMB, for approval or modification. Agencies dissatisfied with OMB decisions on their budget requests may appeal them to the president, although they are not very likely to be successful. Indeed, the president may make further reductions in requests when he reviews the OMB recommendations. In December and early January the budget is put in final shape, fiscal policy issues are given final consideration, the budget message is prepared, and in the middle of January, the budget is officially submitted to Congress for its consideration. This time schedule, it should be noted, is approximate; it may vary somewhat from year to year. Nonetheless, budget preparation is both systematic and extensive in nature, and it also attempts to predict the future.

The ability of the president and top-level executive officials in making budget decisions is limited by the fact that around three-fourths of expenditures are "uncontrollable," at least in the short run, in that they represent continuing obligations and commitments. Illustrative are entitlement programs (such as, Social Security, Medicare, and veterans' pensions), grant-in-aid payments to the states, and interest on the national debt. A large proportion of the funds that are controllable fall in the area of national defense where major budget changes, especially in the form of reductions, are unlikely to occur. Because of factors such as these, even when the budget totals over $700 billion, the executive will have to struggle to secure reductions. (The Reagan administration's efforts to reduce the budget will be discussed in a later section.) The pressures for increased spending to improve programs, to meet new needs, are ever-present. Budget reductions do not come easily as a consequence.

## Congressional Authorization of the Budget

Until a few years ago, the budgetary process in Congress was rather chaotic and fragmented in nature. For purposes of legislative enactment the president's budget was broken up into a dozen or so separate appropriations. These were considered in committee and passed individually with little concern for the overall size and shape of the budget. Budget surpluses or deficits (much more likely) were "accidental figures" resulting from the sum of the various appropriations bills. Fiscal policy considerations had little direct impact on congressional budgetary action.

The Congressional Budget and Impoundment Control Act of 1974, which was brought about by such factors as dissatisfaction with the way Congress was handling the budget and conflict between Congress and the Nixon administration over the impoundment of appropriations, was intended to make substantial changes in the congressional budgetary process.[20] In the words of the statute:

> The Congress declares that it is essential: to assure effective Congressional control over the budgetary process; to provide for the Congressional determination each year of the appropriate level of federal revenues and expenditures; to provide a system of impoundment control; to establish national budget priorities; and to provide for the furnishing of information by the Executive Branch in a manner that will assist the Congress in discharging its duties.

To accomplish these goals the act did several things: First, budget committees were established in the House and the Senate. They have the task of determining priorities and overall limits on spending and needed increases or decreases in revenues. Second, a congressional budget office was created to appraise the state of the economy and its impact on the budget, to improve the quality and availability of budgetary information, and to analyze the costs and effects of alternative government programs. Next, a timetable for congressional budget action was established (see table 2–4) and the fiscal year was changed from July 1 to June 30 to October 1 to September 30 to give Congress more time to work on the budget. Lastly, procedures to control presidential impoundment of funds were provided, which will be discussed in the next section.

We will focus here on a few aspects of congressional action on the budget under the new procedure. On the basis of such data as the current services budget (that is, what would be required to fund existing programs at their current levels for another year), the president's budget, and congressional committee recommendations of appropriations needs, the budget committees develop a budget resolution (to be adopted by May 15), which sets targets for appropriations for various functional areas (e.g., foreign aid, agriculture), total spending, and revenues. This is followed by action on the appropriations bills, which includes hearings, consideration, and mark-up by the appropriations committees. Congress is supposed to complete action on all appropriations and revenue bills on or before September 15, at which

**TABLE 2–4  Budget authorization timetable**

| Action to be taken | Date |
|---|---|
| Current services budget submitted to Congress by president | November 10 |
| President submits annual budget to Congress | Middle of January |
| Congressional committees make budget recommendations to budget committee | March 15 |
| Budget committees report first budget resolution | April 15 |
| Congress adopts first budget resolution | May 15 |
| Congressional committees report all authorizing legislation | May 15 |
| Congress begins floor action on all spending and tax bills | After first budget resolution |
| Congress completes action on all spending and tax bills | 7 days after Labor Day |
| Congress adopts second budget resolution | September 15 |
| Congress passes budget reconciliation bill | September 25 |
| Fiscal year begins | October 1 |

time a second budget resolution must be adopted to either affirm or revise the targets set in the first resolution. If the spending targets have been exceeded or estimated revenues are inadequate, a reconciliation bill may be needed. This reconciliation bill, put together by the budget committees, can revise appropriations, change expenditure authorizations, raise or lower revenue, or some combination of these in order to ensure conformity with the ceilings set in the second budget resolution. (The use of the reconciliation process in 1981 by the Reagan administration will be discussed in the section on the Reagan economic program.) The reconciliation bill should be adopted and sent to the president by September 25.

All action on the budget is intended to be completed by October 1 when the fiscal year begins. However, Congress has had difficulty in following the new budget timetable. Indeed, fiscal years 1981 and 1982 began before final action had been completed on *any* of the thirteen annual appropriations bills. Continuing resolutions were required to enable agencies to continue operating until their appropriations were enacted.

Budget decisions still tend to be incremental in nature. In other words, appropriations for most agencies and programs for a given year tend to differ only marginally, whether up or down, from those of previous years. Moreover, Congress is most concerned usually with how an agency's budget request in one year differs from the previous year. Drastic changes in agencies' budgets are not unknown, but they are not especially frequent.

## Execution of the Budget

The departments and agencies are not free to begin spending as they see fit, within the framework of appropriations legislation, once congressional action is completed. If an agency's original budget differs from the appropriation legislation, the agency's budget must be revised accordingly. Then the agency must seek an apportionment from the OMB, which is an authorization to expend funds at a specified rate (for example, a certain percentage of the agency's appropriation may be spent during each quarter of the fiscal year). This is intended to prevent the agency from running out of funds before the end of the fiscal year. Also, the OMB may require agencies to set aside funds for contingencies or not to expend some funds when changes in needs or increased efficiency permit savings to be effected without detracting from the accomplishment of agency purposes.

The amount of discretion that agency officials have in the expenditure of funds is certainly affected by the nature of appropriations legislation. The more detailed it is, the less leeway agencies have. On the other hand, Congress sometimes provides agencies with "lump sum" or very broad appropriations, as a way of conferring discretionary powers. Clearly, effective management requires some administrative discretion in the expenditure of funds.

Much controversy has been generated by presidential impoundment of funds appropriated by Congress. Presidents have long claimed discretionary authority to prevent the spending of funds for purposes they disagreed with on budgetary or policy grounds. In recent decades, for example, various presidents refused to spend funds for military programs of which they did not approve. Impoundment was usually done on a selective and limited basis; while Congress grumbled, major confrontations were usually avoided.

Following his reelection in 1972, however, President Nixon engaged in the extensive impoundment of funds for such programs as water pollution control, mass transit, food stamps, medical research, urban renewal, and highway construction. Various justifications were given including that impoundment was required to prevent the inflationary effects of "reckless" spending.

One outgrowth of the controversy generated by the administration's actions was the inclusion of controls on impoundment in the 1974 budget reform act. The act provides that a *deferral* of expenditures, in which the executive seeks to delay or defer the spending of funds until a future date when they will be needed, may be imposed unless either house of Congress passes a resolution of disapproval. Then the funds must be released at once. A *rescission* of spending, in contrast, cancels existing budget authority and thus eliminates the expenditure of funds for some purpose. Rescissions become effective only if, within forty-five days of the receipt of a presidential request, both houses of Congress pass a rescission bill. It is, in practice, not always easy to distinguish rescissions and deferrals. The effect of the new impoundment procedures is to give Congress more formal control over budget execution.

President Ford sought to make considerable use of budget deferrals and rescissions in his efforts to hold down government spending. During fiscal years 1975 and 1976 the Ford administration proposed rescissions totaling over $7.5 billion; Congress enacted rescission bills amounting only to approximately $530 million. Most deferrals were not challenged as they involved routine financial transactions. However, thirty-eight deferrals totaling almost $10 billion were disapproved by resolutions. Congress was especially inclined to be negative when policy impoundments were involved; that is, when the president sought to cut appropriations that exceeded his budget requests.[21]

## The Audit

Auditing of agency operations is intended to ensure that agencies, in the obligation and expenditure of funds, follow the provisions of authorization and expenditure legislation. The General Accounting Office (GAO) has the primary responsibility for auditing. The GAO is headed by the comptroller general, who is appointed by the president with the consent of the Senate for a fifteen-year term and can be removed from office only by a joint resolution of Congress. These appointment and removal provisions are intended to make the GAO independent of the executive branch.

In recent years the activities of the GAO have been expanded considerably beyond the traditional focus on the legality of expenditures. Now the GAO is also concerned with the efficiency of expenditures and with policy evaluation activities. The latter concerns often lead to the release of GAO reports with titles such as "The Voluntary Pay and Price Standards Have Had No Discernible Effect on Inflation."[22] (This 1980 report dealt with the voluntary standards developed and administered by the Council of Wage and Price Stability during the Carter administration.) The GAO also has responsibility for monitoring executive compliance with the rescission and deferral procedures under the 1974 budget reform legislation.

## The Budget and Public Policy

The budget is, among other things, a statement of the various policies that will be pursued by the government during the budget year (and beyond, because funds obligated in one year may not be actually paid out until later years). The budget has been aptly described as "a compilation of public policy decisions of great complexity and of far-reaching effect upon the national welfare in terms of total outlay, in terms of the . . . allocation of that outlay among various activities, and in terms of the amount available for any one particular endeavor."[23] Of course, the importance of public policies can not be measured solely by the number of dollars expended in their support. However, the nature, effectiveness, and impact of public policies do depend greatly upon the amount of funds appropriated to carry them into effect. This is so whether one is speaking about food stamps, public housing construction, antitrust enforcement, foreign aid, or synthetic fuel development.

The budget, as we have noted, is also an important instrument of fiscal policy. However, the budget is only partially subject to control by fiscal policymakers on the basis of their preferences. Most expenditures are based on past or continuing commitments and cannot easily be modified. Moreover, notions concerning what is necessary or desirable in domestic or defense policies may conflict with the needs of optimal fiscal policy. Expenditures, in short, cannot be simply raised or lowered for fiscal policy purposes. Beyond this, fiscal policy decisions involving expenditures do not go into effect at the time fiscal policy *decisions* are made. Fiscal policy decisions incorporated into the budget the president submits in January of one year may not be reflected in actual budget behavior until ten to twenty months later during the fiscal year for which it was proposed. By then the economic conditions with which the budget was to deal may have changed considerably. Add to such considerations the difficulties in accurately predicting future levels of expenditures, revenues, and GNP, and one can see that the budget is an imperfect albeit necessary instrument of fiscal policy.[24]

## POLITICS AND STABILITY POLICY

The formation and implementation of stability policy are not merely "technical" tasks performed in a vacuum, although policy experts and economic analysis seem more influential here than in most areas of public policy. Rather, these tasks occur in a highly political environment populated with individuals and groups, official and private, having conflicting values, interests, and expectations concerning the content of policy. Conflict and struggle take place over what instruments to use, to what extent, and at what time. Is there a need for positive action? Should monetary or fiscal policy be stressed? Should a budget deficit be obtained by increasing spending or cutting taxes? What is an acceptable level of unemployment? Of inflation? These are only some of the questions that may arise. What is done in the way of policy action will be affected by the structure of the governmental system, political processes, and political behavior.

### Differences in Policy Systems

To begin with, we should note that fiscal policy and monetary policy are developed within two very different and distinct policy systems. Fiscal policy formation involves the president, Congress, a variety of administrative agencies, pressure groups, the news media, and public opinion, and typically occurs in the macropolitical arena. Monetary policy formation, in contrast, is handled primarily by the FRB, acting in response to whatever pressures or influences its members may feel. Whereas fiscal policy formation is characterized by partisan conflict and the need to mobilize legislative majorities, monetary policy formation, given the independence of the board, takes the form of administrative decision making, largely out of sight of the public. As a result, monetary policy actions typically can be taken much more quickly than fiscal policy actions. One consequence of the existence of these two policy systems is the possibility that their actions may come into conflict. Thus, the restraining effect of the Johnson administration's 1968 tax increase was partially offset by an FRB decision to expand the money supply because of its concern about an economic downturn. Usually, however, the FRB works in reasonably close harmony with the administration in office. It is "independent in but not of the government."

### Fiscal Policy: President and Congress

In the fiscal policy arena, authority over taxation and expenditures is divided between the president and Congress. The traditional rivalry between the two branches is here intensified by the zealousness of Congress in protecting its financial powers against "executive encroachment," particularly when the executive is from a different party than the majority party in Congress. Even when the majority and the president are of the same party, Congress is eager to maintain their powers over taxation. For example, acting on the assumption that if taxation and expenditures were to be most effective for countercyclical purposes, considerable flexibility in their use would be required, a proposal was made by President Kennedy that the executive be given authority "to make temporary countercyclical adjustments in the first bracket rate of the personal income tax." This proposal, which would have required Congress to yield some of its authority over taxes, was never seriously considered by the Democratic-controlled Congress. While the development of the executive budget has strengthened the ability of the president to plan expenditures for stabilization purposes, the need to gain congressional approval remains.

One consequence of congressional consideration of fiscal policy proposals is delay. More than a year elapsed before the tax cut proposed by President Kennedy was enacted into law as the Revenue Act of 1964. And, as we will see, it took even longer for President Johnson to get a tax increase through Congress. Another consequence of congressional consideration is that the influence of group and sectional pressures, operating through Congress, will be fully felt on stability proposals. Here it should be noted that every fiscal policy proposal, because it involves taxes or expenditures, will have other policy implications. It will affect not only the overall operation of the economy but also the interests and welfare of particular groups and individuals. They can normally be counted upon to resist changes in taxes and expenditures which they consider adverse to their interests, and they are especially likely to consider increased taxes or reduced expenditures in that light.

In general, group pressures and existing policy commitments make it more difficult to counteract inflation than recession. Since Congress finds it easier to spend than to tax, fiscal policy has generally had an inflationary bias. Also, it is difficult to reduce expenditures because a large portion of the national budget outlay is "uncontrollable" (at least in the short run) in that it is required under existing law or represents contractual obligations of the government. On this basis, approximately 75 percent of national expenditures for fiscal years 1980 and 1981 fell in the uncontrollable category. Most "controllable" expenditures are in the area of national defense. But let's assume that taxes are going to be cut, which is usually popular. There remains the question of *whose* taxes are going to be reduced—those of individuals or businesses, or high-income or low-income groups? Or, if expenditures are to be increased, how will they be used? For military, welfare, or general government spending? For public works or for business expansion programs? In any case, various groups and interests will struggle for preferment. Congressional action on stability measures will reflect compromises and adjustments of the demands of conflicting group, sectional, and local interests as well as the requirements of stability policy as such.

## Political Parties

The general policy orientations of the political parties also have importance for stability policy. Though it is often said that the parties differ little on policy matters, there is significant evidence to the contrary. In the stability policy area the parties manifest the following tendencies. Republicans are traditionally more concerned with preventing inflation and maintaining a "sound dollar." They favor the use of monetary policy over fiscal policy, customarily oppose the use of direct controls, and express much affection for a balanced budget. Democrats have been more concerned with combating recession and stagnation and with maintaining a high level of employment. They favor the use of fiscal policy over monetary policy, display more support for direct controls and less support for a balanced budget, want stronger presidential control of the FRB, and have more enthusiasm for job creation programs. These tendencies (they are not, it must be emphasized, hard and fast differences) have been manifested in the policy behavior of the various Republican and Democratic administrations during the past two decades.

## Budget Concerns

Although balanced budgets have been a rarity in recent years, concern over balanced budgets has still acted as a restraint on fiscal policy. Despite the general acceptance of Keynesian economics and much experience with unbalanced budgets, there is still substantial public and official sentiment for a balanced budget. To conservatives in both political parties, budget deficits symbolize greater government intervention in the economy. Moreover, the belief persists that governments, like families, cannot wisely spend beyond their means. Both Presidents Kennedy and Johnson found it necessary to agree to hold down government spending in order to secure tax legislation from Congress. In the mid 1970s, in order to restrict the size of current budget deficits and move toward a future balanced budget, the Ford administration sought to hold government spending below the levels recommended by various experts as necessary to combat high unemployment; and President Carter stated that he expected to have the budget in balance by the end of his first term. Carter soon began to waiver on this, however, and never achieved his goal.

## The Politics of Advice

The formulation of fiscal policy proposals rests mainly with the executive branch and, ultimately, with the president. In formulating these proposals, presidents can and do draw upon various sources of advice: executive branch departments and agencies, presidential staff agencies, personal advisers in the White House, some members of Congress, and private economists from the academic and business realms. There exists, then, what can be called "politics of advice," because these sources may provide differing and conflicting recommendations and struggle to secure their acceptance by the chief executive. To illustrate, we can note that different agencies have "institutional biases," which shape their recommendations. Thus, the Treasury and Commerce Departments tend to be especially concerned with price stability and a favorable balance of payments; the Department of Labor favors low unemployment and economic growth; and the Office of Management and Budget wants to hold down spending. During the Kennedy and Johnson administrations the Council of Economic Advisers was most concerned about economic growth and unemployment and urged an activist fiscal policy. Under the Nixon and Ford administrations, however, the council became less activist and more concerned about inflation. In the last couple of decades the council has been very influential in fiscal policy formation, partly because of its competence, partly because it has no organizational loyalty except to the president, and partly because it has been willing to tailor its advice to the president's philosophy and policy goals.

Conflict among economists and economic advisers, however, is based on more than institutional biases or loyalties. There are also ideological and doctrinal differences that divide them. A familiar division is between liberals and conservatives. Liberals tend to be more supportive of government intervention, fiscal policy, and efforts to combat unemployment, whereas conservatives are more likely to advocate the use of monetary policy and anti-inflationary programs. A somewhat different division exists within the economic profession between the New Economists (who are essentially Keynesians) and the monetarists. The New Economists believe in the use of discretionary fiscal, and monetary, policy to stabilize the economy. The monetarists, who take their lead from Milton Friedman of the University of Chicago, contend that a moderate and steady growth in the money supply would solve the problems of both inflation and unemployment while providing the basis for economic expansion. They point to recent experience as proof that discretionary fiscal and monetary policies are not adequate to the task. Although these characterizations oversimplify the differences between liberals and conservatives, New Economists and monetarists, they reveal that economics is not an exact science and that the sort of advice one gets from an economist on stabilizing the economy will depend partly upon ideological and doctrinal perspectives.

## STABILIZING THE ECONOMY: 1966–1981

In this section some of the efforts by five presidential administrations to stabilize the economy are surveyed. The discussion is intended to provide a better understanding of the problems involved in stabilizing the economy and the use of the policy instruments examined earlier.

### The Johnson Administration and Tax Increase

The 1960s were characterized by sustained economic expansion, which began in 1961 and which, stimulated partly by the 1964 tax cut, continued until the end of the decade. By 1966 unemployment had declined below the 4 percent level widely accepted as a standard of full employment. As the Johnson administration became more deeply committed to the Vietnam War, military spending began to rise and to create inflationary pressures on the economy. The Council of Economic Advisers recommended a tax increase in 1966 to restrain the economy, but President Johnson was not then politically prepared to seek a tax increase from Congress. He later argued that he could not have secured action on such a recommendation. In a speech to the Business Council in late 1968 he stated: "We knew we needed action on taxes in 1966. Many of you in this room will remember what happened when, in the month of March 1966, I asked how much support you would give me. Not a hand went up. And I was told that I could get but four votes in the Tax Committee [House Ways and Means] of the Congress out of 25."[25]

By the summer of 1967, as spending on the Vietnam War continued to intensify inflationary pressures, the president felt compelled to seek a tax increase. In a special message sent to Congress on August 3, 1967, he requested a 10 percent surcharge on personal and corporate income taxes and the continuation of some excise taxes. Without a tax increase, the president stated, the large deficit projected in the national budget would touch off "ruinous inflation." Tax cut legislation of the sort recommended was not passed by Congress until June 1968, and only then after the president agreed to a reduction of $6 billion in government expenditures at the insistence of Rep. Wilbur Mills (D.–Ark.), chairman of the House Ways and Means Committee. This was the price exacted by Mills, who had the support of most of his committee, for reporting the legislation out of his committee and working for its enactment. Most observers agree that the tax increase came too late to have been most effective. Inflation was under way, and it was to plague the economy through the next decade.

Several factors seem to have contributed to the difficulties of the Johnson administration in getting the tax increase adopted. Tax increases are never popular with the public. This one was made more unpopular because many people viewed it as necessitated by the administration's Vietnam policy, which was coming under increasing criticism. Many members of Congress could not see why expenditure reductions would not work as well as a tax increase to restrain the economy. Moreover, within Congress there was not full acceptance of the use of fiscal policy to stabilize the economy. Finally, in 1966 and early in 1967 the "evils" that a tax increase was designed to combat "were forecasts rather than facts."[26] To be most effective, stability policy must be anticipatory; action must be taken *before* a recession or inflation gets under way. To many, however, the economy *seemed* to be operating satisfactorily; so why, they asked, should the government take action that might be unnecessary or even disruptive?

## The Nixon Administration and Direct Controls

The Nixon administration came into office determined to quickly suppress the inflation it had inherited from the Johnson administration. Fiscal and monetary restraints were used; these brought the boom of the 1960s to an end and pushed the economy into a recession in late 1969. Even though unemployment rose to the 6 percent level in 1970, prices and wages continued to move upward. In 1971 the Nixon administration shifted to an expansionary fiscal policy to end the recession.

During 1970, as inflation continued, various critics urged the administration to adopt some kind of wage and price controls. Moreover, Congress adopted the Economic Stabilization Act of 1970, which gave the executive branch broad authority to impose price and wage controls to combat inflation. The act was stoutly opposed by the Nixon administration, which contended that it neither wanted nor would use the authority provided. The legislation was passed primarily at the behest of liberal Democrats, who could thus take credit for wanting to do something about inflation and at the same time embarrass the administration.

During the spring and summer of 1971 Nixon administration officials steadily denied any intention to use price and wage controls. Inflation persisted, however, as conventional policy instruments seemed inadequate to bring it under control. On August 15 the president surprised most of the nation with his announcement of his New Economic Policy, which included a ninety-day price-wage freeze. This set off a three-year adventure with direct controls (or what some call an "incomes policy"), the various phases of which will be outlined here.[27]

In Phase I (August 15, 1971 through November 13, 1971), all prices (except for raw agricultural commodities), wages, and rents were frozen. As one would expect, prices and wages rose very little during this time.

In Phase II (November 14, 1971 through January 10, 1973), the freeze was replaced with mandatory price and wage controls, which were administered by a complex administrative structure including a Pay Board and a Price Commission. General guidelines were set: 5.5 percent per year for wage increases and 2.5 percent for price increases. (Profit rates were not subject to control.) Large corporations and unions were subject to more stringent controls than smaller ones, and had to obtain prior approval for price and wage increases. Although the effectiveness or impact of the controls are a matter of controversy, the controls did restrain inflation, especially as measured by the upward movement of the consumer price index. The administration's economic policies, including the controls, also contributed to Nixon's landslide reelection in November 1972.

In Phase III (January 13, 1973 through June 13, 1973), which began a few days after the inauguration of his second term, President Nixon unexpectedly ended most mandatory price and wage controls (excepted were three "troublesome" areas: food prices, health costs, and the construction industry). For most of the economy a system of voluntary guidelines was established. These were backed up by the threat that the government would intervene to roll back price or wage increases considered inflationary. There was considerable talk by administration officials concerning the "club in the closet" which would be used to "clobber" offenders, but little clobbering was done. The lifting of controls unleashed inflationary forces; and prices, especially for food, spiraled upward. Many members of Congress and many economists attacked the administration for abandoning controls, while conservatives generally expressed approval.

Why were mandatory controls abandoned in favor of voluntary controls when the former seemed to be working? A reasonable explanation is offered by Robert Lanzillotti and colleagues:

In retrospect, political considerations appear to have played a more significant role than did pure economic considerations in both the institution of the freeze and the dismantling of the wage-price controls program. Over time, the apparent success of Phase II increasingly became a source of economic embarrassment to administration officials, who had been driven to adopt direct controls out of political pressures but who opposed this approach on ideological grounds as well as from a severe conviction that such measures are inherently counterproductive in efficient economic processes. . . . From an inside perspective . . . it appeared that [with] the presidential elections out of the way, it remained only to prepare a quiet grave for the controls apparatus.[28]

During Phase IV (June 14, 1973 to April 30, 1974), inflation continued to plague the economy. In response to congressional and other pressures for action, on June 13 the president announced a sixty-day freeze on prices. New mandatory controls were developed for prices and wages during the freeze period, and their administration was assigned to the Cost of Living Council, which had been set up during Phase III to replace the Pay Board and the Price Commission. These controls went into effect on August 15. The administration had little enthusiasm for the new controls, however, and in the fall an industry-by-industry decontrol process was started. In the spring of 1974 all controls were ended, except for those on oil prices, which had soared because of the actions of the OPEC cartel (see chapter 3).

In his last months in office, President Nixon returned to action based on his "old-time religion" beliefs and emphasized the need for tight money and budgetary restraint to offset inflation. Along with much of the public, he was disillusioned with direct controls.

### The Ford Administration and Stagflation

At the time Gerald Ford became president, in August 1974, prices were rising at an annual rate of nearly 12 percent. One of his early actions as chief executive was to call a "summit conference" on inflation to consider what could be done. Most of the economists at the conference, which met in late September, concluded that inflation was the prime problem, even though the economy appeared to be facing a recession. In October President Ford called for a tax increase as part of his anti-inflationary program. Spending cuts were also contemplated to reduce the budget deficit. The economy, however, descended into a recession, and by May 1975 unemployment rose to the 9.2 percent level. Inflation continued even though, according to standard economy theory, high unemployment and inflation should not occur together. (The term *stagflation* has been used to describe this condition.) As a consequence of the high unemployment, the administration shifted gears, and in January 1975 the president requested a tax cut to stimulate the economy. Congress responded with a $22.8 billion tax reduction in March.

Confronted with the problem of having to deal simultaneously with high rates of inflation and unemployment, the Ford administration subsequently chose to deal most strongly with inflation while moving more slowly to reduce unemployment. Thus, in early 1976 President Ford called for another tax reduction plus action to hold down government spending. This was a part of his "steady-as-you-go policy," intended to produce moderate economic expansion without touching off inflationary expectations. Under this policy substantial unemployment was expected to continue for several years.[29] Public employment legislation to create jobs, which is popular in Democratic circles, was strongly resisted by the president, who preferred to rely on the private sector to produce economic growth. On the whole, the economic stability policy preferences of the Ford administration were about what one would expect from a rather conservative Republican regime. The Ford policies did have some of the intended effect. By January 1977, the inflation rate had temporarily declined to 5 percent while the unemployment rate stood at 7.8 percent.

### The Carter Administration's Dilemma

Since his election the previous November, there had been speculation about Carter's specific proposals for dealing with the economic situation. When Carter's administration took office on January 20, 1977, members of Congress, mayors, governors, and business and labor spokesmen all provided the new president with varying and conflicting recommendations on how to stimulate the economy. A basic difference of viewpoint was between the spenders (governors, mayors, union officials, etc.) and the tax cutters (businessmen, many economists, etc.). One commentator described Carter's dilemma in these terms: "So Carter has faced a classic problem of trying to reconcile conflicting goals: to reduce unemployment rapidly without triggering a new burst of inflation; to preserve his flexibility to finance new programs without plunging the budget into massive, perpetual deficits; and to satisfy spending demands from members of Congress, mayors, unions, and governors without irrevocably committing scarce future resources."[30]

Late in January the Carter administration proposed a $31.3 billion package of economic stimulants to cover a two-year period.[31] For fiscal year 1977 the package included $13.8 billion in tax cuts and rebates ($50 per person on a "one-shot" basis) and $1.7 billion in spending for public works, public service jobs, and job training. The tax rebate was intended to give a quick boost to the economy by stimulating consumer spending.

Although the administration's stimulus package, and especially the tax rebate proposal, encountered considerable criticism, it was passed by the House in March; and by the middle of April it was ready for consideration on the Senate floor. Some alterations had been made by the House, but the administration's package was essentially intact. Then, on April 14, in a surprising move, the president announced that he was abandoning the proposed $50 tax rebate, the business tax credit for hiring new employees, and the increase in the investment tax credit. Both economic and political factors contributed to this reversal in policy. In the early months of 1977 unemployment had declined, retail sales had expanded, industrial production had risen, and a threat of increased inflation had appeared. The abandoned proposals thus seemed unnecessary because the economy was expanding and because they might fuel inflation. Business and banking interests had opposed the rebate proposal as inflationary and now applauded its withdrawal; however, they still wanted the increase in the investment tax credit. In the Senate the Carter proposal faced substantial opposition, partly on its merits and partly because the president's proposed elimination of many water projects from the federal budget had offended many senators. Given his view of the lessened need for the rebate, the president apparently was not willing to expend the political capital required to win Senate approval. The president continued to support the remaining portions of his stimulus package as necessary to "guarantee us durable growth." Carter's economic package cleared Congress in May and was signed into law, although Congress did retain the tax credit for hiring new employees. (As mentioned earlier, policies intended to help create jobs are usually popular among the Democrats in Congress.)

The Carter administration continued to be concerned with reducing unemployment more than combating inflation for the remainder of 1977 and most of 1978. A tax cut proposed in early 1978 to stimulate the economy was subsequently scaled back and delayed in order to reduce the size of the budget deficit and counter growing concern about inflation. By the latter part of 1978, however, it had become clear that inflation was the dominant economic issue. To deal with inflation the Carter administration now instituted voluntary wage and price guidelines, to be implemented by the Council on Wage and Price Stability, in October 1978. This action was followed in January 1979 by the submission of a budget to Congress which was described as "lean and austere." Monetary policy was also tightened and, in 1979, some credit controls were imposed in further efforts to hold down inflationary pressures. None of this worked very well and the inflation rate continued to move upward to double-digit levels.

In 1980 the administration manifested some more indecision when it first submitted the annual budget (for fiscal year 1981) to Congress calling for a $15.8 billion deficit (proposed receipts and outlays were $600 billion and $615.8 billion, respectively). Criticism of this budget from Congress and the business and financial community led the administration, in unprecedented fashion, to withdraw the budget and announce that it would work with Congress to balance the budget. The forthcoming presidential primaries and general election were also undoubtedly on the minds of administration officials. A few weeks later the president resubmitted the budget. This time, because of reductions in expenditures and proposed tax increases, a surplus of $16.5 billion was projected for fiscal year 1981. Action in Congress, however, fell considerably short of Carter's proposals. This, coupled with higher than expected levels of spending because of inflation, a short but sharp recession, and other factors, resulted in a budget deficit of over $50 billion at the end of fiscal year 1981. By then Carter was no longer in office, having been defeated in his bid for reelection by Ronald Reagan. Dissatisfaction with the state of the economy was a major factor in his rejection by the voters.

The ambivalence and problems of the Carter administration illustrate two characteristics inherent in economic policymaking: the uncertainty that underlies the development of economic stability policies and, second, the blending of politics and economics in policy formation and adoption.

## Reaganomics

The economic program proposed by the Reagan administration soon after taking office in January 1981 represented a significant departure from and rejection of the economic policies that had been followed in the post–World War II era. The Reagan program consisted of four interrelated parts.

1. *Tax cuts.* Marginal personal income tax rates (those people pay on additional dollars of income) were to be reduced by 30 percent over a three-year period and depreciation write-offs were to be accelerated for new business investments in buildings, equipment, and vehicles. The administration intended to propose other tax changes at a later time.

2. *Expenditure reductions.* The president proposed reductions of $48.6 billion in the 1982 fiscal year budget which had been presented by the Carter administration. These were to be focused on domestic programs; at the same time Reagan proposed substantial increases in national defense spending. Budget reductions were to be even larger in subsequent fiscal years, with a balanced budget being projected for fiscal year 1984. A budget deficit of $45 billion was initially estimated for fiscal year 1982. (It later turned out to be $110 billion.)

3. *Regulatory reform.* Excessive government regulation of business was viewed by the administration as a cause of lessened growth and productivity in the economy. Hence, through the increased use of cost-benefit analysis and other means, the amount of regulation was to be reduced.

4. *Monetary policy.* The growth in the money supply was to be held at a slow and steady rate by the Federal Reserve Board in order to bring down the rate of inflation. The administration believed that this would also have the effect of lowering "inflationary expectations."

The Reagan program reflected several strands of thought: a conservative view of the appropriate role of government in economy and society; a monetarist economic policy; and "supply-side economics." Because of its novelty (it came into prominence only in the late 1970s) and its importance as part of the rationale for the Reagan program, some discussion of supply-side economics is in order.[32]

In contrast to Keynesian economics, which emphasizes the use of fiscal policy to influence aggregate demand and thereby stabilize the economy, supply-side economics stresses the need for fiscal policy to take account of the impact of tax rates on the incentives of people to work, save, and invest. If tax rates are too high (and it was contended by supply-siders that they had been for many years), these incentives would be reduced and a fall-off in productivity and economic growth would result. In such circumstances properly constructed tax cuts would not only increase incentives to work, save, and invest, they would increase productivity and economic growth and, in the view of some of the more enthusiastic supply-siders, reduce inflationary pressures in the economy. Most supply-siders did not worry about budget deficits as productive of inflation, since they believed that inflation was a monetary phenomenon and could be effectively dealt with by holding down growth in the money supply. More orthodox conservatives and Republicans, it should be noted, still worried about the effects of budget deficits, and they were not without influence in the Reagan administration.

Once the Reagan program was announced, speculation quickly arose as to how successful the president would be in securing its enactment by Congress. As it turned out, he was very successful. Before turning to the tax and budget cut actions, a few words are in order concerning the monetary and regulatory aspects of the program. The FRB, which had begun to restrain the growth of the money supply during the latter part of the Carter administration, continued on this course during 1981–1982, with the general approval of Reagan administration officials. Reduction of regulatory activity was achieved by budget reductions for regulatory agencies, the requirement that cost-benefit analyses be made of major proposed regulations, and the appointment of many persons to regulatory agency positions who were not inclined to be vigorous regulators. Now we turn to the tax and expenditure cuts.

The expenditure reduction effort was spearheaded by David A. Stockman, Reagan's appointee as director of the OMB. Rather than try to reduce expenditures in piecemeal fashion through the regular appropriations process, Stockman and some Republican congressional leaders decided to use the congressional budget reconciliation process. Reconciliation was used for the first time in 1980 to trim the fiscal year 1981 budget deficit by $8.2 billion through spending cuts and revenue increases. The first budget resolution, adopted in May, directed twenty-nine House and Senate legislative committees to save some $36 billion by making changes (mostly reductions) in many existing domestic program authorizations. The actions of these committees were then combined in a single comprehensive reconciliation bill. Passed handily by the Senate, which, as a consequence of the 1980 elections, was controlled by the Republicans for the first time in a quarter of a century, the reconciliation bill encountered more difficulty in the Democratic-controlled House. Here too, however, the administration prevailed with the support of conservative Democrats and, in early August, the president signed into law the Omnibus Reconciliation Act reducing spending by an estimated $35.1 billion. Although President Reagan did not secure all the expenditure reductions he wanted, he nonetheless had obtained a major change in the direction of government and a slowdown in federal spending.[33]

The tax cut proposal submitted to Congress by the Reagan administration took the form of a "lean" bill limited largely to reductions in marginal personal income tax rates and accelerated depreciation allowances for business investments. Once this bill was passed the administration indicated that a second bill would be introduced which would make a variety of lesser changes or reforms in the tax laws. By this strategy the administration hoped to prevent its major supply-side bill from being slowed in enactment by controversy generated by a multitude of particular provisions. The administration did not have much difficulty in getting essentially what it wanted from the Senate. In the House, however, a major controversy developed. The Democrats on the Ways and Means Committee proposed an alternative to the administration bill which, while similar in many respects, provided greater tax relief to persons earning less than $50,000 annually. To attract votes of southern conservatives the Democrats included in their bill provisions providing substantial tax breaks for the oil industry. The White House and the Republicans responded with a revised tax package which included larger tax breaks for the oil producers, annual indexation of tax rates to offset inflation, increased charitable deductions, and a variety of other provisions designed to win votes. "Both Republicans and

Democrats admitted their bills were more products of a political bidding war than blueprints for sound economic policy."[34] A couple of days before the crucial House vote on the tax measure, President Reagan went on nationwide television to appeal for public support. The administration bill was approved by a 238 to 195 vote when forty-eight Democrats gave their support to the president.

As enacted, the tax reduction legislation, officially titled the Economic Recovery Act, represented another major political victory for the Reagan administration. The act provided for a 25 percent reduction in individual income tax rates to be phased in over 33 months beginning October 1, 1981. Beginning in 1985 tax rates were to be annually adjusted to offset the effects of inflation. Other provisions provided greater depreciation of business investments in new assets, reduced taxes on oil production, exempted most estates from taxation, reduced the top marginal rate on investment or "unearned" income from 70 to 50 percent (this also had the effect of lowering the tax rate on capital gains from 28 to 20 percent), and increased deductions for charitable contributions. It was estimated that taxes would be lowered by about $38 billion for individuals and businesses in fiscal year 1982; for the three-year period 1982–1984 the total reduction was put at $280 billion.

Why was the Reagan administration able to achieve these major tax and expenditure changes? Several factors seem important. One was President Reagan's popularity and political skill. When he needed to bargain or make adjustments to win votes he did not hesitate to do so. Another was unity within the Republican party. Almost without exception all the Republicans in Congress supported the president on major votes. In the House, for example, only one Republican voted against the administration's revised tax bill. A third factor was the support the administration received from a phalanx of conservative House Democrats (mostly from the South and known as the Boll Weevils). Finally, there was the fact that more orthodox economic policies had not been especially effective in dealing with inflation and unemployment. Why not give something different a try?

Thus, in August 1981, the Reagan economic program was in place, substantially as the president intended.[35] The initial reaction to it, however, was adverse. Early predictions were that the budget deficit for fiscal year 1982 would be substantially in excess of the official estimate of a $42.5 billion deficit. Moreover, many were concerned because the prime lending rate (the rate at which banks lend to their best customers) was hovering around the 20 percent level. This was said to reflect expectations of continued inflation along with doubt that the Reagan program would be successful. In late September President Reagan announced that, in order to meet his budget deficit target, the administration would seek $13 billion in additional budget cuts plus $3 billion in increased taxes for fiscal year 1982. In his view these additional proposed savings would keep the economy on the "firm, steady course" that he had charted earlier in the year. Only $2 billion of the proposed cuts were in the national defense area, where members of Congress believed larger cuts should be made. Resistance grew in response to further cuts in social programs and ultimately Congress approved in December 1981 additional reductions of only $4 billion in domestic programs.

In all, economic developments in 1981 did not take the shape hoped for by the Reagan administration. Although the rate of inflation was reduced, interest rates remained high and in mid-1981 the economy lapsed into a deep recession. Unemployment shot upward, it was to exceed 10 percent in the fall of 1982. By the end of 1981 predictions were common that budget deficits would run well over $100 billion annually for the next several years.

The proposed budget for fiscal year 1983 presented to Congress by President Reagan called for additional reductions in domestic expenditures, more increases in defense spending, some limited tax increases, and a balanced budget by fiscal year 1984. Although his advisers had urged a major tax increase (or deferral of some of the 1981 income tax cuts) to reduce the deficit in the 1983 budget, their advice was rejected by the president. Consequently, the president's 1983 budget proposed outlays of $758 billion, receipts of $666 billion, and a deficit of $92 billion.

Skepticism quickly arose concerning the realism of this deficit figure. The Congressional Budget Office, for instance, predicted that the deficit would be in the $140 to $150 billion range. Pressure for action to reduce the budget deficit in 1983 and later years began to build, leading the administration to support a major increase in tax revenues. Support for such action was especially strong among Senate Republicans. A tax bill written by the Republican-controlled Senate Finance Committee and attached to a minor House bill provided for $98 billion in increased tax revenues over a three-year period. The House Democratic leadership chose to go to conference with the Senate on this tax bill without trying to pass a regular House bill. (This produced contentions that the tax bill violated the constitutional requirement that all the legislation must originate in the House.) The conference measure agreed to after lengthy deliberations largely followed the outline of the Senate bill.

A major campaign of pressure and persuasion was undertaken by the administration to secure enactment of the tax legislation. Many members of Congress were reluctant to vote for a major tax increase in an election year. Unhappiness with the tax bill was especially strong among Republicans in the House. Supply-siders argued it ran counter to the administration's mandate to cut taxes. Others opposed particular provisions in the bill. The unity which characterized the House Republicans in 1981 was not to be found. However, the House Democratic leadership gave full support to the bill in the name of fiscal responsibility. In mid-August, with substantial support from moderate and liberal Democrats, the House passed the tax bill by a vote of 226 to 207 (for, 123 Democrats, 103 Republicans; against, 120 Democrats, 87 Republicans). The Senate acted favorably soon afterward by a fairly partisan 52 to 47 vote. Eleven Republicans opposed the bill while nine Democrats supported it. Although viewed as an important legislative victory for the Reagan administration, the bill was signed into law by the president without a public ceremony.

Called the Tax Equity and Fiscal Responsibility Act, the legislation provided for $15 billion in expenditure reductions and an extension of unemployment benefits (which likely won some votes for it) as well as the estimated $98 billion in revenue increases during the period 1983 to 1985. The revenue increases were to be generated by stricter or more effective enforcement of existing tax laws, the reduction or closing of some tax loopholes (as for medical care expenses and corporate tax leasing), and increased taxes (as on cigarettes, telephone services, and airline tickets). No change was made in the 1981 income tax reductions as this was strongly opposed by the president. However, some of the 1981 business tax reductions were eliminated.

Whether the tax legislation, by reducing prospective budget deficits, would have a beneficial effect on the economy remained a question for the future. It certainly did constitute a shift away from supply-side economics and back toward more traditional Republican concern with budget deficits, which the president now acknowledged would persist until at least late in the decade. By late 1982 supply-side economics seemed an idea whose time had both come and passed.

## CONCLUDING COMMENTS

In 1966 Walter Heller, then chairman of the Council of Economic Advisers, proclaimed "the Age of the Economist," because economists had been so successful in influencing economic policy formation.[36] He also expressed enthusiasm over the ability of economists to "fine-tune" the economy. A few months earlier Milton Friedman, a leading conservative economist, had announced that "we are all Keynesians now."[37] There was, in short, substantial agreement and confidence concerning the ability of policymakers, with the advice of economists, to use government programs to maintain stable economic conditions.

This confidence and certainty have diminished in the face of the combined inflation and unemployment of the 1970s and early 1980s, and the inability of the government to deal successfully with them. The standard Keynesian approach to the maintenance of economic stability, which dominated thinking for so long, no longer seems adequate to many people. Supply-side economics emerged as an alternative to Keynesianism but seems to have had its day. Economic theorists are in disarray and many policymakers are in a quandary as they face the problem of how to achieve low inflation and, at the same time, low unemployment—particularly since there is disagreement as to why the economy is experiencing both substantial inflation and high unemployment simultaneously. Uncertainty generally prevails, although given individuals may have their own clear solutions for the economy's problems.

One thing, though, is certain. There exists widespread expectation of and support for government action to attempt to maintain economic stability. The president and party that fail to take effective action to deal with severe economic disturbances are likely to receive harsh treatment at the polls. The election of 1932 was long the prime cited example; it is a lesson that was renewed with the experience of Jimmy Carter in 1980. Given the monetary and fiscal means at the disposal of the government, the chances that either severe depression or runaway inflation will develop seems unlikely, although some would so characterize the "double-digit" inflation and 8 to 10 percent unemployment of the late 1970s and early 1980s. When inflation and recession—especially the former—are mild, there will undoubtedly continue to be controversy as to what discretionary action, if any, should be taken, and when, by the government. What is done will be shaped by both economic and political considerations. The price of inaction, or unsuccessful action, may be paid at the polls.

## NOTES

1. A prominent economist in 1969 wrote about the "obsolescence of the business cycle pattern." He seems to have been unduly optimistic, given the later performance of the economy. See Arthur M. Okun, *The Political Economy of Prosperity* (New York: Norton, 1970), pp. 31–36.
2. Robert Aaron Gordon, *Economic Instability and Growth: The American Record* (New York: Harper & Row, 1974), p. 3.
3. Quoted in Gordon, *Economic Instability*, p. 22.
4. See Herbert Stein, *The Fiscal Revolution in America* (Chicago: University of Chicago Press, 1969), pp. 31–38.
5. Cf. Francis M. Bator, "Money and Government," *Atlantic* 209 (April 1962): 116–117.
6. An excellent discussion of the enactment of the statute appears in Stephen K. Bailey, *Congress Makes a Law: The Story behind the Employment Act of 1946* (New York: Columbia University Press, 1950).
7. Stein, *Fiscal Revolution*, p. 204.
8. Gordon, *Economic Instability*, p. 106.
9. Michael D. Reagan, "The Political Structure of the Federal Reserve System," *American Political Science Review* 55 (March 1961): 65.
10. Ibid., p. 64.
11. We should note that *money*, as the word is used here, includes both currency and coins, as well as demand deposits at commercial banks. This definition of *money* (there are various others) is referred to as M1 by economists.
12. Quoted in *Wall Street Journal*, July 31, 1970, p. 1.
13. Barry M. Bleckman, Edward M. Gramlick, and Robert W. Hartman, *Setting National Priorities: The 1976 Budget* (Washington, D.C.: Brookings Institution, 1975), p. 21.
14. See the account of this episode in Theodore Sorenson, *Kennedy* (New York: Harper & Row, 1965), pp. 443–459.
15. Cf. George P. Schultz and Robert Z. Aliber, eds., *Guidelines: Informal Controls and the Market Place* (Chicago: University of Chicago Press, 1966); and George L. Perry, "Wages and the Guideposts," *American Economic Review* 57 (September 1967): 897–904.
16. Gordon, *Economic Instability*, p. 146.
17. *Economic Report of the President, Together with the Annual Report of the Council of Economic Advisers, 1968* (Washington, D.C.: U.S. Government Printing Office, 1968), p. 119.
18. On economic forecasting within the government, see Lawrence C. Pierce, *The Politics of Fiscal Policy Formation* (Pacific Palisades, Calif.: Goodyear, 1971), chaps. 3–4.
19. Okun, *Political Economy*, p. 103.
20. For good discussions of the Congressional Budget and Impoundment Control Act, see Joel Havemann, *Congress and the Budget* (Bloomington: Indiana University Press, 1978); and James P. Pfiffner, *The President, the Budget, and Congress: Impoundment and the 1974 Budget Act* (Boulder, Colo.: Westview Press, 1979).
21. Dennis S. Ippolito, *The Budget and National Politics* (San Francisco: W. H. Freeman, 1978), pp. 146–147.
22. GAO (Washington, D.C.: U.S. Government Printing Office, December 1980).
23. John D. Millett, *Government and Public Administration* (New York: McGraw-Hill, 1959), p. 358.
24. This paragraph draws on Aaron Wildavsky, *The Politics of the Budgetary Process*, 3rd ed. (Boston: Little, Brown, 1979), chaps. 7–11.
25. Quoted in Okun, *Political Economy*, p. 71.
26. Okun, p. 71.

27. Detailed accounts of various aspects of the controls can be found in the following works: Arnold R. Weber, *In Pursuit of Price Stability: The Price-Wage Freeze of 1971* (Washington, D.C.: Brookings Institution, 1973); Robert F. Lanzillotti, Mary T. Hamilton, and R. Blaine Roberts, *Phase II in Review: The Price Commission Experience* (Washington, D.C.: Brookings Institution, 1975); *Inflation and Unemployment* (Washington, D.C.: Congressional Quarterly Inc., 1975).

28. Lanzillotti et al., *Phase II,* p. 196.

29. Leonard Silk, "Ford's 'Steady' Policy," *New York Times,* January 28, 1976, pp. 41, 45.

30. Robert J. Samuelson, "Carter's Early Economic Choices—It's as Simple as 2 + 2 = 5," *National Journal* 9 (January 8, 1977): 59.

31. The Carter proposal is discussed in *Wall Street Journal,* January 28, 1977, p. 3; and *New York Times,* January 28, 1977, pp. 1, 12.

32. Cf. James R. Barth, "The Reagan Program for Economic Recovery: Economic Rationale," *Economic Review* (Federal Reserve Bank of Atlanta), September 1981, pp. 4–14; and John A. Tatom, "We Are All Supply-Siders Now!" *Review* (Federal Reserve Bank of St. Louis) 63 (May 1981): 18–30.

33. *Congressional Quarterly Weekly Report* 39 (August 1, 1981): 1337.

34. Ibid., (July 25, 1981): 1323.

35. For some useful background on the Reagan program see Joseph A. Pechman, ed., *Setting National Priorities: The 1983 Budget* (Washington, D.C.: Brookings Institution, 1982).

36. Walter W. Heller, *New Dimensions of Political Economy* (Cambridge, Mass.: Harvard University Press, 1966).

37. Quoted in *Time,* December 31, 1965, p. 65.

## SUGGESTED READINGS

Bailey, Stephen K. *Congress Makes a Law: The Story Behind the Employment Act of 1946.* New York: Columbia University Press, 1950.

Gordon, Robert Aaron. *Economic Instability and Growth: The American Record.* New York: Harper & Row, 1974.

Okun, Arthur. *The Political Economy of Prosperity.* New York: Norton, 1970.

Pechman, Joseph A., ed. *Setting National Priorities: The 1983 Budget.* Washington, D.C.: Brookings Institution, 1982.

Pierce, Lawrence C. *The Politics of Fiscal Policy Formation.* Pacific Palisades, Calif.: Goodyear, 1971.

Stein, Herbert. *The Fiscal Revolution in America.* Chicago: University of Chicago Press, 1969.

Tufte, Edward R. *Political Control of the Economy.* Princeton, N.J.: Princeton University Press, 1978.

# Chapter 3

# Energy Policies

## THE ENERGY CRISIS

News reports of blackouts, natural gas shortages, and rising prices for gasoline, home heating, and air conditioning have made it clear to even the most politically unaware citizen that energy supply has sweeping ramifications. In the last decade energy policy in the United States has changed to meet the problems generated by the energy crisis. For the first time since the 1930s the rate of growth in energy usage has declined: in early 1982 we used less foreign oil than we did in 1975. In general, America's energy policy has shifted from the traditional policy of unlimited use at cheap prices to restricted use at high prices. The policy changes were the result of a major upheaval in the politics of energy.

The old politics of energy—pre-1974—was an example of subsystem politics in which a narrow range of actors made minor adjustments in policy, and producer-state interests dominated the process. Each of the major energy sources—coal, oil, natural gas, electricity, and nuclear power—were organized differently in order to participate in the political process.

The new politics of energy is characterized by vastly increased participation. Participation, in the words of Charles O. Jones, "has expanded *up* institutional hierarchies, *out* to citizen groups, *over* to other nations, and *across* from one resource subsystem to others."[1] The range of interested parties now includes consumers, environmentalists, representatives, and senators from states other than energy-producing states. The federal government has structured and restructured itself anew in attempts to deal with increased participation. The Reagan administration has proposed to abolish the Department of Energy (which was Carter's organizational effort to deal with increased participation) and redistribute its programs. Thus the political process rolls along in what Jones aptly calls "crisis response politics."[2]

The new politics of energy has changed America's energy policy and energy habits. Whatever else the future holds, dynamic change in energy policy is a certainty during the next decade, and the new policies must grapple with the same question that policymakers faced in the 1970s: how to assure America's energy future without compromising the present.

Neither the energy policy of the 1970s nor future policies can be comprehended or imagined without an understanding of America's traditional energy policies. The central tenet of energy policy in the past was unlimited use of energy by industry, government, and the consumer. In 1920 Americans used 20,000 trillion British thermal units (Btu's) per year; in 1980 that figure exceeded 78,000 trillion Btu's. This figure is all the more remarkable when one considers that Americans comprise 6 percent of the world population but use over 30 percent of its energy. Some experts have predicted that by the year 2000 we will be using two to three times the present energy output. Even the most optimistic forecasters agree that by the year 2000 Americans will use about twice as much energy as they now use. Turning away from the notion of unlimited use proved to be difficult since the major contributors to the use of energy are motor vehicles, air conditioners, refrigerators, freezers, and so on—items considered necessary by the well-off and desirable by the not so well-off in our society.

Governmental policy until the mid-1970s reflected this attitude of profligate use and unlimited growth. Walter Heller, former chairman of the Council of Economic Advisers, said in 1971, "I think of growth as a source of the problem, but also as a solution. We're doing a bad enough job in the face of growth. An absence of growth would be a corrosive factor."[3] According to economist Arthur Okun, America needs a 4 to 4.5 percent per year growth rate in order to absorb the increasing work force, and in order to have a growth economy, energy production and thus consumption must increase.[4] In order to sustain this growth, the federal government has refrained from regulating or interfering with the sources of energy production. Even in the area of natural gas, where field prices are regulated, there has been very little restriction on the amount of natural gas produced. In fact, legal decisions and governmental policy have encouraged drilling for oil and gas and strip mining for coal.

The practice of encouraging energy source discovery, or at least not discouraging it, has been maintained even when such policies were extremely wasteful of natural resources. For example, in Texas prior to the mid-1920s, more than a billion cubic feet of natural gas were wasted each day because only the heavy hydrocarbons were retained, and the other gases vented and flared, or burned off. Court decisions on oil rights increased the probability of waste by encouraging production before a neighboring well could be built to drain off the original pool. (That situation is discussed in detail later in the chapter.) Regulation that did occur in this policy area was designed to prevent surpluses and thus stabilize the market. State regulatory commissions prorationed the amount of oil to be produced in each state. That is, the commissions determined how much oil could be produced in a state in a given time period by ascertaining how much oil production was needed for markets and how much oil could safely be taken without harming available oil resources or depressing the market price for crude oil. Thus, prorationing was determined by interpretations of both market and conservation criteria. It is clear that unchecked growth and unlimited use have characterized our behavior as consumers of energy and our government's policy regarding energy.

In this chapter we begin by examining the present energy situation in the United States. We then examine traditional energy policies, giving special attention to the ways in which past policies affect present policies on coal, oil, natural gas, and nuclear materials. One of the most important points to be illustrated is that America does not have one comprehensive energy policy but rather several energy policies, which change as the energy area changes (for example, coal, oil, and gas). It can be shown that the energy crisis changed the politics of energy and thus energy policy, as we consider energy policy in the 1973 to 1981 period.

The current energy situation is essentially the result of a search for an American consensus on issues brought to a focal point during the 1973–1974 Arab oil embargo. These issues included overreliance on foreign oil, rising costs of energy, and the high price of readjusting lifestyles and politics to the new energy situation. In 1979, 45.6 percent of all the oil used in the United States came from foreign sources. The cost per barrel of oil to refiners jumped from $9.07 in 1974 to $27.05 in 1980, and the average price of gasoline at the pump went from 56 cents per gallon to $1.36 over the same time period. The combination of price increases and dependence on foreign oil supplies meant that America's traditional energy policy—"use much, pay little"—had changed and was still in flux. Whether there will be adequate production and a relatively decreased consumption is the central question facing America's energy policymakers.[5]

### Fuel Shortages

Natural gas, which is the cleanest fossil fuel, presents one of the most critical energy questions facing the country. Over the last few years and particularly in the winters of 1976–1977 and 1981–1982, reports of schools and factories closing because of natural gas shortages have increased. The federal government reported that curtailments of natural gas from suppliers to customers were increasing—from 350 billion cubic feet in 1971 to over one trillion cubic feet in 1978. Production of natural gas in the United States peaked in 1975 at 24.7 trillion cubic feet, and since 1968 production has exceeded additions to reserves. In short, since 1968 the United States has been dipping into its gas reserves to meet production goals. Thus, in an effort to expand its gas supplies, the United States has been forced to negotiate with the Soviet Union and other countries that are net exporters of natural gas. The severe winters of 1976–1977 and 1981–1982 demonstrated the inadequacy of domestic supplies.

Coal at first glance would appear to be one answer to the energy crisis. It is by far the most abundant of the fossil fuels, with over 500 years of potential supply available in the United States. However, as the Ford Foundation's energy study puts it, "There are two things wrong with coal today. We can't mine it and we can't burn it."[6] The mining of coal, whether by strip or shaft methods, is objectionable because of human hazards and environmental concerns. Burning coal presents another problem, since 80 percent of supplies are high in sulfur content and emit harmful pollutants. Beyond this, coal is expensive and unwieldy to transport. Efforts to reduce the pollutants released from burning coal are being made, but the technology to cleanse coal is not fully developed. The technology to process coal into natural gas and oil is available but is far too expensive to be an economical solution over the next decade.

The technology necessary for using nuclear fuel to solve the energy crisis also is inadequate. America's nuclear trump card is the fast breeder reactor, which theoretically can generate more fuel than it consumes over a twenty-year period. However, the first commercial demonstration unit has not been opened for operation as of late 1982; moreover, the breeder creates radioactive wastes which must be safely disposed. Even by the most optimistic account it will be the twenty-first century before nuclear energy produces around half of our electrical capacity. Moreover, recent opposition to nuclear energy development has been strong enough to delay plans for new nuclear facilities.

Because of these problems with gas, coal, and nuclear materials, oil—the present mainstay of American energy—will have to suffice in the immediate future. Oil is a versatile fuel capable of running the family car or huge electrical generators. In 1980 oil carried about 50 percent of America's energy burden. Unfortunately, the United States exhausted its known reserve production capacity in 1970 and will, short of a miracle, be unable to meet its oil needs solely from domestic sources. There is a possibility that the increased exploration undertaken in the late 1970s will increase our reserve capacity.

The increased dependence on imported oil has resulted in trade deficits, dollar instability, changing relations with Israel, and a dollar flow to the Middle East. More important, there has been a shift in power from big oil companies, who supplied the United States and Europe, to the oil-producing nations. The vehicle for this shift in power has been the Organization of Petroleum Exporting Countries (OPEC), which controls half the world's oil production and 90 percent of exports.[7] Through coordinated actions these countries have managed to raise by tenfold the price of oil since 1969. Thus, even though world reserves are sufficient to see us through to at least the twenty-first century, it is clear that American energy policy cannot be dominated by the doctrine of unlimited growth and unplanned use. Questions concerning the need for new sources of energy, cutbacks in energy use, and energy versus environmental concerns now dominate the energy policy area.

### Proposed Solutions

Possible solutions to the energy crisis fall into three relatively clear-cut patterns: scientific-technological, economic, and political.

The scientific-technological solution is to increase energy supplies through stepped-up research into solar and geothermal energy, synthetic fuels, and new nuclear fission and fusion possibilities. Lawrence Rocks and Richard Runyon have advocated a crash program to develop coal-based synthetic fuels.[8] Richard Post of the Lawrence Radiation Laboratory in Livermore, California, claims, "We've got two really good horses to ride [nuclear fission and fusion], and we ought to ride them both."[9] The crux of the scientific-technological argument is that while America—and, in the long run, the world—cannot count on the supply of fossil fuels, we can count on our technology and science. Thus, solving the energy crisis is a question of renewed funding and support for scientific endeavors to generate efficient and reliable sources of energy.

The economic solution to the energy crisis is to ensure more rational allocation of energy by the market mechanism or by taxation. For example, if the price of gasoline is allowed to rise, in theory the result is a decrease in the amount of gasoline used, because marginal buyers (that is, those who can do without or use other forms of transportation) will conserve gasoline. Variations on this theme are to impose a higher federal tax on gasoline or a heavier import tax on foreign oil, with the federal revenues thereby generated being rebated to the poor and otherwise redistributed to those most affected by the price increases. However one puts it, such a policy allocates energy by increasing prices, which theoretically forces consumers to use energy more wisely. Conservative economists favor using the market mechanism for allocating energy supplies. Liberal economists are likely to express less faith in the market and advocate government actions (even rationing) to improve the performance of the market.

The political answer to the energy crisis is to balance the interests of energy users—consumers as well as producers. Thus, if gasoline for automobiles is a consumer necessity of top priority, the government can act in a number of ways (for instance, by tax incentives to producers or by price controls) to subsidize the consumer's interest and keep the price low. The crux of this argument is that, since a large number of interests are involved in the energy area, a dependence on the market mechanism means that certain interests are not included or represented in the making of energy policy. Certainly until the last few years, energy politics and thus policy was dominated by the producers of energy and the senators and representatives of the major energy-producing states at the expense of various consumer interests. Currently, no representative in Washington can afford to be ignorant of energy policy, because his or her constituents will surely be affected.[10]

## TRADITIONAL ENERGY POLICIES

We have seen that the traditional American attitude toward energy use changed because of increasing rates of consumption and decreased domestic production of fossil fuels. We now turn to the more specific question of governmental policy regarding the primary energy sources of coal, oil, gas, and nuclear energy.

Traditional governmental policies on energy have varied from industry to industry. The basic choices available to the government are public utility regulation and antitrust regulation. Public utility regulation favors consumer interests, and the policy is generally to keep supplies available and prices at a reasonable level. Regulation of the industry, from an antitrust perspective, has tended to promote policies favorable to producer and operator interests. In general, oil and coal policy has favored producer-operators while natural gas policy has favored consumer interests. However, as we shall see, these general categories do not fully describe governmental policy in the energy area.

## Coal

Since the 1920s the demand for coal has declined relative to other energy sources, as has total quantity used. The coal industry was not sufficiently organized and controlled to restrict production and keep prices high. Coal offers one of the rare examples of an industry characterized by nearly pure competition. From the turn of the century to the present there have been many producers, and no one producer or cartel has been able to affect market prices. Since coal is plentiful, entry into the market is relatively easy, and production can be expanded quickly. The combination of plentiful supplies, many producers, and decreasing demands has made coal "a sick industry." Government policy toward the coal industry has been geared toward the elimination of the excesses of competition.

Production in the coal industry expanded rapidly throughout the nineteenth century but began its long decline in the 1920s, when other fuels were easily substituted for coal and when coal consumption became increasingly inefficient. The problem of imbalance between supply and demand flared in World War I. During the war a large number of new mines were opened and old mines reopened in an attempt to increase coal production for the war effort. During this period the government's policy was to fix maximum coal prices, allocate shipments, and adjust labor disputes. The Lever Act of 1917 gave the United States Fuel Administration the right to fix prices and allocate shipments. In 1919 price controls were ended, but, because of increasing labor-management problems, price controls were subsequently temporarily reinstated. Respite from labor disputes in 1922 brought the industry out of the era of shortages and onto the long path toward depression—oversupply and lower prices. For example, from 1923 to 1932, the number of coal mines and miners was reduced by over 40 percent, while the price of coal per ton fell from $2.68 to $1.31. Given the changing economic situation, the government was under mounting pressure to change policies. In other words, governmental policy during the World War I shortage was to protect consumers from high prices and to assure consumers a reasonable supply; when the economic situation shifted from shortages to oversupply, the government's response was to protect producers from "too much competition."[11]

In the period of decline after 1923, the problem for the coal industry was to control the supply of coal, thereby assuring higher prices. The two groups that could control supply were the miners themselves, through the United Mine Workers (UMW), and voluntary organizations of coal operators.[12] That is, if the union had been strong enough to limit (as do bricklayers) the number of hours they worked or the amount of coal produced, or if the owners had joined together to limit production, then prices could have been maintained. The influence of the UMW was weakened in the South following the 1922 strike settlement. The fact that southern miners worked for less money caused producers to move southward, and by 1927 this movement had severely weakened the UMW in the North. Thus, miners were not strong enough to limit production. Efforts of owners at voluntary cooperation to control production were equally unsuccessful. Antitrust laws ruled out binding agreements, and other organizational forms were too weak to withstand the forces of competition. In short, neither miners nor operators were successful in controlling production. As a result, over the 1923–1932 period, pressure for government action increased.

**Government regulation of coal.**    The first government attempt to regulate the coal industry was the Bituminous Coal Code, formed under the National Industrial Recovery Act (NIRA) of 1933, which generally authorized the establishment of industry codes of "fair competition." In essence, the code exchanged labor concessions for restrictions on competition. Minimum prices were fixed for coal in each of five geographic regions; the boards which set prices had to have union representation by a fixed time period. Under this code the miners and the owners both benefited. The UMW organized over 90 percent of the industry, child labor in mines was eliminated, and a 35-hour week became standard. Yearly wages rose by one-third, while the number of workers only slightly increased. Prices per ton rose from $1.31 in 1932 to $1.86 in 1935, and in many cases producers were able to show a profit. However, by 1935 there was an increasing dissatisfaction with the system as both small and large producers and northern and southern coal interests battled each other over code provisions. Then, in 1935, in the *Schechter* case, which involved a challenge to the poultry industry code, the Supreme Court declared the NIRA unconstitutional, thus also eliminating the Coal Code.

Later in 1935, however, at the behest of coal interests, Congress passed the Guffey Act. The Guffey Act created a five-member National Bituminous Coal Commission with authority to set minimum prices and to regulate labor conditions. Again the purpose of the bill was to provide stability for both coal miners and mine owners, and unions were allowed to organize freely and to bargain collectively. Because of another Supreme Court decision concerning the labor clauses of the Guffey Act, an amended Bituminous Coal Act was passed in 1937. This statute expanded the commission to seven members and authorized it to set prices. Through an unbelievably complex process, over four hundred thousand prices were to be established. The commission's attempts to set prices caused immediate controversy. Small operators, large buyers, and certain regions claimed that the commission favored large operators. In 1939 President Roosevelt transferred the commission's functions to the Department of Interior, thus ending regulation from within the industry. The Guffey Act was extended through 1943 but then allowed to die.

Since 1943 the UMW effectively controlled the supply of eastern coal. The increased demand for coal in World War II and the willingness of the UMW to use strikes to gain power and high wages resulted in market control. That is, since wages make up over half of the total cost of coal, there is a real limit on price reductions, and some less efficient mines have closed. Since World War II the union has been "ready and willing" to call for work stoppages whenever supply seemed about to cause problems. For example, in 1978 the UMW started a 110-day strike that stopped production during a boom period. In sum, from World War II until the energy crisis the UMW has privately regulated the coal industry.

**Strip mining.**    With the advent of the energy crisis in the 1970s and especially with the Arab oil embargo, coal gained much greater prominence as a source of energy. Coal production amounted to 840 million tons in 1980 and is expected to rise to one billion tons by 1985. Much of this increased production will occur in the western states since 55 percent of the United States' coal reserves, much of which is low in sulfur content, is located west of the Mississippi River. In 1970, for example, Montana produced only 3 million tons of coal; by 1980 its output had risen to 26 million tons. Because the western coal reserves lie close to the surface, strip mining is the most efficient form of production. And under these conditions the United Mine Workers have little effect on productivity because the UMW dominates in underground coal field operations. In areas where coal can be strip-mined by machine the union is ineffective.

While governmental officials generally agree that coal reserves must be developed, they also express concern over the effect that strip mining will have on the environment. Fears that grazing land would be destroyed, that revegetation may take many years, that underground water supplies may be disrupted or polluted, and that power-generating or coal gasification plants will cause air pollution, contributed to the passage of the Surface Mining Control and Reclamation Act of 1977. This act was designed to lessen the environmental effect of strip mining, by requiring industry to restore the mined land to a reasonable approximation of its original contours by replacing top soil and replanting the land with native plants (see chapter 4).

Another concern is over the effect of coal mining on western towns and cities. Gillette, Wyoming, located in a major coal producing area, had a population of 1,000 in 1970; by 1980 its population had grown to over 20,000 because of employment and business generated by mining. Similar boomtowns, with mobile homes constituting large portions of their dwellings, deficient city services, and alarming social problems, such as crime, alcoholism, divorce, and suicide, have appeared in mining and refining areas of the West. Westerners deplore these effects in other communities that may experience the same boom, disruption, and ugliness patterns.

A third problem concerns transporting the energy represented by coal to distant markets where it is needed. Suggestions include huge "unit trains" consisting of a hundred or more cars; use of generating plants located near mines, which would supply high-voltage transmission lines; coal gasification plants; and use of slurry pipelines, which would carry a mixture of powdered coal and water. Each of the alternatives has its advocates and opponents. No agreement seems forthcoming.

## Oil

Historically, the government regulated the petroleum industry in an effort to prevent excessive competition in the market. Specifically, production was controlled both to help maintain the price of crude petroleum and to conserve petroleum as a natural resource. The initial regulation was requested by the producers and was affected and shaped by legal and physical peculiarities in the production of oil.

The exploration of oil sites requires advanced technology and large capital outlay. Ownership of land overlying oil pools is normally divided into numerous holdings unrelated to the oil pools. Oil is present in a complex physical blending of gas pressure, water pressure, and structural geologic pressure. Maximization of production from oil reservoirs requires that the natural pressures which keep oil's viscosity high be utilized efficiently. Therefore, it is necessary to carefully space the wells in an oil field to maximize recovery of oil below ground.

Early Supreme Court decisions concerning ownership had the effect of encouraging inefficient utilization of oil. Since the land above the oil pool was normally owned by several private individuals, there was a proliferation of wells as individual owners attempted to extract as much oil as possible before neighboring plot owners drilled wells that drained the reservoir. As a result, depending on geological formation, as little as 10 percent of a field potential might be recovered. The Supreme Court decided that oil was like underground water and that owners could "capture" as much oil as possible.[13] These decisions resulted in either highly unstable gluts or market shortages in the 1920s, as well as a terrible waste of the resource. Thus, oil was an industry susceptible to boom and bust periods in its early stages.

The initial regulatory policy was threefold: First, state regulatory agencies, such as the Texas Railroad Commission, prorationed the amount of oil to be produced in each state. This involved control of production on a producer-by-producer basis to bring supply and demand into balance. Next, in 1935 the Interstate Compact to Conserve Oil and Gas provided for collaboration between oil-producing states. Finally, the federal government assisted the states in determining production quotas and in forbidding interstate shipments of oil and oil products produced in violation of state laws. Each of these forms of government policy was created during a time when oil production was, or was presumed to be, excessive. However, as stated earlier in this chapter, there is now little danger of overproduction of domestic oil, meaning that present oil policy differs markedly from past policies.

**Government regulation of domestic production.**    The first attempt at government intervention in the oil industry was concluded in 1911, when under the Sherman Antitrust Act the Rockefeller Standard Oil Company was found guilty of monopolization and restraint of trade, and its component parts were made independent companies. As a result of this action, the companies that had previously refined oil or distributed it now found it desirable to acquire wells and pipelines, which made for more competition but less effective control of the market.

The government's next major policy decisions came during World War I. Because the war had generated tremendous demands on oil production, President

Wilson created a Petroleum Advisory Committee to coordinate the industry's war efforts. The committee was dominated by oil producers seeking preference for their companies. In response the United States Fuel Administration was formed in 1917 to pool production, promote conservation, and allocate supplies. Again, however, the policy followed the interests of the private companies.

Immediately after the war there was a predicted shortage of oil; the head of the United States Geological Survey, for instance, said that we would run out of reserves in ten years. It is against the background of predicted oil shortages that the depletion allowance was passed in 1926. The logic was that just as machinery runs down and can therefore be depreciated, oil wells run dry and become worthless; therefore, something similar to a depreciation tax break was necessary. However, it was not easy to determine the life span of a well. The Republican Senate passed a 30 percent allowance while the Republican House passed a 25 percent allowance; a compromise 27.5 percent depletion allowance was made law in 1926. The law permitted an oil company to deduct 27.5 percent of its gross income as long as this figure did not exceed 50 percent of net income.[14]

The discovery of the Oklahoma and East Texas fields in 1929 and 1930, respectively, flooded the market with oil and drove the price down to as low as 10 cents a barrel. Violence flared in Texas and Oklahoma after both President Hoover and the Supreme Court refused to allow state agencies to restrict production.[15] However, without agreement from the other oil-producing states, Texas and Oklahoma could not effectively maintain national prices by restricting production in their states. The solution to this problem came in 1935 under the New Deal, when the Interstate Compact to Conserve Oil and Gas was formed: the oil-producing states agreed to cooperate to regulate production and to keep oil prices up. Against the backdrop of state-regulated production and producer-state cooperation on production, the federal government's role was to supplement this arrangement by having the Bureau of Mines make monthly forecasts of demands for oil products at current prices and then convert these forecasts to crude oil production equivalents on a state-by-state basis. Another supplemental federal activity involved the Connally "Hot Oil" Act of 1935, which prohibited shipment in interstate commerce of oil produced in violation of state production control laws.

**Government regulation of oil imports.**    Public policy toward importation of oil shifted as America's dependence on imported oil rose. In the first fifteen years after World War II, the problem of restricting imports was handled by voluntary means. That is, imports were held to approximately 15 percent of total oil usage by an informal agreement among the giant international companies, such as Texaco, Gulf, and Standard Oil of New Jersey; they were careful to keep import levels low enough to prevent Congress from legislating restrictions. However, during the mid-1950s, independent oil companies (such as the Getty Oil Company) began to import oil, and the percentage of imported oil used crept higher. This, of course, stimulated domestic producers to ask the president and Congress to restrict import levels, lest domestic prices be depressed by competition from lower-priced foreign oil. In 1955 President Eisenhower and Congress agreed to a government-coordinated program to restrict oil imports. It proved difficult to implement, and by 1958 the program was more mandatory than voluntary. The formal switch to a mandatory program came during the recession of 1958, when oil-field production time in Texas and Oklahoma was reduced to eight days a month. The decrease in production resulted in domestic unemployment and lower profits for domestic oil corporations. The pressure from unemployed workers and from the corporations resulted in mandatory restrictions on imported oil. This mandatory program was continued (with the amounts of imported oil increasing incrementally) as an uneasy fulcrum between cheaper imports and more expensive domestic oil.

However, as the demand for oil increased rapidly during the late 1960s and early 1970s, the amount of imported oil rose dramatically to meet demand from 20.5 percent in 1964 to 29 percent in 1973 to 44 percent in 1978. After the Arab oil embargo, government policy changed to meet the new circumstances. In spite of successive presidents' policies for energy independence, present policy is to assure a steady supply of oil to meet demand, and the major actors are the multinational companies and the OPEC countries. Of course, policies that were once useful in controlling supply are not now feasible because of the present energy situation. The major difference is that state agencies, oil compact, and federal shipments have much less significance in a situation where America's own production meets less than two-thirds of national demand. (Specific policy changes are discussed later in this chapter.)

### Natural Gas

Until the development of high-pressure welded pipelines in the 1920s, natural gas was not an important source of energy. Often discovered in conjunction with oil, large quantities of gas were vented or flared (burned) at the wellhead. After World War II, long-distance transmission pipelines introduced gas into major new markets, especially in the northern and eastern parts of the country, and consumption of natural gas expanded greatly because of such factors as low price, cleanliness, and convenience. The low price of natural gas was essentially the result of government regulation, which began in the 1950s.

**Government regulation of gas.**    The natural gas industry encompasses three basic economic functions: production and gathering of gas in the field; transmission of gas to the market area; and distribution of gas to the ultimate consumers. A series of Supreme Court decisions placed the first and third functions within the scope of state regulatory power. Much of the transmission of gas, however, takes place in interstate commerce and therefore falls under the jurisdiction of the national government.[16] State utility commissions established to protect consumer interests could regulate the prices charged to local consumers but not the wholesale prices at which gas was sold to local distributing companies by interstate pipeline companies. The lack of power to regulate these wholesale rates greatly handicapped the states in their efforts to regulate and hold down the prices charged to ultimate consumers.

This jurisdictional gap was filled when Congress enacted the Natural Gas Act of 1938, partly in response to abuses in the operation of interstate pipeline companies. The act empowered the Federal Power Commission (FPC) which became the Federal Energy Regulatory Commission (FERC) in 1977 to regulate the transportation and sale of natural gas in interstate commerce. The important role that administrative agencies can play in policymaking, and the broad discretion that they may have, is amply illustrated by the commission's natural gas rate setting.

The commission was directed to ensure that all sales of gas within its jurisdiction were at "just and reasonable" prices. Production and gathering of gas, direct sales to industrial users, and the local distribution of gas were exempted from control by the commission. A problem soon arose, however, because the act did not make clear whether field prices of natural gas (the prices charged by producers and gatherers to pipeline companies) were sales in interstate commerce and subject to FPC control or were a part of production and gathering and thus beyond its power.

At first the commission held that it did not have jurisdiction over field (or wellhead) prices charged by "independent" producers. Then, in 1943, the commission reversed itself and claimed such jurisdiction. This decision was quickly challenged by the gas producers, but the Supreme Court upheld the FPC, ruling that all sales to interstate pipeline companies were sales in interstate commerce and thus within the commission's jurisdiction. Efforts were made in Congress at the behest of gas interests to exempt independent producers from FPC regulation. These culminated in the passage of the Kerr Bill in 1950, which was vetoed by President Truman. (The bill was named for its sponsor, Sen. Robert Kerr of Oklahoma, who was an owner of the Kerr-McGee Gas and Oil Company.)

The FPC now became the primary focus of the regulatory struggle. While the Supreme Court had held that the commission was authorized to regulate the prices of independent producers, it had not said that the commission was *required* to do so. In 1954, in the *Phillips Petroleum Company* case, the FPC again changed its mind and held that the exemption of production and gathering included sales by independent producers to pipeline companies.[17] Consumer interests, represented by the state of Wisconsin and several cities, quickly challenged this action. The Supreme Court reversed the FPC's decision and directed it to regulate independent producers' wellhead prices. The effect of the Court's action was to increase substantially the responsibility of a reluctant commission. In 1956 and 1958 the gas industry sought legislation from Congress to exempt independents from regulation, but both attempts failed to become law.

The commission initially sought to discharge its new responsibility by regulating producers' prices on an individual basis.[18] It was, however, swamped by the large volume of cases (nearly eleven thousand rate requests in the first year) generated by this effort. In 1960 the commission ceased trying to set rates on a case-by-case basis and shifted to a system of area pricing under which the country was divided into several producing areas for rate-setting purposes. The first area rate proceedings, involving areas of West Texas and New Mexico, was completed in 1965. A two-tiered system of rates was developed. One set of rates applied to "old" gas from wells in production before 1961. Gas from wells coming into production after January 1961, and which was produced in conjunction with oil, was covered by a higher set of "new" gas rates. The higher rates for new gas were intended to encourage increased production and to make more gas available in the interstate market. Rate proceedings for other areas were completed in subsequent years.

**Attempts at deregulation.** By the early 1970s a shortage in the supply of natural gas had developed, as evidenced by the inability of many gas users to secure all the gas they wished to use. Two general, and conflicting, explanations for the natural gas shortage have been put forward. To critics of rate regulation, the low rates set for gas by the FPC were the problem. They say these low rates discouraged exploration and production and caused more gas to be sold in intrastate markets, where prices have been considerably higher. The solution, contend the critics, is to "deregulate" the price of natural gas. An opposing explanation holds that the shortage is partly the result of substantially greater demand for natural gas and partly a consequence of the prospect of deregulation and higher prices, which caused producers to produce and sell less gas in the interstate market. Advocates of this position maintain that eliminating uncertainty about the future of regulation would help alleviate the gas shortage.

In 1975 and 1976, a major effort was made in Congress, with the support of the Ford administration, to enact legislation eliminating the FPC's authority to regulate natural gas rates. A bill to accomplish this was passed by the Senate. In the House, however, supporters of regulation were successful in amending the bill so as to continue regulation of large gas producers and extend federal regulation to intrastate sales, while exempting thousands of small producers from controls. This bill was unacceptable to the gas industry and its supporters, who wanted complete deregulation. The bill subsequently died without being brought to conference.

In the summer of 1976, when it became obvious that Congress was not going to act, the FPC took major action on gas rates. Area pricing was abandoned in favor of a nationwide price for natural gas of $1.42 per thousand cubic feet, with annual escalations.[19] This rate was nearly three times as high as the previous maximum rate. The commission majority said that this higher rate was necessary to induce producers to engage in expanded exploration, production, and sale of gas. They did not guarantee, however, that domestic production of natural gas would actually register an increase. Where once the commission had been primarily concerned with protecting consumers, its focus had shifted to the interest of gas production (and gas producers). The commission's new policy thrust, while providing for substantial deregulation by administrative action, did not halt the campaign for legislation that would provide total deregulation. In 1978, after a long fight, the Congress passed the Natural Gas Policy Act. This law extended federal control into intrastate natural gas pricing, which, of course, allowed the government to set the same limits on pricing across all fifty states. In addition the 1978 act enabled the government to phase out price controls on new gas discoveries and on some interstate gas by 1985. (More specific aspects of natural gas policy will be discussed later in the chapter.)

## Atomic Energy

American nuclear policy has had two stages of development. During the first stage, 1946 to 1954, atomic energy was viewed as primarily military in nature, and policy was dominated by military interests. Atomic material was controlled by the government, and research activity was devoted to improving atomic weaponry. A second aspect of military atomic energy policy was to prevent foreign powers from learning the secret of the atomic and hydrogen bombs. The second stage saw a shift from a government monopoly to a combination of public and private control of energy as nuclear power came to be viewed as an important peacetime energy source. At present atomic energy policy emphasizes research for both peaceful and military uses of nuclear materials, and the regulation of special nuclear materials used in private and public production of energy.

The Atomic Energy Act of 1946 created the Atomic Energy Commission (AEC), which continued the government monopoly of atomic energy begun with the development of the atomic bomb. The act of 1946 established civilian rather than military control of the AEC, although, to be sure, the military interests were represented in the AEC. In the 1946–1948 period the AEC was run by the General Advisory Council, composed of scientists who had built the bomb. Policy during this period was to rapidly develop military uses of atomic energy to provide national security.

The Russian explosion of an atomic bomb in 1949 precipitated new congressional interest in the AEC and atomic energy. The long-range effect of growing congressional interest was to expand emphasis on the atom's potential for generating electrical energy. The pressure to find peaceful civilian uses of atomic energy and the need for international cooperation on atomic research led to the passage of the 1954 revision of the AEC's charter. Private energy companies did not want such a high-potential fuel solely under government control, and the military had good reason to believe that international cooperation would allow it to better monitor other nations' atomic progress.

The 1954 legislation divided up the new atomic industry according to a pattern almost identical to that of the electric power industry. That is, private enterprise would dominate generation and distribution of nuclear-produced energy while government would have control through licensing, regulating rates, and assured access to AEC experimental plants. The most important difference between nuclear fuel and electrical power was that the AEC would continue to own all fissile materials and would lease to the private utilities what was needed.

Since the passage of the 1954 revisions, some policy disagreements have arisen over whether or not private industry was progressing at a sufficient rate to provide sufficient electrical power to meet future energy needs. Public power advocates have pushed for legislation creating publicly owned nuclear power plants, while private power advocates have insisted that progress in this area was sufficient.

Policy disagreements today are mostly concerned with the safety of nuclear power. Early in the 1970s objections to nuclear power began to take shape. A major event occurred on March 28, 1979, when the water pumps used to cool the nuclear fuel rods at the Three Mile Island nuclear plant in Harrisburg, Pennsylvania, broke down and the core melted. While the radioactive materials did not leak into the environment, similar close calls and the resultant public outcry spawned an antinuclear power protest.

Opposition to nuclear power continues unabated. In September 1981, thousands of antinuclear power protesters converged on Diablo Canyon in California to attempt to block construction of a nuclear plant. Similar events in New Hampshire, Texas, and other states attest to the growing ranks of the antinuclear power protesters. In New York City, in spring 1982, a massive demonstration against nuclear power drew the largest crowds ever for an event of this kind. The Reagan administration has pledged support of America's nuclear industry, but few companies are planning to build nuclear plants given the rising costs—both economic and political—associated with nuclear power. Plants scheduled to be completed by 1985 will in all likelihood be constructed, but not without significant opposition.[20]

One result of the burgeoning opposition to nuclear power in the 1970s was the reorganization of the Atomic Energy Commission. How can safety standards be enforced in nuclear plants, and how can the government safeguard against illegal uses of nuclear materials once nuclear power is a mainstay of energy? The approach has been first to develop nuclear power and then to assure safety in its use. In 1974 the AEC was abolished and two new agencies were created. The first was the Energy Research and Development Administration (ERDA), which consolidated all federal agencies dealing with energy research. The second was the Nuclear Regulatory Commission (NRC), which took over the AEC's regulatory functions. The creation of the NRC was testimony to the impact of nuclear safety as a political issue. Moreover, the emergence of public pressure groups, seeking either to eliminate nuclear energy sources or at least to curtail their use, is becoming an important concern. In a number of states such groups have succeeded in getting proposals limiting nuclear energy on the ballot as referenda. Thus far, none has been successful, but continued attempts to limit nuclear energy are assured.

## NEW ENERGY POLITICS

This section on new energy politics is organized around three general questions: How does the new energy politics differ from the old energy politics? How has the new politics changed policy? Our strategy is to present a case study demonstrating how the new politics changed policy in the field of oil, rather than to review each of the energy areas separately. The primary reason for adopting this approach is that an underlying political phenomenon cuts across all of the energy areas; that is, the "energy crisis" has vastly expanded the numbers of individuals, groups, agencies, and officials who are interested and involved in energy politics and policy. Moreover, as Schattschneider showed, when a conflict is expanded, the nature of politics and policy is changed.[21] A second reason for taking a case study approach is that the creation of the Federal Energy Administration in 1974 and ultimately the Department of Energy under Carter reflects the fact that *energy,* not just coal or oil or nuclear energy, has become the overriding concern.

In the new energy politics, then, the number of individuals and groups participating in the policymaking process has rapidly expanded. Because of widening participation, new and diverse viewpoints are relevant and must be figured in the policy equation. As a result, the issues in energy politics have shifted dramatically, from limited fuel production to all-out production, from simple energy growth to energy versus the environment, and from providing cheap energy to achieving national energy independence.

The major factor precipitating expanded participation, and thus the changed issues, was the energy crisis. The Arab oil embargo of 1973–1974 forced upon the United States full recognition of its energy dependence. The crisis had been building for a number of years as petroleum consumption had outstripped domestic production. However, it was the oil embargo that clearly brought home the facts of energy dependence to most Americans. At that time such matters as national dependence, investment credits, multinational corporations, the depletion allowance, windfall profits, and energy conservation became pressing issues. In short, the problem moved from the shadows of subsystem politics into the spotlight of macropolitics (see chapter 1). No longer were congressmen from Texas, Oklahoma, and Louisiana the only ones concerned about energy. Consumer-state congressmen felt obliged to be informed about these matters as their constituents waited in long lines to pay twice as much for gasoline. In addition, after an extensive oil spill off the coast of Santa Barbara, California, in 1969, and other such disasters since, environmentalists became concerned about the effects of energy production on natural resources. As both environmentalists' and consumers' demands were being incorporated into the policy process, politicians were prevailed upon to respond. As mentioned before, when the number of participants increases, the issues—and ultimately, the policy—are changed.

## New Participants

In the old energy politics specific participants varied across energy areas, but the general pattern was for the politics to be dominated by a narrow combination of producers' groups, the relevant government department or commission, and a small number of representatives and senators from producing states. There were, to be sure, variations on this theme, but they were minor and usually fuel-related. The politics of coal, for the reasons given earlier, included the United Mine Workers, whereas the politics of natural gas dictated the creation of commissions to regulate prices at the distribution points. Given these variations, the old regulatory politics had essentially the same purpose: to stabilize the energy industry by controlling production—either through labor union control or through state regulatory commissions. Stabilization was often achieved with the aid of congressional committees dominated by representatives and senators from producing states.

Just who participated in the old energy politics can be briefly summarized by energy area. In coal the mine owners and the UMW were the major participating groups. The agencies most directly involved in coal politics were the Department of Interior (and its Bureau of Mines), the Department of Labor, and, peripherally, the Department of Health, Education and Welfare. At the congressional level the House and Senate Interior Committees, as well as the Labor Committees and related subcommittees, were involved. In the politics of natural gas the traditional group participants were the producers and the local utility commissions who regulated prices and distribution points in the consumer's interest; the FPC dominated interstate regulation of the industry, while the Department of Interior and its Geological Survey was of aid to producers. In Congress the Ways and Means Committee in the House and the Interior Committees in the House and Senate were the main battlegrounds for natural gas. In oil policy the American Petroleum Institute and the major oil corporations long dominated policy. Regulation came primarily from producing-state commissions, which prorationed oil production. The Department of Interior and its Geological Survey and Division of Oil and Gas were also involved in a supporting role. In Congress the Ways and Means Committee was the major oil policy battleground. Atomic energy was controlled by the combined interests of the major energy-producing corporations (oil companies, General Electric, and Westinghouse)—the Atomic Industrial Forum, the AEC, and the Joint Committee on Atomic Energy.

Although the participants in the old energy politics varied somewhat, one central point stands out. In most cases the only effective participants were producer interests directly involved in and affected by policy decisions. Participation was by a small select group, and oil policy clearly reflected the dominance of producer groups. In natural gas policy, consumer groups and interests were more prominent than they were in oil politics. However, in the last decade producer interests have gained much more influence over natural gas policy.

Table 3–1 shows how the energy crisis precipitated an increase in participation, the formation of new agencies to deal with the crisis, and a renewed and broadened congressional interest in energy as well as a changed congressional policy stance. Consumer groups and western-state congressmen are now heavily involved in energy politics. Numerous federal agencies (and ultimately the Department of Energy) were created to deal with the problems involved and to process the demands placed on the energy system. Furthermore, OPEC now dominates in an area where as late as 1971 the multinational corporation held sway. As the available supply of energy at low costs diminished, the politics of the unlimited-use policy could not remain stable. Accelerating gas and oil prices more than anything else forced the public to become aware of the problem. In light of increased public awareness, new consumer group demands, and disputes with oil-producing nations, the old energy politics were displaced.

## The New Oil Policy: A Case Study

The purpose of oil policy in the United States traditionally was to ensure the oil industry a stable market for its products, with attention also given to oil conservation. The result of this policy was cheap energy prices to consumers and unlimited use. Close cooperation between government and industry was evident: the oil industry had its major contact with the government through the Department of Interior and its Geological Survey and Division of Oil and Gas. The staff of the Oil and Gas Division was small. When asked how such a limited staff could do all that was necessary, its director replied, "The secret of our success lies in government and industry cooperation. Each year through advisory committees and personal contacts the federal government obtains thousands of man hours of invaluable assistance from hundreds of outstanding leaders and technical experts in this industry."[22] It is not surprising, under this arrangement, that government policy and industry policy became intertwined.

The Interior Department in the past was advised on oil policy through a number of commissions and advisory groups, which were staffed by industry representatives. The relationship was more than advisory, in that the Oil and Gas Division took the position that it should not have authority to make policy for the industry. In the words of the Oil and Gas director, "We would lose effectiveness if we had any authority. We are not authorized to establish federal policy with respect to oil and gas."[23]

At the congressional level the oil industry's major contacts were with Interior Committees and the Ways and Means Committee in Congress. The Ways and Means Committee was important because tax policy is made in that committee. (The Public Works and Finance Committees have sometimes also been involved in oil matters.)

Prior to the new oil politics, committee decisions were made, with industry cooperation, in a closed situation. In 1950–1951 and in 1962–1963 presidential attempts to decrease the depletion allowance were defeated in the House Ways and Means Committee without public votes by either committee members or the whole House; and, in general, partially because of the closed nature of the policy process, representatives and senators from oil-producing states were able to control legislation in the Congress. That is, in most cases attempts were being made to change existing policy, and preserving the status quo is easier when the number of interests involved is restricted. In oil politics prior to the late 1960s, moreover, the policy process was dominated by the American Petroleum Institute (API), a trade association of oil companies, including both large and small companies. Through its members' service on the advisory boards and commissions of the Interior Department, the API substantially controlled Department of Interior policy regarding oil. At the congressional level the industry was able to resist policy changes because of public apathy and a lack of organized counterinterests, which allowed decisions to be made in relative obscurity. This closed subsystem form of politics began to change in the later 1960s.

**TABLE 3-1.** Congressional and governmental participants in the old and new energy politics

| | Old politics |
|---|---|
| Governmental and Congressional | Department of Health, Education, and Welfare |
| | Department of Interior |
| | Department of Labor |
| | House Committees: |
| |   Interior |
| |   Labor |
| |   Ways and Means |
| | Senate Committees: |
| |   Finance |
| |   Interior |
| |   Labor |
| | Atomic Energy Commission |
| | Federal Power Commission |
| | Joint Committee on Atomic Energy |
| | State and local regulatory commissions |
| | Members of Congress from oil-producing states |

| | New politics |
|---|---|
| Governmental | Agencies and Corporations: |
| |   Civil Aeronautics Board |
| |   Environmental Protection Agency |
| |   Federal Maritime Commission |
| |   Federal Trade Commission |
| |   International Development Cooperation Agency |
| |   Interstate Commerce Commission |
| |   National Aeronautics and Space Administration |
| |   National Science Foundation |
| |   National Transportation Safety Board |
| |   Nuclear Regulatory Commission |
| |   Tennessee Valley Authority |
| |   U.S. Railway Association |
| | Departments: |
| |   Agriculture |
| |   Commerce |
| |     Census |
| |     International Trade Administration |
| |     Bureau of Standards |
| |   Energy |
| |     Energy Regulatory Administration |
| |     Federal Energy Regulatory Commission |
| |     Regional Power Administration |
| | Housing and Urban Development |
| | Interior |
| |   Bureau of Mines |
| |   Office of Surface Mining |
| |   Reclamation |
| |   Geological Survey |
| |   Water and Power Resources Administration |
| | Justice |
| | State |
| | Treasury |

**TABLE 3-1**
(*continued*)

| *New politics* |
| --- |

| | |
| --- | --- |
| **Governmental** | Transportation |
| |   Federal Aviation Administration |
| |   Federal Highway Administration |
| |   Federal Railroad Administration |
| |   National Highway Transportation |
| |   Safety Administration |
| |   Urban Mass Transportation Administration |
| | Executive Office of President |
| |   Council on Environmental Quality |
| |   Domestic Policy Staff |
| |   Office of Management and Budget |
| |   Office of Science and Technology |
| **Congressional** | |
| **House:** | Agriculture |
| |   2 subcommittees |
| | Appropriation |
| |   3 subcommittees |
| | Banking Finance and Urban Affairs |
| | Budget |
| | Education and Labor |
| | Goverment Operations |
| |   2 subcommittees |
| | Interior and Insular Affairs |
| |   4 subcommittees |
| | Interstate and Foreign Commerce |
| |   3 subcommittees |
| | Merchant Marine and Fisheries |
| |   2 subcommittees |
| | Public Works and Transportation |
| |   2 subcommittees |
| | Science and Technology |
| |   4 subcommittees |
| | Select Committee on Outer Continental Shelf |
| | Small Business |
| | Ways and Means |
| **Senate:** | Agriculture, Nutrition, and Forestry |
| |   2 subcommittees |
| | Appropriations |
| |   2 subcommittees |
| | Banking, Housing, and Urban Affairs |
| | Budget |
| | Commerce, Science and Transportation |
| |   3 subcommittees |
| | Energy and Natural Resources |
| |   5 subcommittees |
| | Environment and Public Works |
| |   4 subcommittees |
| | Finance |
| | Governmental Affairs |
| | Labor and Human Resources |

Transformation in the politics of oil began with the rise of environmentalism as a political issue. Such matters as oil spills and pollutants in the air and water became the concern of more than a few individuals in environmental interest groups. National attention focused on the deterioration of the environment. People began to speak of the concept of "spaceship earth," recognizing that the conditions for human life depend on the conservation of natural resources. Environmentalists, western-state officials, concerned biologists, and college students became active participants in energy politics and advocates of strong federal legislation to control the effects of pollution in the environment. Everyone has seen television commercials or read advertisements that promote big-energy interests at the expense of extreme environmentalists. For the first time oil companies have had to appeal to the general public for understanding and support of their situation.

The creation of the Environmental Protection Agency (EPA) in 1970 was partly in response to public pressure and this affected oil companies. The EPA was empowered to establish standards and penalize corporations and others who violated these standards. In order to dump pollutants the oil companies had to justify such disposal to the EPA as well as demonstrate that pollution abatement methods were being developed and used. Congress demonstrated that it favored a change in environmental policy by passing EPA legislation. With the Congress and the executive branches of government favoring new environmental policy, the oil industry was forced to turn to the public for support. The advertising campaigns mentioned above were indicative of a changing politics of oil: under increased public scrutiny and participation, the politics of oil was no longer able to operate within a closed system. The conflict expanded, and the politics changed.

The major factor accounting for the expanded politics of oil was the OPEC oil embargo of 1973, which caused shortages in gasoline and heating oil as well as increased prices for these and other petroleum products. Thus, the average American waited in long gasoline lines, turned down the thermostat at home, and paid more to use less. Public opinion focused on the oil companies and their "windfall" profits (increased profits due to abrupt price increases). Congressmen from consumer states were pressed by constituents to explain rising prices and diminishing quantities of fuel. Senate and House investigating committees claimed that the oil shortage was an attempt by the major companies to force independents from the marketplace. Elected representatives never before concerned about the politics of oil became involved because their constituents were interested. The oil industry now had to justify the depletion allowance and the foreign investments credit tax (a tax break whereby foreign investments are deductible from American income taxes) to the Senate and House committees. First the Federal Energy Office, then the Federal Energy Administration, and finally under Carter (1977), the Department of Energy became responsible for policy concerning oil (and gas) interests. Production, transmission, and distribution of oil had become a macropolitical issue, no longer dominated by a select group of producers, oil state officials, and friendly bureaucrats. Differences in approaches to the problem among Democrats and Republicans, industry, environmentalists, and consumers, independent and major producers, became prominent. In the 94th Congress (1975–1976) the president proposed one oil policy while House Democrats proposed another, and each Democratic presidential hopeful in the Senate sought his own singular solution. Oil had to turn to the public to justify windfall profits and a number of other industry policies. As Bruce Oppenheimer concluded, "The new public stance the industry has taken is not a sign of strength, but a symptom of weakness."[24] We can predict that the politics of oil will not be easily controlled by the industry, and compromise with consumer and environmental interests will be forthcoming, just as consumers and environmentalists will have to compromise and comprehend the oil industry's problems.

The politics and policies of natural gas, coal, and nuclear energy have followed the pattern observed for oil. The increased participation of environmental and consumer groups has not been limited to oil. Coal, natural gas, and nuclear energy have their fair share of conservation and consumer groups actively involved in the policy process. Today most congressmen are informed on the problems of strip mining, gas shortages, radioactive pollution, and the like. In sum, energy politics in all areas has "gone public," with the result being a change in who gets what.

There is, however, no consensus regarding energy policy. Large portions of the consuming public are not prepared to accept the fact that energy can no longer be unlimited in supply and cheap in cost. This problem is further compounded by the fact that in mid-1982 gas and oil were readily available; the Arab countries have reopened the pipelines and Americans are using less energy. Producers, oil corporations, and government officials who warn that the crisis has not passed are not accorded a good deal of attention by the American public. In politics wherever there are constituents, there are political representatives; therefore, there are spokesmen for producers, consumers, internationalists, isolationists, regions, and others. In short, there is no agreement as to how the goals of energy policy should be achieved. Moreover, since energy is an important policy area that has been shifted from subsystem to a macropolitical level, a myriad of groups and interests are involved.

## ENERGY POLICY GOALS

It is by now obvious that oil will have to bear an increasing share of America's energy burden. Until some time in the twenty-first century, when nuclear or solar power will perhaps be able to replace oil as the main source of American energy, oil will probably continue to account for about 50 percent of all energy used in the United States. The Arab oil embargo in 1973 hit the United States at a time when demand for petroleum products was growing rapidly and domestic supplies remained constant at 1970 levels. The cutback in oil supplies and subsequent price increases thus defined the nature of the problem in the energy crisis. In the context of the energy crisis with its expanded politics, government energy policy is primarily concerned with four problems: (1) protecting consumers and businesses against short-run energy shortages resulting from foreign (essentially OPEC) initiatives; (2) long-range protection of natural resources—assuring energy sources for the future; (3) protecting the environment from damage caused by energy production, consumption, and waste disposal; (4) assuring a "proper" distribution of income between producers and consumers.[25]

### Protection from Foreign Initiatives

There were essentially two strategies available to the Nixon and Ford administrations regarding dependence on imported oil. The first alternative was to institute policies that would assure self-sufficiency by a certain date. The second strategy, the insurance policy, was to continue oil imports as long as they were cheaper than domestic oil but, at the same time, to protect the economy from embargoes and price increases. The self-sufficiency policy meant increased prices while the insurance policy emphasized lower prices. The Nixon-Ford administration policy stressed self-sufficiency and entailed raising oil prices to cut back on energy consumption. For example, President Ford in early 1975 placed a $3 per barrel tax on imported oil and raised taxes on all oil. (The $3 per barrel tax was subsequently removed.) The increased price of foreign oil was to encourage domestic production as well as decrease dependence on imports. However, the policy did not decrease dependence and was subsequently dropped.

### Resource Protection

Although the United States has an estimated 50 to 100 years' supply of natural gas and oil, over 100 years of oil shale, and over 500 years of coal, it is clear that fossil fuel supplies are in finite supply. Given finite supplies, some people have argued that the free-market mechanism encourages present rates of consumption at future expense and that, therefore, the government should pursue a policy that limits present production levels. However, the Nixon-Ford policy of trying to ensure domestic self-sufficiency encouraged short-run expansion of United States output even though it depleted reserves for the future.

### Protecting the Environment

The process of producing and consuming energy creates effects that are often not reflected in the market price of energy commodities. For instance, coal can be produced quickly and cheaply by strip mining, but unless the strip-mined land is restored, the environment suffers. Likewise, gasoline used in automobiles contributes to heavy air concentrations of carbon monoxide and smog, and offshore oil drilling risks spillage and pollution. Neither the costs of auto-emission damage nor offshore spillage is reflected in the market price of oil and gasoline. Economists call these side effects *externalities* because the market price does not include the cost of polluted land, air, and water. Thus, in the area of externalities or side effects, governmental policy must make sure that these costs are included in energy prices.

Government policy can achieve this end by either prohibiting certain activities or utilizing various taxes and other charges so that social costs are included in the energy prices. Outright prohibition of activities emphasizes the incompatibility of preserving the environment and increasing energy consumption, because in order to get more cheap energy, pollution risks are increased. However, in some areas, such as urban mass transit systems, the goals of preserving the environment and of encouraging efficient use of energy are compatible. Accordingly, policy is more easily agreed upon—for instance, the 1975 budget included increased subsidization of mass transit.

Of course, in many areas the two goals of protection and consumption come into open conflict, and in these fields policy has changed rapidly according to circumstances. For example, prior to the 1973 oil embargo the Nixon administration had moved ahead forcefully in protecting the environment through the creation of the Environmental Protection Agency and other actions. With the advent of the oil crisis and the onset of the 1974–1975 recession, the Ford administration's policy shifted to increased energy production and economic stimulation at the price of environmental controls. In 1975 the EPA's timetable for pollution devices on automobiles was delayed for five years due to economic pressures.

### Distribution of Windfall Profits

The size and durability of the market for fuels is so large that disruptive events, such as the OPEC oil embargo or a great increase in world oil prices, can create windfall profits for oil and gas companies. Correspondingly large costs to consumers in all income brackets occur. Government policy will determine who will pay the increased fuel costs. Market solutions place a disproportionate share of the burden on the less well-to-do, while regulatory decisions place a heavier burden on energy companies. Debates over windfall profits, taxes, and deregulating natural gas prices all testify to the continuing importance of this problem. For example, early in 1982 President Reagan decided not to push for deregulation of natural gas prior to 1985 because Republican representatives did not wish to campaign for reelection with consumers bearing the brunt of increased heating costs. Government policy that seeks to redistribute cost burdens can follow one of two broad strategies. On one hand it can let energy prices rise and tax away profits. The other avenue is to prevent a price rise by wage and price controls.

### Policy in the Nixon-Ford Era

The Nixon-Ford policy toward income redistribution as a result of large profit taking by energy companies was to allow prices to increase without severely taxing oil and gas companies. A windfall profits tax and a decrease in foreign investment credits were the major tax-increasing proposals in Ford's 1975 State of the Union message. Public policy regarding the redistribution of income from energy profits was in 1975 an important area of disagreement between the Democratic Congress and President Ford.

The Nixon-Ford administration responded to the energy crisis by creating the Federal Energy Administration (FEA) in 1974. The authority of the FEA was to manage the federal response to energy shortages. In addition, the government succeeded in passing a $20 billion research effort concentrating on conservation, solar energy, coal gasification, and other energy resources. The Congress also passed a 55-mile-per-hour speed limit law, a bill restoring standard daylight time for the winter months, and extended for half a year the Emergency Petroleum Allocation Act of 1973. This last act authorized the president to control supply allocations and pricing of oil. Conflicts between environmentalists, those favoring price ceilings, and free-market advocates characterized the policy debates. Presidents Nixon and Ford vetoed energy legislation which they felt was not in accord with their policies. For example, Nixon vetoed the Energy Emergency Act because of its low price ceilings, while Ford pocket-vetoed a strip-mining bill that the coal industry favored. Both Nixon and Ford backed bills that would have deregulated natural gas, but due to Democratic majorities in the House and Senate, their efforts met with failure.

### 1975 Energy Act

In 1975 President Ford signed the Energy Policy and Conservation Act. The most important aspect of the bill was the continuation of oil price controls. Ford had earlier opposed price controls but signed the bill when Congress agreed to phase out controls over time.

The 1975 energy legislation reflects the diversity of interests in energy policy. Six House committees and nine Senate committees worked on parts of the bill; for example, the Commerce Committee in the House was responsible for the rollback in oil prices, while the Ways and Means Committee worked on taxation measures such as the depletion allowance. In the Senate the Armed Services Committee dealt with energy matters related to defense, while the Interior and Commerce Committees handled consumer-related aspects of the bill. Besides these committees there were alliances of congressmen politicking for the interests of their regions, investigating committees, and policy papers by the hundreds. Obviously everyone wanted a say regarding energy. There was no shortage of policy proposals and recommendations.

Sharp differences arose between the Republican president and the Democratic Congress over the direction of energy policy. The Nixon-Ford approach tended to favor a market solution (that is, to let prices rise), along with the goal of seeking energy independence by 1985. Many Democrats favored price rollbacks and more government regulation and control of the oil industry.

The 1975 Energy Act was therefore the product of compromises between President Ford and the Democratic Congress. An omnibus act, it contained provisions for energy conservation, production stimulation, income distribution, and measures to insulate the nation from the impact of a sudden termination of foreign supplies. The energy bill had five parts, which are outlined below.

Coal production was encouraged by allowing the FEA to order major fuel-burning plants to switch to coal and to loan money to develop underground coal mines, which produce fewer pollutants.

Standby power was given to the president for use in energy crises. Specifically, the president could restrict imports and allocate scarce supplies, require gas and oil production increases, and require gas and oil corporations to maintain and distribute certain levels of oil and petroleum products. Moreover, it was specified that the United States shall create a reserve of one billion barrels of oil and petroleum (a three-month supply of imports) by 1980. The United States had by late 1982 met this reserve requirement.

Fuel economy standards were set for automobiles, as were energy efficiency tests and standards for major appliances, and efficiency measures were established for states, industries, and the federal government. As an example of standard setting, automobiles were to average 18 miles per gallon by 1978 and 26 miles per gallon by 1985.

A fourth section rolled back domestic oil prices from $8.75 per barrel in December 1975 to no more than an average of $7.66 a barrel. The president could adjust the price of various categories of domestic oil as long as the average price does not exceed $7.66 per barrel. In this averaging procedure old domestic oil was priced lower than new, recently discovered, oil ($5.25 per barrel for old oil; $11.28 for new oil in 1977). This average price was, of course, far below the price of OPEC oil ($13.50 a barrel in 1977) and was criticized by oil producers as a serious restraint on the free-enterprise system. Proponents argued that the rollback assured the American consumer that oil prices would not double in a two-year period as they did in 1973–1975. These price controls were slated to last forty months, at which time market considerations would be applied.

Finally, the act provided for congressional review of presidential actions and authorized the GAO (the auditing and investigating arm of Congress described in chapter 2) to audit energy producers and distributors.

In sum, the energy policy in the act of 1975 was meant to encourage the substitution of coal for oil, set energy conservation standards, redistribute income by controlling domestic oil prices, and provide for a billion-barrel petroleum reserve.

## Natural Gas Deregulation

Further consideration of the struggle over natural gas deregulation helps in understanding energy policy in the Nixon and Ford administrations. As we have seen, interstate natural gas was in short supply and federally regulated. As a consequence the wellhead price for new natural gas consumed by many Texans in 1974 was $2.20 per thousand cubic feet while the price for gas sent to New Jersey was $1.42 per thousand cubic feet. People in Texas paid more but were usually assured of a continuing supply, while those living on the East Coast paid less but experienced shortages of gas. The problem of equal allocations of both prices and supplies became serious.

In 1975 the Senate passed a natural gas bill dealing with short-term shortages by setting priorities for curtailment in use. When the bill came to the House floor in early 1976, a major amendment was proposed by Rep. Robert Krueger (D.–Tex.). This amendment would have ended price controls immediately for onshore natural gas and after five years for offshore gas. However, opponents of deregulation, mostly northern Democrats, managed to substitute for the Krueger proposal an amendment that deregulated several thousand small independent producers but retained controls on twenty-five to thirty major producers and extended the controls to the intrastate sales of these producers. The amended measure passed the House by a narrow vote of 205 to 201. It was strongly opposed by those who favored deregulation, including President Ford.

Later in 1976, the Senate Commerce Committee approved a compromise bill, which would have permitted gas prices to rise considerably while retaining federal controls. Although the prospects for this bill looked good, no floor action was taken, and the 94th Congress ended without the enactment of any deregulation legislation—partly because proponents of deregulation, such as Representative Krueger, refused to budge from their advocacy of total deregulation. During the 1972 presidential campaign, both Carter and Ford favored deregulation.

## ENERGY POLICY IN THE CARTER ADMINISTRATION

### Strategy

On April 20, 1977, President Carter proposed his comprehensive energy policy to a joint session of Congress. As suggested earlier in this chapter, solutions to the energy problem could be either economic, political, or technical in nature. President Carter's proposed policy was essentially political in nature, with some economic and technological components. The president sounded a theme of sacrifice for all Americans—no group or individual would get an unfair advantage. The policy attempted to balance interests among concerned parties; thus, for example, consumer needs were balanced against producer needs, and midwestern and eastern states were more likely to have stable energy sources but would have to pay more. The specific policy theme was conservation of energy. The energy problem, as perceived by Carter and James Schlesinger, his top energy adviser, was that the world is fast running out of traditional fossil fuel energy sources. A Central Intelligence Agency study predicted severe shortages, demand outrunning supply, by 1985—far too early, in Carter's opinion, for either nuclear, solar, or geothermal sources to fill United States energy requirements. Given these perceptions the Carter administration formulated a policy of strict energy conservation, which would reduce energy consumption so that the United States could buy time to move into the nuclear-solar age. The specific provisions were designed to encourage conservation through tax rebates and other incentives and, if necessary, to enforce conservation through higher prices.

### Policies: The National Energy Act

In the Carter policy package the major features that encouraged conservation of energy were tax breaks and rebates to those individuals who conserve energy, for instance, by insulating their homes or installing solar units. Energy would be conserved because the government, through rebates, would reward conservation practices. However, the most controversial segments of the proposed policy were those that sought to enforce conservation—most notably, the proposed federal tax on gasoline at the pump and the tax on "gas-guzzling" cars (those averaging 12 miles per gallon or less). The tax on large cars, which could rise to as much as $600, met immediate opposition from car manufacturers in Detroit. The intention was to encourage Americans to buy smaller and more efficient cars by giving rebates to small-car buyers while taxing big-car buyers. The proposed tax on gasoline at the pump contained an escalator clause allowing the president to increase the tax, thereby ensuring a rise in price, if gasoline consumption was too high. Opposition to this tax was substantial, especially in Congress, because the tax hit consumers in their pocketbooks, and there were millions of voting consumers who demanded lower prices. This part of the policy proposal was quickly rejected by the House Ways and Means Committee.

The economic component of the president's energy policy featured raising the interstate price of natural gas to $1.75 per thousand cubic feet and allowing the prices of both new and hard-to-recover oil to rise to the world price. Although the Carter administration regarded these price increases as inducements to increase exploration, the oil and gas companies did not share that view. (It should be noted that later in his administration Carter no longer supported total deregulation of natural gas, as he had during the 1976 presidential campaign.)

Objections to Carter's natural gas policy were immediate. The major objection was that the $1.75 price for interstate sales represented a price increase, but that $1.75 for previously unregulated intrastate gas represented a decrease in price, so that natural gas companies that had been selling gas at up to $2.25 per thousand cubic feet in producing states (Texas, Louisiana, Oklahoma) would get a lower price. Oil companies objected to Carter's oil policy because it did not, in their view, encourage exploration for new sources. In short, oil and natural gas companies did not get the deregulation policies that they favored. The major objection to the policy from producers was that it did nothing to stimulate exploration and production.

Another part of the president's policy was the conversion of industrial facilities from natural gas and oil to coal. The goal was to more than double coal production and usage by 1985. In combination with the energy conservation measures the conversion to coal would (at least in Carter's view) reduce our dependence on foreign energy sources.

President Carter's energy policy also included a technology component, but it was a surprising one in that the president in effect wrote off breeder reactors. Many nuclear experts have said that the breeder is our best energy hope because it generates more nuclear materials than it uses. However, because of the dangers associated with fabricating and processing plutonium, the Carter policy favored reactors that used uranium. The uranium reactors are safer, but, like fossil fuels, uranium is an exhaustible fuel. Besides favoring uranium over plutonium, Carter promised that licensing and building of uranium reactors would be accelerated. Solar energy production was to be encouraged through a tax rebate to those installing solar units in individual heating units.

There are, of course, other aspects of the detailed policy not mentioned above, but the major thrust of the policy was clear. In sum, President Carter's policy asked Americans to pay more and use less energy. Actually getting a policy that asked for sacrifice and higher prices through Congress proved to be beyond Carter's leadership ability.

To facilitate consideration of the Carter proposal in the House, Speaker O'Neill established a thirty-seven member Energy Committee. It handled the Carter proposal as a single package once the component parts were considered by the appropriate standing committees. By handling the proposal in this centralized fashion, the leadership restricted "log rolling" on the various taxes, rebates, and price controls and produced a comprehensive, integrated piece of legislation. The special Energy Committee membership represented all regions and special interest groups and was somewhat weighted in favor of consumer interests and against drastic changes, such as total deregulation of oil and gas prices. While the ad hoc committee changed Carter's proposal somewhat, the final package had Carter's stamp of approval.

In the Senate the Carter administration's energy package was divided into a number of separate bills, dealt with in separate committees, and debated individually on the Senate floor. Moreover, the Senate leadership did not give the administration the close support accorded it by the House leadership. As a result, senators from producing states like Russell Long (D.–La.) were able to greatly alter the Carter proposals and make them more in accord with petroleum industry interests. For example, producing-state senators were able to win a narrow vote providing for deregulation of natural gas prices. Generally, more emphasis was placed on incentives for increased production of oil and gas than on conservation in their use.

On the whole, the Senate version of energy legislation was more congruent with producer rather than consumer interests. Several factors contributed to this. First, the decentralized division-making process in the Senate gave producing-state senators more opportunity to affect action. Second, the Senate "overrepresents" producing states because of the two-senators-per-state rule. And, President Carter did not effectively manage his interests during Senate consideration.

The final energy package was shaped by a House-Senate conference committee. The result was a compromise, giving producer interests more incentives and deregulation than proposed by the Carter administration but less than they wanted, while the administration got some conservation measures but less than they requested. In October of 1978 the Congress finally presented the president with an energy bill which, as passed, contained only remnants of Carter's original proposals. The five major areas of the National Energy Act concerned natural gas, coal conversion, utility rates, conservation, and taxes.

The Natural Gas Policy Act allowed the prices of newly discovered gas to rise about 10 percent a year until 1985 when the controls would be lifted. In addition special pricing categories were set which made industrial users pay higher prices until a certain cost was reached.

### Coal Conversion Act

New plants (industrial and utility) were required to utilize coal or fuels other than gas or oil. Already existing plants were to switch away from oil and gas by 1990 and on an individual basis the Secretary of Energy could order plants to change from gas or oil before 1990.

### Public Utility Regulatory Policy Act (PURPA) and Utility Rates Act

State regulatory agencies and utility commissions were to formulate policies to save energy. For example, they could choose to price energy at lower levels during off hours. Further, utility commissions were to cease giving discounted rates to heavy users, and the Secretary of Energy was empowered to intervene in the regulatory process in order to conserve energy.

### Energy Policy and Conservation Act

Utility companies were required to disseminate information to customers on ways to conserve energy. However, said utilities were not allowed to sell or install energy-saving devices. Schools and hospitals were to receive $900 million to have energy-saving devices installed. Home appliance industries were required to meet mandatory efficiency standards by the mid-1980s.

### Energy Tax Act

Homeowners and businesses would receive tax credits for installing energy-saving devices. New cars that used fuel inefficiently were to be taxed to discourage sales. In 1980 cars getting less than 15 miles per gallon would be taxed $200, by 1986 the taxes and standards would be higher such that a car averaging 12.5 miles per gallon would be taxed almost $4,000. As a result American automobile manufacturers have met these standards by producing lighter more fuel-efficient cars.

The National Energy Act finally passed in 1978 was not what President Carter sought when he introduced the legislation in 1977. The 1978 act was a patchwork of legislative provisions that reflected the bargaining necessary to pass any act. The president signed the act rather than vetoing it because he felt that no better bill was possible given the diversity of opinion and policy preferences regarding energy policy in the United States. Regional, sectional, ideological, partisan, and producer-consumer differences were severe and intense. Once again, policy was changed because energy politics now involved macropolitics instead of subsystem politics. The wide representation of all the relevant interests in Congress assured that all parties would have access to and influence on energy legislation. The result could only be a watered-down compromise policy.

If the president did not get what he wanted in the National Energy Act, he fared much better with legislation creating a Department of Energy. The Department of Energy was created in 1977 and brought together over sixty federal agencies and programs. Its purpose was to encourage energy production, efficiency and conservation. Box 3–1 outlines the organization and powers of the Energy Department.[26]

---

**BOX 3-1    Brief Summary of the Organization and Powers of the Department of Energy**

Titles 1 and 2 declared that the energy situation could best be dealt with through a Department of Energy and established such a department. The Department of Energy was given cabinet status and given broad functional responsibility over which the assistant secretaries would have control. These areas include: fuel supply, research and development, environment, international energy policy, competition and consumer affairs and nuclear waste management among others. These titles included the establishment of an Energy Information Administration.

Title 3 transferred to the Secretary of Energy all functions previously the responsibility of the FEA and ERDA. In addition the energy functions held by other government agencies were also transferred to the Department of Energy.

Title 4 created the Federal Energy Regulatory Commission which was given the right to set rates on natural gas, prices for oil transportation by pipe, and oil prices. These provisions eliminated the FPC's basic pricing functions.

Titles 5, 6, and 7 established the administrative procedures and rules necessary to run the department.

Title 8 required the president to submit to Congress a biennial energy plan summarizing the nation's energy goals for the next five and ten years.

Titles 9 and 10 provided for the initiation and review of the new Department of Energy.

---

Other important energy legislation passed during the Carter administration were the amendments to the 1953 Outer Continental Shelf Lands Act, the Windfall Profits Act, and the Synthetic Fuels Act. The amendments to the Outer Shelf Act were passed in 1978 and were designed to increase competition in bidding for oil and gas leases, increase the states' role in determining leases, and protect the environment.

In 1980 the Congress passed the Crude Oil Windfall Profits Tax Act, which established a federal tax on the income produced from domestic oil production. The bill also provided incentives to conserve energy and set up a program to aid poor families. The origins of the legislation lie in the successful effort to decontrol oil. The rationale was that as oil was decontrolled, prices would increase and oil company profits would increase. Thus a "windfall tax" which would then be redistributed to those who could least afford the rising prices.

In mid-1980 the Congress passed the Energy Security Act. The act contained eight titles, the most important of which were the synthetic fuels and conservation sections. The synthetic fuels section authorized expenditure of $20 billion to encourage private development of synthetic fuels. The act created a Synthetic Fuels Corporation to allocate the monies to private companies for research. The conservation section of the act allowed consumers to borrow up to $3,500 to improve energy efficiency. The total amount authorized was $375 million. Other sections of the act concerned solar energy, biomass, and alcohol fuels and renewable energy sources.

The Carter presidency was a period in which energy legislation dominated the congressional agenda. Many other energy bills not discussed here passed Congress during these years, for example, the Naval Oil Reserves Act, the Gasoline Rationing Act, and the Utility Rates Act. In addition many energy-related bills were proposed but not finalized.

The Carter answer to the energy problem fits into the "political" category of solutions. That is, the thrust of the policy was deregulation of oil and natural gas *over time,* with safeguards built in to lessen the economic shocks. Policies such as research and use of synthetic fuels and windfall profits tax point to the political nature of the Carter policies. The Carter view emphasized conservation of energy over the remaining two decades of the twentieth century, which would buy time until nuclear, solar, coal, and other alternative sources could be made feasible. Later, the original Carter proposals were changed by Republican and Southern Democrat interests toward the direction of faster deregulation.

## ENERGY POLICY UNDER REAGAN

With the election of Ronald Reagan as president, America's energy policy shifted dramatically. Reagan changed the deregulation timetables by deregulating oil and gas prices ahead of schedule. In September of 1981, President Reagan proposed the dismantling of the Department of Energy. The basic rationale behind early deregulation and dismantling the Department of Energy was that the market mechanism was the best way to conserve energy. Reagan believed that if prices are allowed to rise to meet market conditions then energy companies would invest capital to discover new oil and gas fields. In line with this policy, Interior Secretary James Watt announced the Reagan administration's intentions to make public lands (especially in the West) more accessible to energy companies. This policy would also include more exploration of the continental shelf. Market solutions to energy problems rest heavily on the assumption that there are energy resources available for development if prices are high enough to encourage exploration. Drilling deeper and in heretofore inaccessible locations for natural gas and oil, finding new technologies to recover oil from old fields, and gasification of coal and other techniques, would, according to Reagan's reasoning, provide sufficient energy resources for the future.

Given their strategy for coping with energy problems, the Reagan administration's policies of dismantling the Energy Department, early deregulation of prices, and making exploration easier on public lands make sense. It is clear that the Reagan energy policy favors market solutions. One factor that worked in Reagan's favor was the so-called oil glut: since about March 1981 there was a glut on the oil market caused by decreased usage by Americans and Saudi Arabia's continued high levels of oil production at lower prices, a policy that many OPEC members do not favor. This combination created an oil surplus which caused prices to stabilize at a lower rate than projected. The Reagan solution to energy problems was thus proposed at a most opportune time, namely, during a period of lowered stable prices. However, the new politics of energy has placed restrictions on pure market solutions. The severe winter of 1981–1982 resulted in increased use of natural gas, which heats 60 percent of American homes. Reagan had originally planned to ask Congress to decontrol natural gas prices before the 1985 Carter phase-out date (about one-half of natural gas would be decontrolled in 1985 under the Carter plan). Decontrol of natural gas would have caused a sharp price rise at a time of high usage and the cost would have been borne across the board by most Americans. This situation was not deemed desirable by Northeastern Republicans beginning to campaign for reelection in 1982; thus, in early February, Reagan announced that decontrol would not be pushed by his administration during the 1982 session of the 97th Congress. Since American politics does not allow for pure solutions to problems, it is more accurate to say that Reagan tended toward market solutions while Carter favored regulatory ones.

## CONCLUDING COMMENTS

Until the Arab oil embargo of 1973, American energy policy had featured unlimited use at cheap prices. As stated earlier, Americans use about one-third of all the energy generated and pay lower prices than anyone else in the world. Government energy policy was formed during energy crises, and in each case the policies sought to stabilize markets by controlling energy supplies. In the case of coal, the government supported the UMW's demands for shorter work weeks and limited production, thereby controlling supplies. In the case of natural gas and oil, government policy supported the producers' ability to control supply either directly, as in the case of oil, or indirectly, as in natural gas. In short, government policy traditionally was geared to the anticipation of oversupply. The subsystem politics of energy during the era of oversupply was characterized by few participants and well-established big-business lobbies.

Two major events changed both the nature of energy questions and the politics of energy. The first event was the environmental protection movement touched off by the oil spill in Santa Barbara, California, in 1969. The net effect of the environmental protection movement was to increase the number of participants in energy politics and to advance the question of clean energy sources. The more important event was the OPEC oil embargo of 1973–1974. The OPEC policy made it clear that the United States no longer controlled its energy future. As long as OPEC is able to keep its policy unanimous, America faces higher energy prices and the spectre of energy shortages. Thus, the new problem in energy is how to assure supply in the face of increasing demands, rather than how to control supply itself.

During the 1970s the politics and policy of energy were in dramatic flux. Both the changed politics and policies were responses to the "crisis" of the Arab oil embargo. Jones has observed that "whereas a perceived crisis often encourages a demand for coordination, comprehensiveness, and rationalism, expanded participation in decision making, so common in crises, ensures that the demand will not be met. Further, just when speedy action is presumed to be required, the normal system is slowed to a crawl by organizational adjustments, new information, citizen involvement, and media attention."[27] In the years since the original oil embargo, America's political process has been characterized by "crisis-response politics" instead of anticipatory actions. Policy solutions that are beyond the government's ability are demanded by all participants.

It appears that oil will remain America's primary energy source until the twenty-first century. Maintaining a steady supply of foreign oil imports looms as a major problem. The largest suppliers of foreign oil are the Middle-Eastern nations, an area fraught with constant turmoil. Successive presidents have sought both to maintain a steady flow of Middle-Eastern oil to the industrial West and to assure Israel's continued existence as a nation—policies beset with increasing uncertainty. The relationship between American Jews and Israel, increasing Islamic revolutionary zeal and instability, worries over Soviet influence in the Middle East, the fate of the Camp David peace talks since the death of Anwar Sadat in Egypt, the Iran-Iraq war, the invasion of Lebanon by Israel, the PLO and Palestinian question—all are pressing policy questions. Maintaining peace in the Middle East is paramount to ensuring stable energy supplies. Policymakers continue to convince Israel to make more concessions to Arab and Palestinian interests in order to assure peace. Shifting Arab alliances and changing sentiments about the United States' relationship with Israel and the Middle East make the situation even more tenuous.

One might logically expect the United States to tap the rich oil resources of our nearest neighbors to the north and south—Canada and Mexico. While there will be some increase in the supply of oil from these nations, neither can be counted on to solve our dilemma. Canada and especially Mexico need sizable energy reserves for their own purposes. Mexico must use its oil wisely in attempting to transform its economy from an underdeveloped economy into a modern one, while the Canadians have serious regional and cultural differences to overcome; without an expanding economy their problems will be exacerbated.

Technological solutions such as solar power, oil shale reserves, wind power, coal gasification, synthetic fuels, and nuclear energy all have assorted difficulties—both political and technological. Reagan's Secretary of Energy James Edwards, for example, has supported government participation in the development of certain synthetic fuels, whereas David Stockman of the Office of Management and Budget favors letting free-market forces determine energy alternatives. In early 1982, Secretary Edwards seemed to have won Reagan's support for the Synthetic Fuels Corporation. The development of solar, coal gasification, and other technological solutions are long-range solutions. Moreover, their development as regular energy sources depends upon their profitability and higher traditional energy prices. Accordingly, technological solutions, while advancing, are not likely to solve America's energy problems in the next decade.

The American political process itself creates problems for solutions to the energy crisis. Kash and his colleagues have described the problem in this fashion: "The energy policy system ... suffers from all the problems associated with pluralism and fragmentation. Pluralistic politics requires an often difficult process of compromise between competing interests—a process which governmental institutions with fragmented and overlapping responsibilities and ad hoc modes of operation are often ill-equipped to handle."[28] The demand for well-planned long-range solutions is not easily incorporated into a system based on subsystem politics. As we have shown, each energy source generates its own problems, interest groups, and congressional and governmental structures. Thus organization and reorganization (and even dismantling) are features of the government's response to the energy crisis. Since major changes in the structure and process of American politics are not expected, the policy process in the 1980s will be characterized by congressional, presidential, and bureaucratic compromises in a piecemeal fashion. One should not expect an overarching, well-planned response to continuing energy problems; rather, a case-by-case approach to the bundle of problems loosely labeled energy.

In spite of the perplexities outlined above, Americans are now more conscious of energy problems than in the mid-1970s. By 1982 we reduced the amount of imported oil to pre-1975 levels. In general, Americans are aware of the dilemma and are using less energy. Cars are smaller and homes are warmer in summer and cooler in the winter, synthetic and alternative fuels are being developed. The higher cost of energy has in fact caused us to use less while paying more. That such a situation has resulted from the mid-1970s crisis is in itself an encouraging development.

Finally, it is important to note that those who offer utopian solutions to the energy problem fundamentally misunderstand the American political process. It is a process characterized by a pluralism of interests and fragmented power centers dealing with a series of ill-assorted problems. Thus, unless there is a major restructuring of the American political process, policy will continue to be piecemeal, experimental, and responsive to short-run problems.

## NOTES

1. Charles O. Jones, "American Politics and the Organization of Energy Decision Making," *Annual Review of Energy* 4 (1979): 105.
2. Ibid., p. 101.
3. Quoted in John Noble Wilford, "Nation's Energy Crisis: It Won't Go Away Soon," *New York Times,* July 6, 1971, p. 24.
4. Ibid.
5. In discussing the energy situation, we find it helpful to proceed by considering, in turn, each of the fossil fuel categories. The first authors to use this approach were Merle Fainsod, Lincoln Gordon, and Joseph Palamountain, in their *Government and the American Economy* (New York: Norton, 1959). Howard Davis, *Energy Politics* (New York: St. Martin's Press, 1978), also uses this approach. In the next section, we rely on these works, particularly Fainsod et al.
6. *Exploring Energy Choices: A Preliminary Report* (New York: Ford Foundation, 1974), p. 45.
7. OPEC was created in 1960. Member countries are Algeria, Ecuador, Gabon, Indonesia, Iran, Iraq, Kuwait, Libya, Nigeria, Qatar, Saudi Arabia, United Arab Emirates, and Venezuela.
8. Quoted in William D. Smith, "Energy Crisis: Shortages among Plenty," *New York Times,* April 17, 1973, p. 26.

9. Quoted in John Noble Wilford, "Nation's Energy Crisis: A Nuclear Future Looms," *New York Times,* July 7, 1971, p. 24.

10. G. Garvey, *Energy, Ecology, Economy: A Framework for Environmental Policy* (New York: W. W. Norton, 1972), and S. D. Freeman, *Energy, the New Era* (New York: Vintage, 1974) have overviews of this position. J. C. Fischer, *Energy Crisis in Perspective* (New York: Wiley, 1974) offers a balanced summary of energy alternatives.

11. This section relies on Fainsod et al., *Government and the American Economy,* chap. 20.

12. A description of the struggle between workers and owners can be found in Morton Baratz, *The Union and the Coal Industry* (New Haven, Conn.: Yale University Press, 1955); and George S. McGovern and Leonard Cuthridge, *The Great Coalfield War* (Boston: Houghton Mifflin, 1972).

13. The court case that first made use of the "capture" theory was *Medina Oil Development Company* v. *Murphy,* 233 S.W. 333 (1921). The capture theory rests on the assumption that oil percolates below the surface much as wild animals and birds roam upon the surface. Oil belongs, then, to those who can capture it.

14. Davis, *Energy Politics* (1974), pp. 48–51.

15. Fainsod et al., *Government and the American Economy,* chap. 20.

16. For background on natural gas regulation, see the excellent discussion by Ralph K. Huitt, "National Regulation of the Natural-Gas Industry," in Emmette S. Redford, ed., *Public Administration and Policy Formation* (Austin: University of Texas Press, 1958), pp. 53–116.

17. *Phillips Petroleum Company* v. *State of Wisconsin,* 347 U.S. 672 (1954).

18. The following discussion draws on Daniel J. Fiorino, "Regulating the Natural Gas Producing Industry: Two Decades of Experience," in James E. Anderson, ed., *Economic Regulatory Policies* (Lexington, Mass.: Heath, 1976), pp. 89–103.

19. Richard Corrigan, "FPC Boosts Gas Rates to Raise Production," *National Journal* 8 (November 13, 1976): 1626–1631.

20. See A. W. Murphy, ed., *The Nuclear Power Controversy* (Englewood Cliffs, N.J.: Prentice-Hall, 1976).

21. E. E. Schattschneider, *The Semi-Sovereign People* (New York: Holt, Rinehart and Winston, 1960).

22. Quoted in Robert Engler, *The Politics of Oil* (New York: Macmillan, 1961), p. 291.

23. Ibid., p. 290.

24. Bruce Oppenheimer, *Oil and the Congressional Process* (Lexington, Mass.: Heath, 1974), p. 151.

25. See Sam H. Schurr and others, *Energy in America's Future: The Choices Before Us* (Baltimore: Johns Hopkins Press, 1979), for a good overview.

26. Bruce Oppenheimer, "Policy Effects of U.S. House Reform: Decentralization and the Capacity to Resolve Energy Issues," *Legislative Studies Quarterly* (February, 1980): 5–30.

27. Jones, "American Politics," p. 100.

28. D. E. Kash et al., *Our Energy Future: The Role of Research Development and Demonstration in Reaching a National Consensus on Energy Policy* (Norman: University of Oklahoma Press, 1976), quoted in Jones, "American Politics," p. 100.

## SUGGESTED READINGS

Commoner, Barry. *The Poverty of Power, Energy and the Economic Process.* New York: Bantam Books, 1977.

Davis, David. *Energy Politics.* New York: St. Martin's, 1978.

Engler, Robert. *The Brotherhood of Oil.* Chicago: University of Chicago, 1977.

Freeman, David. *Energy, the New Era.* New York: Vintage, 1974.

Jones, Charles, "American Politics and the Organization of Energy Decision Making," *Annual Review of Energy* 4 (1979): 99–121.

Oppenheimer, Bruce. *Oil and the Congressional Process.* Lexington, Mass: Heath, 1974.

Sanders, Elizabeth. *The Regulation of Natural Gas.* Philadelphia: Temple University, 1981.

## Chapter 4

# Protecting the Environment

For most of our history, Americans have thought of their land as having unlimited natural resources which were there for the taking. Water was abundant and free and could be used to turn the wheels of industry and to carry away wastes. Wind was also free and would disperse the soot and other emissions belched forth by homes and factories. Timber could be cut without concern about reforestation or erosion. Minerals could be extracted from inexhaustible reserves with no consideration for the consequences for those living downstream from or near slag heaps. Farmland and grazing lands could be exploited with little attention given to using the land so as to retain its productivity. When the minerals or timber had been stripped from the land or the productive capacity leached out, one simply moved to areas that had not been exploited.

Careless disregard for the consequences of exploitative practices remained possible as long as we were a nation of farmers scattered with low density across the map. Now, however, we can no longer ruin the environment in one area and then escape the consequences of our action by moving further into the wilderness.

During the latter half of the 1960s public concern about environmental conditions became widespread. Large oil spills, dirtier air, the rape of the land by strip miners, and other factors combined to draw attention to problems long ignored. Newspapers printed more stories about environmental conditions, and between 1965 and 1970 the Gallup Poll showed that concern about air and water quality was the fastest-rising item on the public agenda.[1] By 1970 pollution control was the second most frequent problem cited by Americans. It was mentioned by 53 percent of the public, more than three times more frequently than five years earlier.

In response to public concern, the government changed its policies regarding environmental exploitation. After protracted debate, Congress enacted legislation that discouraged the unthinking abuse of our resources. This legislation (which will be discussed later) made it less economical to pollute water and air.

Industry has generally opposed legislation designed to clean up the environment. Industry opponents have argued that compliance with pollution standards will increase costs of production. Thus, if strip miners must heal the scars inflicted by their giant scoops, or steel mills must reduce the smoke from their stacks, or chemical plants must filter their wastes, or automobile manufacturers must purify the gases contained in exhaust, new and often costly technology will be needed. Small, inefficient concerns sometimes warn that they cannot afford to make extensive changes and that therefore stringent pollution control standards will force them out of business.

Critics counter that environmental costs are a component of production costs and therefore should be added to the price of goods. They contend that to act as if there were no costs involved in degrading the environment results in nonusers having to bear a disproportionate share of the burden. Allowing factories to send plumes of smoke into the air may reduce the quality of life for people living in the vicinity. In some instances the emissions from factories may contain deadly substances, such as the Kepone dust which was emitted for several years during the 1970s in Hopewell, Virginia. In many communities pollutants cause diseases and shorten the lives of residents. Allowing toxic wastes or untreated sewage to flow into streams makes life more than simply unpleasant for people living downstream, necessitates more expensive purification systems for downstream communities which take their water from the river, destroys wildlife, and puts some fishermen out of work. Although difficult to calculate in dollars, certainly there is a value in being able to use a stream or lake for boating, fishing, swimming, and water skiing.

Rather than focus on the state of the environment or some of the more serious abuses to nature, this chapter looks at the current state of national public policy in this sphere. The greatest attention will be given to policy initiatives dealing with water and air quality, the National Environmental Policy Act, and the controversy over use of public lands.

## CLEAN AIR AND WATER LEGISLATION

As the dangers to health and the ecology have become more widely recognized, removing pollutants from the air and water has become a major objective of environmentalists. Several major pieces of legislation have been passed to improve water and air quality. And as the federal role in environmental regulation broadened, the Environmental Protection Agency (EPA) was created in 1970 to oversee the expanding environmental responsibilities. The EPA was assigned responsibility for both air and water quality programs. This section describes the most significant pieces of legislation on air and water pollution and then discusses the EPA's efforts to enforce the legislation.

### Pure Water

Waterborne pollutants are of three main types: waste and sewage, heavy metals, and toxic organic compounds such as pesticides. The extent to which sewage and animal feedlot runoff are degrading water conditions is measured in three dimensions: level of fecal coliform bacteria, dissolved oxygen levels (which determine the capacity of water to sustain fish and other animal life), and phosphorus levels (which produce algae blooms when too abundant). Deadly heavy metals such as mercury work their way into the food chain by accumulating in fish. Some pesticides and other chemicals which wash into streams are carcinogenic.

Efforts to remove pollutants from the nation's streams and lakes have relied chiefly on two techniques. One strategy has been to reduce the amount of pollution emptied into the water by setting effluent controls for the amount of pollution allowed in streams. The second strategy has been to provide grants to communities to encourage them to construct sewage treatment facilities.

**Early legislation.**    Until the mid-1960s, the federal government acted only halfheartedly to reduce water pollution.[2] Legislation passed in 1956 sought to do little more than alert the public to problems in this sphere. Federal authorities sponsored conferences to discuss problems of pollution. Although these conferences could ultimately lead to a Justice Department suit against a polluter, only one suit was ever filed and it had little effect.[3] The 1956 legislation also launched a federal grant program which made funds available to communities to help finance construction of sewage treatment plants. Federal funds could be used for a maximum of 55 percent of the facilities' cost. For the most part, pollution control was left to the states.

**Water Quality Act, 1965.**    The 1956 legislation failed to significantly improve water quality; in 1965 the Water Quality Act marked the first step toward establishment of specific standards for water quality. However, rather than mandating nationwide criteria, the legislation left it up to each state to devise its own standards. These were to be submitted to the Department of Health, Education and Welfare (more recently to the EPA) for approval.

In the absence of vigorous federal guidelines, states displayed little interest in forcing resident polluters to clean up their discharges—largely because state officials worried that setting tight limitations on pollution would make production more costly in their state, perhaps inducing some manufacturers to relocate in less demanding states and discouraging the location of new industries within their borders. Responding to federal urging that water quality not deteriorate further, most states set standards that simply reflected current conditions. However, states with relatively pure water often balked at setting standards higher than those of states with dirty water. Thus, conditions in states with the poorest-quality water became the norm nationwide. Federal authorities did little to force development of more demanding standards.

**Water Pollution Control Act, 1972 and 1977 amendments.**    Heightened public awareness of pollution problems resulted in passage of amendments to the Water Pollution Control Act, in which the federal government moved to correct the weaknesses of earlier legislation. In place of the state-developed standards called for in 1965, Congress set nationwide objectives. The goals set in the amendments of 1972 were very high: to make all streams safe for fish and swimming by 1983 and to eliminate all discharges of pollution into navigable streams by 1985. To achieve these objectives, all private concerns discharging wastes into streams were to adopt the "best practicable technology" for waste treatment by 1977 and the "best available technology" by 1984. Economic feasibility, or cost, could be considered in meeting the 1977 standard but would not be relevant in determining the adequacy of a corporation's pollution abatement efforts after 1983. Since determinations of economic feasibility include considerations of the expenses relative to the emissions reduction achieved and the age of the machinery included, the EPA would have to make numerous case-by-case determinations of what steps would be necessary for an installation to achieve compliance.[4] Less demanding standards were set for public sewage treatment facilities. There was to be secondary treatment of wastes (that is, removal of 85 percent of the pollutants) by 1977, and the "best practicable technology" was to be in use by 1983.

The 1972 legislation also established a nationwide discharge permit system and empowered the EPA to set water quality standards for interstate streams. Applications for discharge permits specified the amount of effluents allowed to be released by the installation and the steps to be taken to comply with the 1977 deadline. The EPA was to administer the permit system in each state until the state developed an acceptable set of standards and could assume administration of the program under general EPA supervision. The EPA could also establish standards for intrastate waters if states failed to do an adequate job. To correct the problems encountered in earlier legislation, permit standards were to be the same nationwide for each industry, so that states could not use water quality standards as a bargaining device in attempting to lure industry. To help communities meet their obligations, federal aid for the construction of municipal sewage treatment facilities was expanded. The size of the maximum federal contribution was raised from 55 to 75 percent.

**Progress in achieving water standards.**    While the EPA authorized $33 billion for sewage plant construction between 1972 and 1981, much remains to be done to meet water pollution control standards. Estimates place the additional needed costs at between $90 and $106 billion.[5] The Reagan administration has indicated a desire to reduce federal appropriations by almost 75 percent. The financial implications of this proposal for state and local governments are serious. Unless the deadlines are delayed or the standards for water quality weakened, states and localities will be confronted with a staggering bill for sewage treatment.

Latest evidence indicates that there has been some but not great progress in making waterways swimmable and fishable. As shown in table 4–1, the frequency with which excessive amounts of the three chief sewage-related forms of pollution are found has remained constant or increased slightly. Moreover, most cities continue to exceed standards for untreated sewage discharge at least occasionally. In part this stems from insufficient treatment capacity and in part from a failure to maintain and operate treatment plants properly. Nonetheless, the president's Council on Environmental Quality (CEQ) concluded that "the fact that the nation's surface water has not deteriorated despite a growing population and an increased gross national product is an accomplishment for control efforts."[6]

**TABLE 4-1   Frequency of violations in river water quality**

|                         | 1975 | 1978 |
|-------------------------|------|------|
| Dissolved oxygen        | 3%   | 6%   |
| Fecal coliform bacteria | 37   | 38   |
| Phosphorus              | 47   | 47   |

SOURCE: U.S. Bureau of the Census, *Statistical Abstract of the United States, 1980* (Washington, D.C.: U.S. Government Printing Office, 1980), p. 218.

That conditions have not deteriorated may be due to success in getting 80 percent of the major nonmunicipal dischargers of wastes and 40 percent of municipal dischargers to meet the standards set for 1977.[7] Many of those who failed to comply were sued.

A scarcity of data makes it difficult to assess the adequacy of the EPA's other water-related responsibilities. Although there is some indication that the quality of drinking water supplied by municipal systems is declining slightly, the EPA has done little to establish the national standards which it was directed to set in 1974.[8] The EPA has also paid little heed to legislative directives to ensure the quality of the ground water which most cities rely on.

### Clean Air

Much of the justification for imposing pollution standards has been premised on public health concerns. Table 4–2 reports the sources and health-related problems of major air pollutants. Substances that the EPA has banned altogether, such as asbestos, have been shown to have fatal consequences.

Although the items for which the EPA has set primary standards (that is, levels necessary to protect public health) are less lethal than those banned, the former, by contributing to emphysema and other health problems, can reduce life expectancies. It has been estimated, for example, that sulfate pollution plays a role in the premature deaths of one-hundred-fifty thousand Americans annually.[9]

Federal efforts to improve air quality largely paralleled initiatives in the sphere of water pollution. In 1955 Congress made a tentative move, registering largely symbolic concern for air quality by authorizing federal officials to study the problem and to make information available to states wishing to take corrective actions.

**Clean Air Act, 1963.**   A more promising federal initiative came in the Clean Air Act of 1963, which was modeled on the 1956 Water Pollution Control Act. The

**TABLE 4-2**   Major air pollutants and their health effects

| Pollutant | Major sources | Characteristics and effects |
|---|---|---|
| Carbon monoxide (CO) | Vehicle exhausts | Colorless, odorless, poisonous gas. Replaces oxygen in red blood cells, causing dizziness, unconsiousness, or death. |
| Hydrocarbons (HC) | Incomplete combustion of gasoline; evaporation of petroleum fuels, solvents, and paints | Although some are poisonous, most are not. Reacts with $NO_2$ to form ozone, or smog. |
| Lead (Pb) | Antiknock agents in gasoline | Accumulates in the bone and soft tissues. Affects blood-forming organs, kidneys, and nervous system. Suspected of causing learning disabilities in young children. |
| Nitrogen dioxide ($NO_2$) | Industrial processes, vehicle exhausts | Causes structural and chemical changes in the lungs. Lowers resistance to respiratory infections. Reacts in sunlight with hydrocarbons to produce smog. Contributes to acid rain. |
| Ozone ($O_3$) | Formed when HC and $NO_2$ react | Principal constituent of smog. Irritates mucous membranes, causing coughing, choking, impaired lung function. Aggravates chronic asthma and bronchitis. |
| Total suspended particulates (TSP) | Industrial plants, heating boilers, auto engines, dust | Larger visible types (soot, smoke, or dust) can clog the lung sacs. Smaller invisible particles can pass into the bloodstream. Often carry carcinogens and toxic metals; impair visibility. |
| Sulfur dioxide ($SO_2$) | Burning coal and oil, industrial processes | Corrosive, poisonous gas. Associated with coughs, colds, asthma, and bronchitis. Contributes to acid rain. |

SOURCE: *Congressional Quarterly Weekly Report*, February 7, 1981, 39, 271. Copyright 1981 by Congressional Quarterly, Inc. Reprinted by permission.

1963 legislation authorized the secretary of HEW to convene conferences of all interested parties to set standards for airsheds. As with water conferences, the impact of the conference approach to improving air quality was far less than the legislation's proponents had hoped. HEW made modest use of its authority to call conferences, hold public hearings, or file suits, despite the fact that by 1970 no state had fully implemented an air quality plan.

**Clean Air Act, 1970 and 1977 amendments.**   In 1970 Congress directed the EPA to establish primary and secondary ambient air quality standards. It was then up to the states to propose plans for meeting the standards and to submit these plans to the EPA for approval. States were slow in developing plans; only five were approved by 1979.[10]

Attainment of primary standards (levels necessary to protect public health) originally set for 1975 were postponed until 1982 and may be delayed still further. Compliance with ozone standards in heavily polluted urban areas has been put off until 1987. Thus far the EPA has established primary and secondary standards for levels of carbon monoxide, hydrocarbons, nitrogen oxides, particulate matter (dust and soot), ozone, and sulfur oxides. In addition, the EPA has prohibited emission of five particularly dangerous items (asbestos, beryllium, vinyl chloride, benzene, and mercury) from both new and existing sources. Secondary standards (levels necessary to prevent damage to materials, vegetation, and so on) are to be met within "a reasonable time."

The 1970 amendments also directed the EPA to set emission standards for about twenty categories of new industrial plants. The EPA now requires that the "best feasible technology" be used in new plants for manufacturing cement, sulfuric acid, nitric acid, and electric generating plants that use fossil fuels.

The implementation of EPA standards for coal-burning power plants built since 1978 has been particularly controversial. These new plants were to remove 90 percent of the sulfur oxides in the coal they burn, regardless of whether relatively "clean" (low-sulfur) or "dirty" (high-sulfur) coal is being used. To remove the sulfur oxides, "scrubbers," which use a spray of water and limestone to filter out the polluting sulfur, must be installed. This requirement has not been popular with the utility industry, whose spokesmen say "scrubbers are costly, unreliable, and likely to cause new problems such as excess sludge."[11]

In addition to specifying the percent of sulfur to be removed, the EPA set maximum levels of pollutants per million Btu's of heat produced. The effect of this second provision is to prevent the burning of high-sulfur-content coal at new generating facilities. Some older facilities have been able to comply with state environmental standards by building tall smokestacks which disperse pollution without reducing quantity. Some power companies find it financially advantageous to continue to operate outmoded plants rather than bear the expenses that pollution control devices add to construction costs for new facilities.

The foregoing discussion illustrates the difference in legislative approaches to new and existing facilities. The EPA can regulate the emissions of new operations, but its influence over existing facilities is indirect. The EPA sets the primary air quality standards. In the course of implementing these standards states may put pressure on the operators of existing facilities to clean up their emissions.

**Guidelines for air quality.**    The EPA has developed three classifications for the 247 air quality control regions into which it has divided the nation. Class I areas, which include national parks and wilderness areas, are to be kept pristine with no diminution in air quality permitted. In Class II areas, some increases in pollution are allowed. The quality of air in Class III areas would be allowed to deteriorate until it reached the national primary standard; no areas have yet been transferred into this category from Class II.

In areas where pollution levels have reached the upper limits set by the EPA, new polluting factories can be built only if the present level of pollution in the area is reduced. In order to offset anticipated emissions from the new facility, some businesses have cleaned up or closed down some of their own nearby dirty operations. Others have bought sources of high emissions for the sole purpose of acquiring an offset by closing the operation!

A second alternative allows a factory to treat its operation as if it were surrounded by an invisible "bubble," with the emissions from the whole operation monitored at a single outlet. This approach has allowed the business flexibility in cleaning up the aspects of its operation which can be most easily improved. For example, steel mills may find it cheaper to reduce particulates by paving their parking lots rather than installing a huge vacuum cleaner in the mill.

A third possibility is that local governments or businesses which reduce their emissions can keep the reduction in the form of a negotiable credit. Cities could offer such credits to lure new industry while private operators might develop a market for exchanging pollution reduction credits.

**Automobile emissions.**   The first federal scrutiny of automobile emissions came in the 1965 Motor Vehicle Air Pollution Control Act. Since the internal-combustion engine produced approximately two-thirds of the country's air pollution, the requirement that new cars meet standards for reducing the emission of hydrocarbons and carbon monoxide by 1968 seemed to hold great promise.[12] However, various weaknesses in the EPA's certification process have dashed many pre-enactment hopes. First, large numbers of cars were approved on the basis of tiny samples; in one instance, 1.2 million cars were approved after only four prototype engines had been tested.[13] Second, even if engines are successful in reducing emissions when the cars roll off the assembly line, tests indicate that cars in use quickly slip below acceptable levels of cleanliness.

When the 1965 legislation failed to substantially reduce the pollution caused by cars, higher auto emission standards were included in the 1970 amendments to the Clean Air Act. This legislation called for a 90 percent reduction in hydrocarbon and carbon monoxide emissions by new cars by 1975. A similar reduction in nitrogen oxides was to be achieved by 1976. Manufacturers could be fined $10,000 for each car not in compliance.

Automobile manufacturers who opposed the 1970 standards on the grounds that insufficient time was allowed for the development of needed technology found the 1973 Arab oil embargo to be a useful bargaining lever in their continuing efforts to modify the standards. In response to Detroit's contention that emission reduction would come only at the price of higher rates of fuel consumption, the EPA has postponed deadlines.

**Acid rain and greenhouse effect.**   While the EPA has concentrated on establishing and monitoring air quality standards designed to protect the public's health, two other consequences of pollution are stirring concern. Rain and snow with the acidity of vinegar can result when moisture joins with sulfates and nitrates in the air in a combination called *acid rain*. The phenomenon is widespread in North America: in New England and New York's Adirondack Mountains the acidity levels from polluted precipitation in many lakes is so high that all fish and most other plants and animals have been killed. Acid rain also harms some crops. Burning coal is thought to be the primary source of the pollutants that cause acid rain. Use of tall stacks to disperse emissions has contributed to the scope of areas affected by acid rain, since pollutants from tall stacks travel further before returning to earth.

Clouds of carbon dioxide from vehicles and stationary sources accumulate in the atmosphere and may produce what is called a *greenhouse effect*. Many scientists fear that high concentrations of carbon dioxide may cause the climate on earth to warm slightly, which could change weather patterns and perhaps melt some of the polar icecap, which in turn would flood many coastal cities.

**Progress in meeting clean air standards.**   Despite frequent industry protests that standards are unreasonable, some progress is being made. Figures compiled in 1979 show that the amount of sulfur dioxide in the air of our cities has decreased by two-thirds since 1964; particulates are down by one-third since 1960; and carbon monoxide has been reduced by one-third since 1972.[14] The president's Council on Environmental Quality reported that "an examination of data from the four or five counties with the poorest air quality in each federal region shows that in most regions, and for most pollutants, the frequency of violations of ambient air quality standards either stayed constant or decreased over the 1974 to 1977 period."[15]

Despite improvements, problems remain with hundreds of areas having concentrations of at least one pollutant in excess of federal standards and with Los Angeles out of compliance on five pollutants.[16] Nonetheless, the National Commission on Air Quality predicts that by the end of the 1980s all but eight urban areas will be in compliance with EPA air quality standards.[17]

While the air in many cities has improved, total amounts of most pollutants emitted nationally have changed little in recent years. Table 4–3 shows that only for particulates has the amount of pollution been substantially reduced across the country. Figures in table 4–4 indicate substantial improvements in cleaning up vehicle emissions. Despite improvements, vehicle emission levels remain higher than the objectives of the 1970 legislation.

When industry-by-industry comparisons are made, there are wide variations in the extent of compliance. For example, industry representatives claim that 96 percent of the members of the Chemical Manufacturers Association meet EPA standards, compared with a quarter of the steel plants.[18] Assessing the impact of legislation designed to reduce air pollution reveals that statistics are often ambiguous. One's conclusion depends on data selected for interpretation; both may be determined by one's values and what one hopes to prove.

TABLE 4-3    Estimated amounts of
air pollutants in the United States
(in millions of tons)

|  | 1970 | 1978 |
|---|---|---|
| Carbon monoxide | 113.1 | 112.5 |
| Hydrocarbons | 31.2 | 30.6 |
| Nitrogen oxides | 21.9 | 25.7 |
| Particulates | 25.6 | 13.8 |
| Sulfur oxides | 32.8 | 29.8 |

SOURCE: U.S. Bureau of the Census, *Statistical Abstract of the United States, 1980* (Washington, D.C.: U.S. Government Printing Office, 1980), p. 217.

TABLE 4-4    Motor vehicle pollution in the United States
(in grams per mile)

|  | 1970 | 1979 | Projected for 1981 | Goal set by legislation |
|---|---|---|---|---|
| Carbon monoxide | 86.9 | 65.2 | 55.5 | 3.4 |
| Hydrocarbons | 12.1 | 7.3 | 5.8 | 0.41 |
| Nitrogen oxides | 4.7 | 3.8 | 3.4 | 1.0 |

SOURCE: U.S. Bureau of the Census, *Statistical Abstract of the United States, 1980* (Washington, D.C.: U.S. Government Printing Office, 1980), p. 217.

## PROBLEMS OF ENFORCING LEGISLATION

In carrying out its congressional mandate to reduce water and air pollution, the EPA encountered a number of obstacles. Several of these stemmed from the detailed nature of the environmental legislation enacted by Congress. Although the members of Congress were motivated by the best of intentions (that is, they tried to specify the corrective actions to be taken, because they feared that administrators might not pursue environmental cleanup with sufficient vigor), some of the requirements written into law by Congress appear to be counterproductive.

First, the water and air legislation set specific timetables. For example, Congress directed that 90 percent of several pollutants were to be eliminated from automobile emissions by a certain date. Similarly, it stipulated that the EPA must bring suit against a water polluter who does not take corrective action within thirty days after receiving notification of a violation. By setting such specific objectives for the EPA, Congress has complicated the agency's operation by reducing its latitude of action. The EPA's ability to improve air and water quality through negotiation and compromise is, thus, somewhat restricted.

Second, in attempting to specify in detail what the EPA was to do, Congress caused some confusion because overlapping requirements sometimes created apparent contradictions or made it difficult to determine which provision was more applicable. Observers have pointed out, "By trying to cover all possible situations, and thus having several provisions dealing with closely related situations and functions, it is frequently left to the administrator to determine which section of the law to apply to a particular polluter or state."[19]

A third problem is created by the requirement that the EPA devise environmental cleanup standards on matters about which relatively little is known. In the absence of scientific testing, the EPA may have little evidence with which to justify imposition of a particular standard on the emissions allowable for a factory or plant. In analyzing a series of legal setbacks for the EPA, it can be seen that "in each of the cases, the court found the burden of proof lay on EPA to show that its standards were based on reliable data and that the available technology had been adequately demonstrated. In most of the cases the court found that EPA could not sustain the burden of proof."[20]

A fourth problem area for the EPA has been its relationship with the states. Although polluted streams and dirty air do not respect state boundaries, environmental policy still leaves a fair amount of responsibility to the states. The EPA sets national standards, but it is up to the states to design the programs that should achieve compliance with the air standards. As mentioned earlier, this has meant that differing amounts of pollution are permitted in differing parts of the country. In the case of automobile emissions, for example, California has more rigorous standards than those found in the rest of the nation.

Fifth, while the EPA can draft plans for achievement of air and water standards when state proposals are inadequate, the federal government is less influential when it comes to the construction of sewage treatment plants. Distribution of federal funds for this purpose is left up to the states, and states have rarely devised comprehensive strategies for cleaning up a watershed. Instead, construction funds for sewage treatment facilities have been distributed to municipalities on a first-come, first-served basis. In addition to the inefficiency of this approach, the waste treatment construction program has been further marred by the absence of standards for the facilities that are built or for their subsequent operations.

Finally, Congress has, at times, called on the EPA to achieve a level of pollution control before the requisite technology has been developed. For example, it has been said that the 1972 water legislation "abounds with technical barricades to implementation."[21] It can be argued that this sort of mandate is useful in that it can force those who are being regulated to expedite the development of new technology. An example is automobile emission control; until technological advances are made, implementation is impossible.

### Criticism of Standards

In retrospect, it appears that the 1970s may mark the furthest advance achieved by the advocates of pure air and water. The oil embargoes and subsequent price increases created a public climate far different from the one in which the amendments had passed with hardly any dissent.

As the Clean Air and Clean Water acts came up for review in the early 1980s, critics attacked them on several grounds and proposed numerous changes. Most of the efforts to weaken the requirements came from businesses, often those which were most affected by the legislation. Eight specific issues were presented to Congress for resolution.

First, industry charged that EPA standards to prevent significant deterioration in air quality unreasonably curb industrial expansion. In place of the EPA approach which would allow a constant increment of additional pollution in Class II areas, regardless of the current level of air quality (for example, an additional 20 micrograms of sulfur dioxide per meter per day is permitted in Class II areas), industry prefers to allow air quality to decline until the national primary level is reached. Environmentalists object since such a policy would result in a general deterioration of air quality. The National Commission on Air Quality questions whether clean air requirements have interfered with industrial growth. If the significant deterioration standard is waived, a consequence could be accelerated departure of industry from the North to the Sun Belt where more additional pollution would be permitted.

Second, critics contend that primary standards are too restrictive. A spokesman for the Business Roundtable summed up his organization's position, "Nobody wants to jeopardize public health. But the question is, how clean is clean?"[22] Current standards prevent levels that endanger the health of the most vulnerable segment of the population—those with chronic respiratory problems. Critics suggest that a "reasonableness" test be substituted, under which some share of the population would be inconvenienced.

In the third place, business would like to see cost-benefit analyses carried out before the EPA establishes standards. The Clean Air Act prohibits consideration of cost or feasibility of attainment when EPA sets primary standards. This is another facet of industry's claim that environmental regulations contribute to the disadvantages faced by business in competing not only for the world market but even for sales at home. Thus pollution control is cited as one cause for America's unfavorable balance of trade. On the other hand, a Carter administration EPA official charged that "anyone who tells you they want to mandate that benefits outweigh costs wants to gut the act."[23]

Fourth, businesses are critical of the requirement that they provide an offsetting reduction in pollution before building a new facility in a polluted area. They favor an arrangement whereby they could pay a fee in return for the right to build. Environmentalists warn that in the absence of offsets, conditions will continue to deteriorate.

The fifth issue concerns projected expenses. The Business Roundtable places the cost of pollution control to industry at $400 billion for the period 1970 to 1987, a factor they say is a significant cause of inflation.[24] On the other side, the National Commission on Air Quality estimates that pollution control has added only 0.2 percent to the annual rate of inflation. Moreover, the CEQ estimated the value of cleaner air at $21.4 billion annually during the 1970s, which goes a long way toward balancing the $27 billion it estimates that environmental cleanup cost during each of those years.[25]

In the sixth item presented by industry, utilities continue to oppose the requirement that 90 percent of the sulfur dioxide be removed regardless of the sulfur content of the coal. They would prefer at most a sliding scale for emission reductions, or better yet that they simply be held to a specific level of emissions per million Btu's produced. Utilities argue that the result would be emission levels within the healthful range and perhaps lower than at present, since cleaner coal would be used whenever that was cheaper than expensive scrubbing devices. Legislators from eastern coal-producing states, led by Democratic Senate leader Robert Byrd (W.Va.), have opposed the substitution of western coal with its lower sulfur content since this would cause higher unemployment in eastern coal fields.

Furthermore, there has been criticism of the absolutist terms of control objectives, such as "zero discharge by 1985." A great deal of the impurities could be removed for relatively modest cost; however, as the proportion of the pollution to be removed increases arithmetically, costs rise geometrically. According to analysts,

> Depending upon the industry or pollutant, going from, say, 97 percent to 99 percent removal may cost as much as the entire effort of going from zero to 97 percent. In one analysis, the total ten-year costs of eliminating 85 to 90 percent of water pollution in the United States was estimated at $61 billion. Achieving 95 to 99 percent freedom from pollution would add *another* $58 billion, bringing total costs to $119 billion. . . . A 100 percent objective (zero discharge) would demand an *additional* $200 billion.[26]

The final criticism in the list is that obtaining permits for new construction is too long and costly. Some claim that to negotiate the red tape and carry out the simulations necessary to estimate the amount of pollution which would be generated may take years and hundreds of thousands of dollars. The EPA is trying to streamline this process, while still protecting the environment.

At the heart of many of the above criticisms is the cost of compliance. In initially setting environmental policy, Congress acted with little appreciation of or concern for how expensive implementation would be. The extent to which standards are ultimately weakened will depend on how accurate industry's cost estimates are, the relative credibility of industry and EPA, and public willingness to pay whatever higher prices result.

### Public Attitudes

Public opinion polls continue to find widespread willingness to pay higher prices in order to curb pollution. A 1978 national sample found five times more people preferring environmental protection regardless of cost than believing that cleanup efforts were not cost-effective.[27] A 1981 CBS-*New York Times* poll found that even in the early days of the Reagan administration's rhetoric about budget balancing, 31 percent of a national sample endorsed higher spending to control pollution.[28] Of eight programs considered, support for higher spending for environmental protection was third to national defense and Social Security. Only 18 percent wanted to reduce federal spending to protect the environment, while 46 percent favored funding at current levels.

Despite continued support for pollution control programs, public enthusiasm has declined. The proportion of national samples endorsing high standards and additional improvement, regardless of cost, dropped from 55 to 42 percent between

1977 and 1980. During the same period, the percentage who felt that "we should now concentrate on holding down costs rather than requiring stricter controls" rose from 20 to 34 percent.[29] Whether these trends continue may be determined less by how well current policy is implemented than by the state of the economy. Spiraling inflation, idle factories and unemployment, unfavorable balance of payments, and widespread perceptions of decline in quality of life may eclipse concerns about environmental protection.

## Alternative Plans

Critics contend that the pollution control strategy being pursued is inefficient. They object to efforts to specify precise standards for the level of emissions to be tolerated, which, according to critics, produces only short-term improvements. Once a city or factory reduces its emissions to the level specified by the EPA, it has little incentive to adopt more efficient control devices. With policies of this type, the air of areas experiencing population and/or industrial growth will, in time, deteriorate until it reaches the maximum tolerated by EPA.

Similarly, couching objectives for reducing water pollution in terms of "best practicable technology" or "best available technology" may actually create disincentives for industry to improve control methods even for new plants, since they fear they might later be ordered to install these devices in all existing facilities. Critics also object to the kinds of penalties assessed for noncompliance. For example, the $10,000 fine for each new automobile that violates emission standards is so large that it will never be imposed, for to do so for even one or two defective models would be an impossible burden for America's already troubled auto industry.

Some economists have recommended that the regulatory approach be replaced by market incentives, which would reward efforts at maximizing pollution reduction. To encourage removal of pollutants, a tax could be levied on each unit of pollution discharged. For example, taxes could be assessed on biodegradable pollutants dumped into waterways on the basis of the pounds of biochemical oxygen demand. Polluters of the air could be taxed on the number of pounds of sulfur oxides, particulates, or other matters they release. Metering devices could be installed on smokestacks and discharge pipes to measure the volume of pollution of each offender. Applying the classical economic formula, polluters would reduce emissions to the level at which costs of further purification exceed the unit tax on pollution. From the beginning, therefore, an emissions tax should substantially reduce discharges, with the extent of reduction being determined by the size of the per unit tax. Emission taxes could be increased in order to create cleaner conditions. Desires by industry to reduce its tax burden create an incentive to develop and install more efficient technology for removing pollutants. Since industries or companies having more thorough pollution control systems will be able to undersell competitors who pay higher effluent taxes, the latter will be encouraged to reduce discharges.

There are additional advantages to the use of effluent charges to encourage pollution cleanup. First of all, a national system of taxes would remove the incentive for industry to relocate to states with more lenient pollution standards. Moreover, effluent charges generate revenue, unlike subsidies for sewage treatment plants, which cost money. By establishing a taxing system, and not simply mandating uniform levels of cleanup to be achieved by all, policymakers acknowledge that some industries and some types of discharge can be more easily cleaned up than can others. In contrast, uniform control standards may prove reasonable for some installations but impossible for others.

Despite its advantages, a system of effluent taxes has not been adopted, partly from a reluctance to make such a major change in approach. Other considerations include the question of whether collection of such a tax would rely on voluntary compliance or be based on a monitoring scheme. A voluntary approach could be easily circumvented, while monitoring may be objectionable as an intrusive form of enforcement. Moreover, it is not clear that the necessary technology for continuous monitoring has been developed.

## OTHER TYPES OF POLLUTION

In addition to the more extensive and historically longer legislative concern about the quality of the air and domestic waterways, there have been congressional efforts to reduce other types of pollution, such as noise, ocean pollution, toxic materials and solid waste disposal, each of which is discussed below.

### Noise

Amid estimates that 40 million Americans risk hearing impairment because of high noise levels and that the homes of 64 million Americans are disturbed by sounds generated by aircraft, traffic, or construction, Congress passed a Noise Control Act in 1972. The legislation called for the EPA to work with the Federal Aviation Administration in setting noise standards for airplanes. In late 1976 the Department of Transportation unveiled standards for jet noise. The Department of Transportation estimated that by 1985, when the requirements become effective, it will have cost between $5.5 and $7.9 billion to bring the nation's jet fleet into compliance.[30] While most planes can be brought into compliance, some older ones will have to be replaced.

During the 1980 campaign Ronald Reagan promised to eliminate most federal noise controls. As president he scheduled the phasing out of EPA's noise control program, with responsibility shifted to the states. The transportation industry favors a continuation of federal standards, fearing that some states and cities may begin to set their own stricter limits for trucks and trains.

### Ocean Pollution

With passage of the 1972 Marine Protection, Research, and Sanctuaries Act, use of the oceans as gigantic cesspools came under regulation. Dumping of radioactive wastes and products manufactured for chemical or biological warfare was prohibited. Ocean disposal of municipal sewage and industrial wastes was regulated by a permit system through 1981. It is unclear whether all ocean dumping will be discontinued in the near future.

## Strip Mining

After a struggle of several years, coal strip-mining legislation was enacted in 1977 (the Surface Mining Control and Reclamation Act). Strip miners were ordered to restore future sites to their premining conditions. Restoration involves grading to achieve earlier contours, replacing the topsoil, and replanting the land. Land that cannot be restored is off limits for all types of surface mining. Funds collected through taxes on coal will be used to restore abandoned strip mines. Coal producers seek to amend the legislation to permit state differences in place of national standards, and have found an ally in Reagan's Secretary of Interior James Watt.

## Hazardous Wastes

Public awareness of the nation's hazardous waste problems was triggered by the discovery of severe health problems in the Love Canal area of Buffalo, New York. This neighborhood, which was built on a chemical dump, was found to have an extraordinarily high incidence of cancer, miscarriages, and birth defects. Although the cause is still being debated, many residents attribute these health problems to the mixture of dozens of chemicals, some of them carcinogenic, which were leaking from the rusted barrels in which they had been buried in the long abandoned canal. In the wake of Love Canal, hundreds of chemical waste sites have been located. A number of these have been abandoned and no one knows what they contain.

In addition to locating dump sites and identifying their contents, the public is concerned with how to clean up existing sites and what to do to prevent future chemical dumps. A step toward eradication came with congressional approval of what has become known as the 1980 Superfund bill. A sum of $1.6 billion, most of it coming from the chemical industry, was established to pay for cleaning up dump sites. No funds have been provided for helping those who lose their health or homes. The Chemical Manufacturers Association claims this is several times over the amount needed while the EPA estimates that the cost may run to between $22 and $44 billion.[31] These funds will be used primarily for detoxifying abandoned dumps, with the government authorized to sue dump operators if their identity is known. The Reagan administration wants to reduce such funding for cleanups.

Prevention of creating new dumps was addressed in the 1976 Resources Conservation and Recovery Act. The EPA was directed to set standards for handling dangerous chemicals from the time they are manufactured until they are disposed of. In addition to making sure that situations similar to what happened at Love Canal do not occur, a second consideration in disposal is that wastes not seep into the nation's ground water supply. Despite this legislation, some share of the hazardous wastes are dumped along highways and in vacant lots by "midnight dumpers," who underbid legitimate disposal operations.

In addition to the problems of illegal dumping are the difficulties caused by the slowness with which EPA has implemented its responsibilities. Only two of ten thousand facilities handling dangerous wastes have received final permits. In the face of such delays, congressional committees were considering legislation in 1982 that would require EPA to issue permits within four years or the facilities would have to close. Environmentalists attribute the delays to budget cutting and what they perceive to be unsympathetic appointees of the Reagan administration.

The provision of safe disposal is made more difficult by strident local opposition whenever location of a site is proposed. President Carter's head of the EPA, Douglas Costle, referred to this as "the backyard syndrome," pointing out, "Everyone wants these wastes managed, but not in his backyard. And our entire nation is someone's backyard."[32]

Local opposition is also an obstacle to finding places for storing radioactive wastes, some of which will be deadly for generations. Storage in natural subterranean salt domes has been suggested, but is opposed by legislators representing areas where such domes are found. Some arrangements will have to be made during the 1980s. One possibility would be to store radioactive materials, such as spent fuel rods from nuclear generating plants, on federal lands.

### Solid Waste

The size of the problem of solid waste disposal is staggering, since only 8 percent of the 148 million tons of residential and commercial waste is recycled.[33] Most of the recycling involves paper; yet, even there, only 20 percent of discarded paper is reused. In the absence of recycling, most solid wastes are burned—contributing to air pollution—or buried in land fills. Both disposal processes place a heavy burden on our natural resources.

Efforts to handle solid wastes have been limited primarily to locally operated recycling programs, usually for paper or aluminum (see figure 4–1). A more permanent solution of part of the problem was pioneered in Oregon when it prohibited the sale of beverages in disposable containers. This legislation, since passed in about eight states, reduced container litter by two-thirds but some claim there were concomitant job losses among container manufacturers. Still mostly in the planning stage are proposals for making some use of the mountains of garbage generated daily. One idea is to fuel steam plants by burning garbage, while recovering reusable metals.

### NATIONAL ENVIRONMENTAL POLICY ACT

Unlike the piecemeal environmental legislation discussed thus far, each of which was aimed at cleaning up one component of the environment, the National Environmental Policy Act (NEPA) was intended to assure that environmental conse-

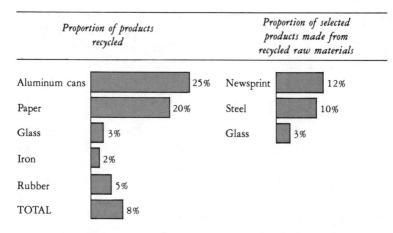

**Figure 4-1** Levels of recycling in the United States. (*Source: Council on Environmental Quality,* Environmental Quality, 1979. *Washington, D.C.: U.S. Government Printing Office, 1979; chap. 4 and p. 685.*)

quences be considered as a factor in all relevant federal policy decisions. The act was signed into law on January 1, 1970, as the first legislation of the new decade, and environmentalists hoped that it would usher in an era of greater environmental responsibility.

### Provisions

The most controversial part of the act is the requirement for environmental impact statements (EIS). Such statements—which are required for all proposed federal actions that might affect environmental quality—must address the following items: (1) the environmental impact of the proposed activity; (2) unavoidable negative consequences that would result from the activity; (3) alternatives to the proposed activity; (4) the relationship between the short-term uses to be made of the environment and the maintenance and enhancement of long-term productivity; and (5) any irreversible commitments of resources that would result if the activity were carried out.

Environmental impact statements are supposed to be prepared well in advance of the initiation of the proposed activity, so that concerned citizens have an opportunity to oppose the project on the grounds that the harmful consequences outweigh the benefits. The statements are filed with an office created by NEPA, the three-person Council on Environmental Quality (CEQ).

### Implementation

In performing its functions, the CEQ has opted for a relatively low profile. It has chosen to rely heavily on persuasion and therefore has tried to avoid antagonizing other agencies. Moreover, its public role seems to be limited to simply collecting environmental impact statements rather than evaluating their adequacy or the merits of projects in light of the likely environmental consequences. Although there are guidelines specifying when an environmental impact statement should be filed, these are often vague; some federal agencies, for example, require statements when "actions are likely to be highly controversial." Even when statements are presented, they may gloss over matters of great concern to environmentalists. Since the agencies generally prefer to carry out programs rather than to question whether some environmental damage may result, they are ill prepared to undertake the introspection called for by NEPA. Consequently, it is not surprising that the CEQ has concluded, "Too often the environmental impact statement is written to justify decisions already made, rather than to provide a mechanism for critical review."[34]

Environmental groups such as the Wilderness Society have interceded when they believed that CEQ was not sufficiently vigilant. By seeking injunctions when they believe that an agency has failed to file a needed EIS, or that its EIS is inadequate, or that the concerns raised in the EIS have not been considered by policy makers, private groups have delayed some projects and secured additional protection for the environment. During NEPA's first decade, private plaintiffs filed 1,200 suits.

While judges have often agreed with conservationists to the extent of requiring statements when none has been filed, they have shown greater tolerance in deciding what constitutes an adequate study. Thus, if an agency has prepared an impact statement, plaintiffs are unlikely to prevent a project unless they can prove that an official has incorrectly interpreted the law.[35] Since NEPA requires only that environmental consequences be considered and does not specify when environmental protection is to take precedence over project objectives, projects may be carried out despite the environmental harm noted in the impact statements.

Although they may ultimately fail to prevent a project, environmentalists have caused delays in 15 to 20 percent of the energy projects where suits have been filed.[36] These delays occur relatively infrequently. An average of more than 1,200 EIS are filed each year; less than 10 percent of these result in litigation. Plaintiffs win only about one-fifth of the cases they file.

The infrequency with which NEPA has obstructed federal projects has been lost sight of because of a few heavily publicized issues, the best known of these being the Alaska pipeline.[37] The point of the 1970s controversy was the desirability of laying an 800-mile pipeline to transport 2 million gallons of oil daily from Alaska's North Slope to the year-round port of Valdez. Conservationists warned that placing the pipeline above ground might impede migratory patterns of the region's wildlife. Even less desirable, they cautioned, would be the practice of burying the pipeline underground. In the first place, they argued, the high temperature generated by the speed of the oil being pumped southward would cause the surrounding tundra to melt, so that the pipeline might sink and rupture. In the second place, earthquakes in the area also could produce a massive spill. Even with the best technology, if the line should break when it was operating at capacity, at least 165,000 barrels of oil would spurt out before the flow could be stopped.

The EIS on the project pointed out that damage would occur to the flora and that scars inflicted during construction would take as long as 150 years to heal fully. Opponents of the pipeline concluded that the damage to the environment would be so severe that it would be preferable to transport the oil by tanker direct from the North Slope, even though ice floes would curtail such shipment for several months each year.

On the other hand, oil companies involved in tapping Alaska's oil reserves pointed to the chronic need for new domestic oil. These needs became quite real to many Americans during 1973 and 1974 as angry motorists queued up to purchase rationed supplies of gasoline. Oil company arguments had already won over the Department of Interior, whose secretary authorized construction of the pipeline.

The critical event leading to congressional participation was an environmentalist suit, *Morton v. Wilderness Society*, decided by the Supreme Court in 1973. The decision blocked construction of the pipeline because it would require usage of more than the 50-foot-wide right-of-way permitted by the 1920 Mineral Leasing Act. In November 1973 Congress passed legislation prohibiting further delays under NEPA or through litigation raising environmental questions. Thereupon the authorization for the pipeline granted by the Secretary of the Interior became effective; and the struggle by environmentalists, which had lasted several years, came to an end. The Trans-Alaska pipeline was completed in 1977.

The response by Congress to the environmentalists' challenge to the Alaska pipeline suggests that, given current needs, energy policy will ultimately take precedence over environmental policy when the two policies clash head to head. On the other hand, although they eventually lost the struggle to prevent construction, the environmentalists were able to secure some important modifications in the design of the pipeline.

## PUBLIC LANDS: CONSERVATION OR COMMERCIAL DEVELOPMENT

The United States government continues to own vast stretches of land, particularly in the western states: most of Alaska is federally owned; in five other states the federal government holds title to more than half the land; and even California, with its sprawling cities, is 44 percent federal land. Where federal holdings are extensive, the health of the local economy often hinges on the uses made of federal lands. If the lands are left as trackless wilderness, they generate no revenue for the local areas. Making some of the land available for recreational use will bring in some local income from the sale of camping supplies, fishing gear, and so on; however, sometimes the greatest income will accrue to the local community if the land is made available to private concerns. Each year individuals and large corporations are permitted to use millions of acres of public lands to make private profits. Mining companies extract valuable minerals from public lands, ranchers lease grazing rights, and timber rights are sold to logging companies.

Opposing the ranchers, miners, and timber companies are environmentalist groups. They counter the proposals for making money from the exploitation of federal lands by extolling the land's natural beauty which once sullied cannot be regained. Environmentalists argue that today's increasingly urban population needs to be able to escape to inspiring vistas, wild streams, and quiet forests. Moreover, they urge that some parts of the nation should be left unchanged for the enjoyment of future generations. Environmentalists also point to the biological function of forests, which provide wildlife habitats and convert carbon dioxide into oxygen.

Representatives of a variety of interests eager to make greater use of federal lands, such as James Watt, President Reagan's Secretary of Interior, charge that the nation is economically handicapped because resources on federal lands cannot be developed. They contend that if we were allowed to extract the petroleum and minerals on federal property it would reduce the balance of payments deficit and reduce our dependence on foreign countries for a number of minerals, such as cobalt, manganese, nickel, and zinc. This dependence, they warn ominously, could become critical in time of war. Timber interests, claiming that timber yields from private lands are approaching the upper limits, want Congress to allow additional logging in national forests. As timber companies are quick to point out, trees are a renewable resource and plastics or metals will be substituted if wood products are unavailable.

Whether to use or conserve national resources has become something of a regional confrontation. Some westerners complain that restrictions on federal lands limit their region's development. They see these restraints as imposed by an eastern-dominated Congress.

Through the 1960s and 1970s the conservationists had the upper hand. Legislation authorizing the protection of wild, free-flowing rivers, designations of wilderness areas in which development was prohibited, and the creation of national seashores was approved (see table 4–5). In addition the amount of land encompassed in national parks and monuments and state parks grew substantially. Passage of the Alaska Lands Act in the waning days of the Carter presidency, which designated 104 million acres as national parks, forests, wildlife refuges, and wild and scenic rivers, may signal the culmination of conservationist efforts.

The Reagan administration is opposed to expanding national park lands. It has also shown itself prepared to tolerate development of the resources on federal lands, including wilderness areas. This suggests that President Reagan's many supporters in the West—the region where he outpolled Jimmy Carter by the largest margins—may have been instrumental in turning the tide in the struggle between users and conservationists.

## THE ENVIRONMENT VERSUS ENERGY: THE TRADEOFFS

In this chapter we have described the major requirements of legislation designed to protect the environment, with special emphasis on efforts to rid air and streams of pollution and to limit emissions from automobiles. The preceding chapter outlined our nation's current energy policy, including the comprehensive program that President Carter sent to Congress in the spring of 1977. In the course of these two chapters we have sometimes noted in passing that some objectives of environmental protection legislation require greater use of energy, or that achievement of some

**TABLE 4-5  Major conservation legislation
and expansions, 1960-1980**

| Legislation/Program | Purpose | Extent |
|---|---|---|
| **New legislation** | | |
| Wilderness Act, 1964 | Restrictive designation for use of federal lands | 94 million acres |
| Wild and Scenic Rivers Act, 1968 | Maintain free-flowing (undammed) rivers | 27 rivers, 700,000 acres[a] |
| National Trails Act, 1968 | Trail preservation and maintenance | 257 trails |
| Endangered Species Act, 1973 | Promote survival of rare plants and animals | |
| Alaska Lands Act, 1980 | Preserve land in Alaska with limited use | 104 million acres |
| **Existing programs** | | |
| National Wildlife Refuges | Protect habitats of wild animals and fowl | Enlarged by 25 million acres[a] |
| National Parks | Preserve natural areas for public enjoyment and recreation | Enlarged by 5 million acres[a] |

[a]Figures exclude lands added in Alaska.

energy goals may necessitate fouling the environment. In this section we deal more explicitly with the conflicts between the policies of these two areas.

One such conflict concerns the increased use of coal. Each of the last four administrations has emphasized the need to increase coal production and the use of coal as a fuel substitute for petroleum products. President Carter urged that annual coal production be increased from 665 million tons to 1.1 billion tons by 1985. Hiking coal production will require more extensive strip mining. But if strip miners are forced to reclaim the land, coal extraction will become more expensive and possibly slower. Since any additional costs would be passed on to consumers, they will not switch from natural gas or oil to coal until petroleum products become even more expensive, so that the conversion from gas and oil will be delayed. It should be noted that deep-pit mining, while a potential alternative to strip mining, has drawbacks of its own: subsidence of surface land, higher cost, and higher incidence of injury to workers.

Even if coal production goals are met, there remain obstacles to the use of this fuel. Large amounts of the coal reserve contain high levels of sulfur. The strictures of the Clean Air Act and the regulations proposed by the EPA prevent the burning of much of this coal in large sections of the country unless steps are taken to reduce the sulfur oxide that is emitted. In areas where "scrubbers" would have to be installed to clean up emissions, the adaptation would be costly. Moreover, there are problems involved in disposing of the sludge from the scrubbers. Dumping it into a nearby river—a popular solution in some quarters—is prohibited by the 1972 amendments to the Water Pollution Control Act.

In addition to coal, hydroelectric power is an energy alternative to petroleum products. While hydroelectric power cannot provide more than a small share of America's energy needs, some environmental legislation limits the extent to which water power can be used to generate electricity. Rivers protected by the Wild and Scenic Rivers Act cannot be dammed. The construction of several other dams has been held up temporarily because of the 1973 Endangered Species Act, which prohibits actions detrimental to rare animals or plants.

A third potential source of fuel is oil shale, which is found in many parts of the West. At present the costs of extracting oil from shale are too high to make it a feasible alternative. Should recovery of oil from this source become economically feasible, there would probably be objections from environmentalists, since the extraction technology requires vast amounts of water—a quantity in short supply in the arid West. Furthermore, the shale residue left after the oil has been removed would, some environmentalists warn, be blown by the winds, producing great clouds of dust, which would pollute the air and the remaining water.

The requirement for environmental impact statements is seen in some quarters as a serious impediment to various activities which would provide some relief to the energy crisis. Environmentalists have often sued to prevent activities when federal agencies responsible for protecting the environment have no objections to the contemplated private development. (The earlier discussion of the Alaska pipeline is an example.) The construction of power plants, especially those that would use radioactive materials, is often delayed for years as power companies seek to overcome judicial challenges brought by environmentalists. New refineries and offshore docking facilities capable of handling supertankers have also been targets of objections based on their potential harm to the environment. Similar challenges to proposed new offshore drilling for oil have been voiced in some parts of the country. Environmentalists have been particularly fearful that offshore transfer or recovery of oil will produce additional devastating spills. Oil companies argue that they take great care to prevent such accidents and they admit that they cannot eliminate all risks but insist that the benefits offset the likely costs.

Finally, efforts thus far to reduce auto emissions have resulted in less efficient use of gasoline. Estimates are that pollution control devices have increased gasoline consumption by approximately 10 percent.

In a number of instances, then, the objectives of environmental protection and conservation of domestic petroleum supplies are incompatible.

## CONCLUDING COMMENTS

Both in his campaign and since inauguration Ronald Reagan indicated that he believes that environmental concerns have received too much emphasis. As a candidate he charged that nature in the form of Mount Saint Helens and even trees and other plants caused far more air pollution than does industry. As president, Reagan quickly began cutting back the scope of federal environmental efforts. The staff of the CEQ was chopped and the Reagan budget cut environmental funding levels to 42 percent below what President Carter had proposed. The president's cutbacks affected all aspects of environmental protection. In terms of water pollution, not only were few funds earmarked for sewer construction but funding was to go only to the larger systems, where it would be available for remedying current problems and not for extending sewer mains. There was also less money for rehabilitating strip-mined land and for cleaning up chemical dumps.

On the issues considered when legislation designed to improve water and air quality was reviewed in the early 1980s, President Reagan usually sided with business. Reagan and his advisers endorsed plans to reduce the influence of EPA as part of their deregulation effort. They have also gone on record in favor of making federal lands more accessible for energy development.

Another aspect of Reagan administration proposals for reducing federal authority over environmental protection is to decentralize decision making. Shortly before taking office President Reagan urged, "we should return to the states the primary responsibility for environmental regulation in order to increase responsiveness to local conditions."[38]

Environmentalists have found little in President Reagan's program to applaud. They plan to monitor closely the actions of the Reagan administration and to see that the positive legislation of the last two decades is not ignored. As a director of the Sierra Club said, "The old rapist days are over. Even the worst that could happen is not as bad as the worst that could have happened ten years ago. We're all expecting to be in court a lot more."[39] Environmental groups may be able to take advantage of the rapid growth in their membership ranks and contributions after the 1980 Republican victories, as frightened environmentalists rallied to the colors.

## NOTES

1. Walter A. Rosenbaum, *The Politics of Environmental Concern*, 1st ed. (New York: Praeger, 1973), p. 14.
2. For a discussion of early federal efforts, see Lettie McSpadden Wenner, *One Environment under Law: A Public-Policy Dilemma* (Pacific Palisades, Calif.: Goodyear, 1976), pp. 71–84.
3. J. Clarence Davies and Barbara S. Davies, *The Politics of Pollution*, 2nd ed. (Indianapolis: Pegasus, 1975), p. 208.
4. Ibid., p. 194.
5. Lawrence Mosher, "Clean Water Requirements Will Remain Even if the Federal Spigot is Closed," *National Journal* 13 (May 6, 1981): 874–878.
6. Council on Environmental Quality (CEQ), *Environmental Quality, 1980* (Washington, D.C.: U.S. Government Printing Office, 1980), p. 100.
7. CEQ, *Environmental Quality, 1979* (Washington, D.C.: U.S. Government Printing Office, 1979), p. 137.
8. CEQ, *Environmental Quality, 1980* (Washington, D.C.: U.S. Government Printing Office, 1980), pp. 86, 87, and 119.
9. Kathy Koch, "Dealing with Environmental, Health Effects of Coal Use," *Congressional Quarterly Weekly Report* 38 (May 31, 1980): 1490.
10. Kathy Koch, "Coming Clean Air Debate Will Reflect Traditional Costs vs. Benefits Quandary," *Congressional Quarterly Weekly Report* 39 (February 7, 1981): 268.

11. Prudence Crewdson, "Congress Faces Hard Choices on Clean Air Act," *Congressional Quarterly Weekly Report* 34 (June 7, 1976): 1172.
12. Rosenbaum, *Politics of Environmental Concern*, 1st ed., p. 155.
13. Ibid., p. 156.
14. Koch, "Coming Clean Air Debate," p. 268.
15. CEQ, *Environmental Quality, 1979*, p. 44.
16. Timothy B. Clark, "A Market for Air Pollution," *National Journal* 10 (August 19, 1978): 1332.
17. Kathy Koch, "National Commission Report Starts Congressional Debates on Renewing Clean Air Act," *Congressional Quarterly Weekly Report* 39 (March 7, 1981): 424.
18. H. Barclay Moxley, "Cleaning the Nation's Air," *National Journal* 12 (November 29, 1980): 2054; Lawrence Mosher, "Big Steel Says It Can't Afford to Make the Nation's Air Pure," *National Journal* 12 (July 5, 1980): 1088.
19. Davies and Davies, *Politics of Pollution*, pp. 196–197.
20. Ibid., p. 93.
21. Rosenbaum, *Politics of Environmental Concern*, 2nd ed. (New York: Praeger, 1977), p. 163.
22. Quoted in Lawrence Mosher, "Clean Air Act an Inviting Target for Industry Critics Next Year," *National Journal* 12 (November 15, 1980): 1928.
23. Quoted in Koch, "Coming Clean Air Debate," p. 270.
24. Ibid., p. 268. The federal OMB estimates that during the 1980s compliance with environmental requirements could cost business half a trillion dollars.
25. CEQ, *Environmental Quality, 1979*, pp. 665–668.
26. Allen V. Kneese and Charles L. Schultze, *Pollution, Prices, and Public Policy* (Washington, D.C.: Brookings Institution, 1979), p. 21.
27. Dick Kirschten, "Something to Cheer About," *National Journal* 10 (December 16, 1978): 2031, quotes poll undertaken by Resources for the Future.
28. CBS News, *New York Times* Poll, released February 2, 1981, p. 13.
29. CEQ, *Environmental Quality, 1980*, p. 407.
30. "Federal Officials Announce Efforts to End Half of Jet Noise by 1985," *Houston Chronicle*, November 19, 1976, section 1, p. 11.
31. Kathy Koch, "Cleaning Up Chemical Dumps Posing Problems for Congress," *Congressional Quarterly Weekly Report* 38 (March 22, 1980): 796.
32. Quoted in ibid., p. 802.
33. CEQ, *Environmental Quality, 1979*, p. 262.
34. CEQ, *Environmental Quality, 1971* (Washington, D.C.: U.S. Government Printing Office, 1971), p. 26.
35. Rosenbaum, *Politics of Environmental Concern*, 1st ed., p. 272.
36. CEQ, *Environmental Quality, 1979*, p. 590.
37. The discussion of the Alaska pipeline is drawn from Gerald Garvey, *Energy, Ecology, Economy* (New York: Norton, 1972), pp. 106–107.
38. Lawrence Mosher, "Reagan and Environmental Protection—None of the Laws Will Be Untouchable," *National Journal* 13 (January 3, 1981): 17.
39. Bill Keller, "Environmental Movement Checks Its Pulse and Finds Obituaries are Premature," *Congressional Quarterly Weekly Report* 39 (January 31, 1981): 214.

## SUGGESTED READINGS

Davies, J. Clarence, and Davies, Barbara S. *The Politics of Pollution*. 2nd ed. Indianapolis: Pegasus, 1975.
Jones, Charles O. *Clean Air: The Politics and Policies of Pollution Control*. Pittsburgh: University of Pittsburgh Press, 1975.
Kneese, Allen V., and Schultze, Charles L. *Pollution, Prices, and Public Policy*. Washington, D.C.: Brookings Institution, 1975.
Rosenbaum, Walter A. *The Politics of Environmental Concern*. 2nd ed. New York: Praeger, 1977.
Wenner, Lettie McSpadden. *One Environment under Law: A Public-Policy Dilemma*. Pacific Palisades, Calif.: Goodyear, 1976.

# Chapter 5

# Welfare, Medical Care, and the War on Poverty

The roots of welfare run deep in our history, even if the fruit produced is not always bountiful. During the last two generations, welfare became increasingly a responsibility of the federal government. Its benefits have been broadened into new areas and distributed through a growing number of programs, and the cost has spiraled ever upward. This chapter first describes the social and political environment in which welfare programs developed. We will then describe the major programs. Some of these provide cash, as does Supplemental Security Income. Others, such as the housing programs, offer a commodity but no money for the poor. Still other programs help the needy obtain specific benefits, such as food or health care, by paying federal dollars directly to the provider rather than to the person being helped. Through the combination of these programs, the federal government provides, at least in rudimentary fashion, for basic human needs.

This chapter addresses: (1) the major welfare programs initiated during the administration of Franklin D. Roosevelt; (2) subsidized housing programs; (3) Medicare and Medicaid programs; (4) programs that emerged as a result of Lyndon B. Johnson's War on Poverty (for instance, Project Head Start, various job-training programs, and Community Action Programs); and (5) the food stamp program. Reforms proposed and implemented by President Reagan for each area will also be noted.

## ALLEVIATIVE PROGRAMS: THE WELFARE STATE

Every society has its orphans, widows, aged, and sick—people who cannot fully care for themselves and must depend on others to some degree. Traditionally, care for the unfortunate was provided locally, primarily by the relatives of the poor; the elderly were cared for by their children, and orphans were taken in by aunts and

uncles, cousins, or grandparents. Then, at about the same time that English coloni-
zation of America began, Parliament passed the first welfare laws. This early legislation provided that poor people who could not be cared for by their families were
the responsibility of the local community. This same pattern—of families caring for
their less fortunate members, with local authorities providing whatever supplemental assistance was available—was adopted in this country.

This approach evidenced little change until the Great Depression of the 1930s.
As the country sank to the nadir of the economic cycle, local and state resources
proved insufficient for the massive levels of unemployment and the widespread
need for income and essential goods and services. With the unemployment rate
exceeding 20 percent, the rudimentary welfare system designed to help widows,
orphans, and the elderly was inundated with millions of able-bodied people who
would gladly work and support their families but could not find jobs.

The Depression placed greater strain on the traditional system of assistance
than had previous financial panics, since during earlier depressions most Americans
could at least provide bare economic necessities for themselves. Until 1920 most
Americans lived on farms, so that even when times were bad many families could
raise their food, continue to live in their homes, and help each other. Moreover,
an opportunity which in the past had helped large numbers of people begin their
economic recovery, namely, cheap land along the frontier, was no longer available.

The lines outside of the Depression soup kitchens raised doubts in the minds of
some Americans about the adequacy of commonly accepted attributes of the nation's approach to poverty. One of the first assumptions to be questioned was the
proposition that the federal government bears no responsibility for the care of the
poor. As it became increasingly clear that local resources, both private and public,
were inadequate to the mammoth tasks confronting them, the federal government
emerged as the only possible bulwark for the needy.

Second, some people began to wonder whether—as had long been assumed—
the poor really were solely responsible for their plight. A widespread belief (not
wholly displaced today) was that poverty is caused by laziness, drunkenness, or
some other personal shortcoming. The joblessness and resulting need of the Depression affected former factory owners as well as former factory workers, pointing
up the fact that poverty could and did touch even those who were most hardwork-
ing and conscientious about setting something aside for a rainy day. No longer
were the old virtues of thrift and diligence sufficient. Individuals no longer controlled their destinies but instead were dependent on corporations and banks, which
succeeded or failed depending on distant fluctuations of the stock market and the
international financial community.

Awareness of these societal changes brought about a growing support for programs that would provide some income and services for the poor and unemployed.
Although millions of formerly middle-class citizens suffered and came to support
the idea of federal welfare assistance, the conservative element in society continued
to oppose federal involvement in this new sphere. They clung to the old myths of
self-reliance and raised the symbol of states' rights as a barrier to federal interven-

tion. If federal revenues were given to the poor, these people said, they would lose all initiative to care for themselves and would grow lazy as they dined at the federal trough. Conservatives also warned that even if the initial programs were modest, they would, in time, be expanded. Therefore, even a small-scale federal program would be a dangerous precedent.

With the election of Franklin D. Roosevelt as president in 1932, proponents of comprehensive welfare assistance gained ascendance among the federal policy-makers. Supported by huge liberal majorities in Congress, the New Deal programs were enacted, ushering in a series of federal programs designed to help those in need.

The relief policies begun during the New Deal were alleviative in nature. Programs, such as Old Age Assistance, were designed to provide small amounts of money to reduce the hardships of poverty for people who for some reason could not work.

The rationale behind alleviative programs is that each citizen is entitled to some minimal level of subsistence; therefore, the federal government will provide a small amount of money or goods with which the recipient is to care for self and family. The money is not, however, simply there for the asking. To get it, one must demonstrate need and also fit into a category which qualifies for aid. The "needs test" is clearly initiated in response to critics who suspect that the indolent and undeserving will try to obtain benefits improperly. Need has been defined in terms of wealth and number of dependents. Thus, a widow with one child must have less income to qualify than would a widow having several dependent children, since the former will have fewer expenses than the latter.

## Cash Assistance Programs

The categories of people who qualified for federal relief programs were the elderly, who could receive Old Age Assistance; widows (and other women without husbands) and their dependent children, who could participate in the Aid to Families with Dependent Children (AFDC) program; the blind; and the permanently and totally disabled. Until 1974 all four categoric aid programs were operated in the same way. That is, federal grants constituted part of the benefits, while the states that operated the programs (under a system of matching funds) also provided some of the funding. In 1974 a major change was made in the programs for the aged, blind, and disabled; that is, the more than 1,000 state and local categoric programs which received federal aid were combined, and their funding was taken over by the federal government. The new creation, called Supplemental Security Income (SSI), introduced uniform minimum benefits throughout the country. Increases in benefits are tied to the cost of living. Beneficiaries in poorer states have received more money as a result of the federalization of these programs. In June 1981 federal payments averaged $107.72 for aged recipients but $170 per month for each blind or disabled person. In most states, the state makes a payment in addition to the SSI grant. In some states—for instance, California and Massachusetts—the state contribution exceeds the federal. Some other states provide only a token subsidy.[1] The AFDC program continues to be administered under the "matching funds" system, which allows even greater disparities in benefits. AFDC payments in 1980 averaged $30 per month in Mississippi per person, compared with approximately $163 per month per recipient in Alaska.[2] The federal contribution constitutes 50 to 77 percent of the AFDC payments made by states.

The SSI program, unlike most others discussed in this chapter, has not experienced soaring increases. Indeed, from 1975 to 1980 there was a gradual decrease in recipients. This is the only entitlement welfare program (entitlement programs are those in which the federal government guarantees benefits to all who are eligible) for which annual costs have grown at a moderate pace—an average of only 6.2 percent a year.

Of the four categories of cash assistance, three have come to be almost universally accepted. The AFDC program, however, remains very unpopular in some quarters. Some critics insist that the program fosters illegitimacy by paying money to unwed mothers, since the larger the family the greater the amount of benefits received. The size of the program also contributes to its unpopularity. It has many more beneficiaries than the other three, approximately 11 million in 1981. In addition to attracting opposition because of its numbers of participants, increases in the cost of AFDC have contributed to its unpopularity among conservatives. As table 5–1 shows, the cost more than doubled between 1970 and 1976, even though the number of participants has remained between 7.0 and 8.1 million since 1970. Another aspect of AFDC has been the disproportionate number of black participants. Although blacks make up about 12 percent of the population, they comprise more than 40 percent of all AFDC recipients.

In short, conservatives criticize the AFDC program for being expensive and poorly designed. As AFDC rolls began to swell rapidly, conservatives in Congress tried several tactics in hopes of curbing expenses. The first strategy was to increase the number of social workers assigned to AFDC families, in hopes that more intensive counseling and supervision would increase the number of families able to leave welfare by becoming self-sufficient.[3] But as the number of AFDC recipients continued to rise, Congress tried a new tactic. AFDC mothers were first allowed and then, in 1971, required, to sign up for work-training programs. (There were some exclusions; mothers of preschool children, for instance, were not forced to participate in work training.) The assumption behind this approach was that mothers who wanted to work could be trained for jobs which would pay enough for them to get their families off welfare. To make work training a realistic possibility for mothers of dependent children, day-care centers were to be provided for participants. Defects in the program have been the failure to create enough day-care facilities, the inadequacy of the training provided, and the low salaries offered many mothers who took jobs after completing the training. Often women would be better off continuing to receive welfare and other benefits, rather than taking the available poor paying jobs and forfeiting public assistance. Beginning in 1967 AFDC recipients lost sixty cents worth of benefits for each dollar earned,[4] but starting in 1982 their benefits are cut by an amount equal to what they earn.

**TABLE 5-1   Aid to Families with Dependent Children Program (AFDC) participation and costs**

| | Participants (in millions) | | Cost (in millions) |
|---|---|---|---|
| | Total | Children | |
| 1960 | 3.1 | 2.4 | $ 1,055 |
| 1965 | 4.5 | 3.4 | 1,809 |
| 1970 | 9.7 | 7.0 | 4,857 |
| 1971 | 10.7 | 7.7 | 5,653 |
| 1972 | 11.1 | 8.0 | 6,710 |
| 1973 | 10.8 | 7.8 | 7,292 |
| 1974 | 11.0 | 7.9 | 7,990 |
| 1975 | 11.4 | 8.1 | 9,211 |
| 1976 | 11.2 | 7.9 | 10,140 |
| 1977 | 10.8 | 7.6 | 10,603 |
| 1978 | 10.3 | 7.2 | 10,729 |
| 1979 | 10.4 | 7.2 | 11,069 |
| 1980 | 11.1 | 7.6 | 11,102 |
| 1981 | 11.1 | 8.0[a] | 6,600[a] |

SOURCE: U.S. Bureau of the Census, *Statistical Abstract of the United States* (Washington, D.C.: U.S. Government Printing Office, annual issues for the years shown).

[a]Estimated figures.

The third attempt by Congress to hold down welfare costs showed the least imagination. The Ways and Means Committee of the House of Representatives put a ceiling on the amount of money available to care for children added to AFDC rolls because of illegitimacy or desertion by their fathers. This placed the burden squarely on the states, since while program registrants would continue to grow, the federal government's contribution to the costs of the program would not. Having exhausted its own supply of remedies, Congress tried to force the states to come up with some ideas. Pressure from the states, which did not want to assume the additional financial burden, quickly forced Congress to relent and remove the ceilings.

On the other side of the political spectrum, AFDC is criticized for providing inadequate benefits. Specifically, critics note that benefits rarely lift families to the federally established poverty level. In 1980 federal officials, using Department of Agriculture estimates of how much income would be needed to inexpensively feed a family (the Orshansky Index), classified a family of four having less than $8,410 yearly income as poor. With the average monthly benefits received by an AFDC family of four being less than $400, this program alone is insufficient to raise most recipients out of poverty. (AFDC critics note that participants in this program typically receive other benefits which, in combination, may suffice to lift a family above the poverty line. We will return to this point shortly.)

Both liberals and conservatives agree that the program is poorly administered. Liberals complain about the red tape and petty rules which may keep some of the eligible from receiving benefits. They deplore the long applications, embarrassing needs tests, and questions about personal matters such as sex life. Some liberal critics charge that some of the regulations are counterproductive. For example, although female-headed households are much more likely to be poor than are those having male heads, some states' AFDC regulations encourage fathers to desert their families. (Although federal matching funds have been available since 1961 to states which extend benefits to families with unemployed fathers, 25 states have exercised this option.) Where the presence of an unemployed male in the home makes the family ineligible for AFDC, a father may decide that his family will be better off if he leaves. Thus, the family is broken up, and a potential breadwinner and needed role model may be gone forever. On the other hand, some conservatives believe that the eligibility requirements are not stringent enough.

Liberal critics of AFDC have urged the federal government to take over the program as it took over the other categoric aid programs. They point out that there would then be equality of benefits among the states, with increases coming in states that are least generous. Moreover, if all states paid the same benefits, there would no longer be an incentive for AFDC families to move from states offering low benefits to states that are more generous. Financially hard-pressed state and local administrators also urge the federal government to relieve them of their welfare burdens. For example, New York City's brush with bankruptcy was in part caused by the huge sums it pays out in AFDC.

The very costliness of AFDC has caused many congressmen concerned about widening federal budget deficits to oppose increasing federal responsibilities for the program. Instead of incurring greater expense and standardizing benefits nation-wide, recent federal laws have attempted to reduce costs. One technique has been to order states to locate fathers who have deserted their children and to extract support payments from them. The Department of Health and Human Services makes Social Security numbers available to states to help locate fathers who have ceased supporting their families. (President Carter convinced Congress to divide the Department of Health, Education and Welfare into a Department of Health and Human Services and a Department of Education.)

Many critical policymakers continue to suspect that the welfare rolls contain large numbers of cheats. These suspicions were fueled by recent studies reporting that 16 percent of all AFDC payments involved errors, costing approximately $1 billion annually. To force the states, which are responsible for day-to-day adminis-tration of the program, to tighten eligibility screening, the federal government has threatened them with loss of a share of the federal matching funds.

**Reagan proposals.**    Liberals charge that President Reagan has tried to balance the federal budget on the backs of poor people. Conservatives respond that "this administration wants welfare to help only people who are down and out."[5] Irrespec-tive of one's value judgment, both sides agree that legislation supported by the Reagan administration has tightened up eligibility standards so as to exclude the working poor. Other changes are designed to force the poor who can work to do so for as many hours as it would take when earning the minimum wage to pay for the benefits received. Many of those who have retained eligibility have lost some benefits.

Changes in the rules made 10 percent of the households which had received AFDC ineligible in late 1981 and cut the benefits of another 7 percent. This was done by reducing the value of assets families could have and still be eligible, as well as the amount a recipient can earn, and cutting the amount of child-care expenses that can be offset against earnings. The impact of cutting back AFDC rolls is magnified since people ineligible for AFDC may also lose Medicaid benefits, a program to be discussed shortly.

The president's budget proposal for fiscal year 1983 calls for further belt-tightening in order to scale AFDC costs back to $5.5 billion, a figure far below any amount spent during the last decade, especially if one adjusts for inflation.

A more revolutionary change than that encompassed in the budget-cutting efforts was outlined in President Reagan's 1982 State of the Union address. He proposed that states assume full responsibility for AFDC and food stamps in return for Washington making Medicaid a wholly national program. This is precisely the opposite of what occurred when SSI assigned three other categoric aid programs to the federal government. Those who speak for the poor oppose giving states full control of AFDC since, they argue, many states have never provided adequate funds. Elimination of a federal role would, they fear, result in even less generous funding than is currently found in some states. In February 1982 the nation's governors voted by a 36 to 5 margin not to take on the AFDC and food stamps programs, although not surprisingly they did favor federal operation of Medicaid.

## IN-KIND PROGRAMS

In-kind programs discussed in this section provide a commodity or service rather than money to the poor. In part this strategy stems from the distrust of the poor which is widespread among policymakers. From the suspicion that the poor are in large part responsible for their plight comes the belief that if they are given money they will spend it foolishly rather than for the commodities which policymakers intended. One way to assure that a program designed to feed the poor does result in food and not "luxuries" being purchased is to give recipients food stamps rather than cash. The creators of the New Deal programs that provide cash believed that beneficiaries would be "deserving" poor who were temporarily down on their luck but could return to self-sufficiency. A more pessimistic view of poor people underlies the programs discussed here.

A second reason for structuring programs so that benefits may only be used for the purpose intended is that poor people are not the sole beneficiaries. Part of the rationale for food programs has been to help farmers by creating additional consumers. Moreover, housing programs have helped the construction industry whose health is vital to the nation's economy.

### Housing Programs

For more than forty years there have been programs to subsidize the housing costs of some low-income families. Federal housing programs have been motivated by two considerations. First, poor housing conditions have been linked to a number of pathologies, particularly sickness and crime. It was hoped that new housing, by eliminating filth and vermin and by providing more pleasant surroundings, would make the poor healthier. Second, because the construction industry is such an important component of the economy, federal aid which spurs new building has wide-ranging economic consequences.

In this section we will discuss the range of housing programs for the poor. We will then evaluate the federal housing efforts and briefly note some of the recent proposals for redirecting efforts to provide decent shelter.


**Public housing.**   For many years the only form of housing assistance was public housing. In this program federal funds are given to local communities for the purpose of building or buying inexpensive rental units. Public housing projects have generally lacked amenities but have been structurally sound. The appeal of public housing has been that units rent for less than what private landlords would charge for comparable shelter. Thus, it allows families who would otherwise be forced to live in rat-infested, dilapidated tenements or shacks to rent a unit with a good roof, air-tight walls and floors, central heat, and, in some new projects, air conditioning. Rents in housing projects are based on the tenants' income and the size of the family. The program was designed for the less affluent working poor. Some income is needed to qualify; however, growing income or declining family size could make one ineligible, forcing a move to privately owned housing.

Since its beginning in 1937, public housing has been erected in hundreds of towns and cities. In smaller communities projects are often composed of duplexes or two-story apartments with only four to eight units per building. Projects often have extensive public grounds, and tenants are allowed to have flower and vegetable gardens. Within a project may be units of various sizes—from efficiency apartments for the elderly to single-family, detached houses with as many as four bedrooms. In some small cities housing projects compare favorably, visually, with private developments designed for moderate-income families. In large central cities, however, public housing has followed a very different design. Exorbitant land costs have prompted erection of high-rise buildings by public housing authorities. Since the main objective was to house a maximum number of people on a minimum of land, little space was left for recreation.

The population density of high-rise projects has drawn a great deal of criticism. The impersonal nature of these developments is blamed in part for the high crime rates found in some of them. In describing high-rise public housing projects, one observer charged, "They spawn teen-age gangs. They incubate crime. They are fiendishly contrived institutions for the debasing of family and community life to the lowest common mean."[6] A study of two adjoining public housing projects in New

York City found that the high-rise one had four times as many robberies as did the low-rise one.[7] In the Pruitt-Igoe Project in Saint Louis—a multibuilding, high-rise project which upon completion had been hailed as the way of the future for urban public housing—crime and vandalism became so rife that people refused to live in the development. Vacant units had windows smashed and plumbing fixtures ripped out. After several unsuccessful efforts to attract residents, Saint Louis authorities gave up on their dream-turned-nightmare and dynamited the buildings.

The high incidence of various forms of antisocial behavior in projects like Pruitt-Igoe has been a factor in making public housing an unattractive program in many circles. The high proportion of black residents (70 percent) in public housing is a second factor in its unpopularity. Further contributing to the relatively low levels of support for public housing has been middle-class distaste for programs to help the poor. While those attitudes have become modified with time, they seem to remain fairly strong where public housing is concerned.

Not only has the public housing program failed to develop a strong clientele who could achieve its expansion in Congress; it has also faced a powerful coalition of opponents. Conservative groups like the Chamber of Commerce have opposed the program on ideological grounds. Some real estate interests, such as the National Association of Home Builders and the National Association of Real Estate Boards, have opposed public housing on economic grounds. They prefer alternatives in which the federal government does not compete with the private section in building and renting apartments.

**Subsidies and supplements: 1960s.**    The unpopularity of public housing led to the development of alternative programs, which allowed a larger role for private industry. Congress authorized participation of profit-making components of the housing industry in the task of sheltering the poor. In two programs launched in 1968, low- and moderate-income families paid a specified proportion of their income for shelter, and the federal government made up the deficit between what the family could afford and the market price of the unit. The rent supplement program (Section 236) required that tenants pay 25 percent of their income toward rent. The government approved apartment developments for participation in the program and regulated the rent which landlords could charge.

In theory at least, all participants benefited from this program. The rent supplement program was less expensive for the federal government than public housing, since private entrepreneurs bore the costs of initial construction as well as management expenses. Tenants escaped the stigma attached to public housing projects, and they would not be forced to move if their earnings rose—as they would in public housing; instead, the size of the federal rent contribution would be gradually phased out as tenant incomes increased. Finally, rent supplements were attractive to private investors, who received tax breaks by depreciating the value of their apartments. Moreover, the federal supplements made it economically feasible to rent to a less affluent clientele, thereby opening a new market to the rental industry.

The other housing innovation of 1968 was the Section 235 Mortgage Subsidy

Program. The intent of this legislation was to permit families earning between $3,000 and $7,000 annually to buy homes. Eligible families were to pay 20 percent of their incomes in mortgage payments on houses selling for $15,000 to $20,000. The federal contribution would be paid to the lending institution and would be used to reduce the purchaser's interest rate to as little as 1 percent (at the time of the legislation, housing interest rates varied from 6.5 to 7 percent). Loans made to participants were guaranteed by the Federal Housing Administration (FHA), which had extensive experience in guaranteeing the home loans of millions of middle-income Americans.

The rationale behind mortgage subsidies was based on the concept of pride of ownership. People working in real estate had long recognized that homeowners tended to take better care of their dwellings than did renters. Owner-occupied homes are more likely to have well-kept yards and better-maintained dwellings than are rented premises. Program supporters hoped that mortgage subsidies would not only allow low- and moderate-income families to build up equity but would also stem the deterioration of many urban neighborhoods where the housing stock was structurally sound. Realtors and builders, who saw a whole new market opening before them, were strong supporters of the program. Chester Hartman says that the 1968 rent and mortgage subsidy programs "were largely the work of the most powerful Washington lobbying group in the housing and urban development field, the National Association of Home Builders, and a broadly based organization of large and small home builders, mortgage bankers, and some land speculators and realtors."[8]

Both the rent and mortgage subsidy programs developed serious problems. While they functioned successfully in some communities, elsewhere they became tainted by scandals, which received wide publicity. In retrospect, the programs relied too heavily on good intentions, with insufficient attention given to drafting precautions to prevent abuses by the unscrupulous and to screen applicants. Section 235 housing proved to be particularly susceptible to exploitation. Dishonest developers bought old houses needing extensive work, but they made only cosmetic improvements—for example, a paint job, a new ceiling, or stop-gap repairs on the furnace. They would then bribe the FHA appraiser whose job it was to establish the fair market price of the house. In this way, a developer might pay $9,000 for a house, spend $1,000 to make it more attractive, pay a $100 bribe, and then have the house appraised at $20,000. The developer would make a huge profit, and the house would be sold to an unsuspecting family that relied on the validity of the FHA's appraisal. After moving in and discovering that the roof leaked, or that rotted walls were crumbling under cheap wallpaper, or that the plumbing or furnace needed to be replaced, many new homeowners decided that the joys of buying were vastly overrated. Unable to pay for costly repairs in addition to the mortgage, many buyers allowed lenders to foreclose. The down payment required was so small—a minimum of $200—that many purchasers had little incentive not to abandon their homes when they encountered difficulties. Since the loans are guaranteed by the FHA, the lender suffered no loss if the purchaser stopped making payments;

the federal government simply paid off the balance of the loan and acquired the property. By mid-1975 the Department of Housing and Urban Development (HUD) had more than 200,000 foreclosed units worth $2.7 billion on its hands. Vandals quickly broke into the foreclosed units, stripping them of copper pipes and plumbing fixtures. Losses to HUD mounted into the hundreds of millions of dollars as vandalized units deteriorated to the point at which they had to be razed.

Overpricing was not the only defect in the mortgage subsidy program. Too little care was exercised in screening loan applicants. Since loans were guaranteed by the FHA, the lender had less incentive to thoroughly check out the credit of applicants. Even reasonable diligence by lenders might have been unavailing in some circumstances, since some realtors doctored the credit records of applicants to make them appear to be good credit risks. Thus, even in the absence of fraudulent pricing, many Section 235 purchasers proved unable to make their payments.

Another cost created by the mismanagement of the mortgage subsidy program is less easily calculable although no less real. The presence of vacant houses owned by HUD provided a haven for transient alcoholics and drug addicts. By attracting undesirables to a neighborhood, Congress's well-intentioned but poorly conceived effort accelerated the deterioration of some of the very neighborhoods it was designed to save.

Poor families who sank their savings into decrepit wrecks and the American taxpayers were the big losers. Some dishonest realtors, developers, and appraisers were the only winners. Not surprisingly, HUD substantially altered the Section 235 program.

**Subsidies: 1974.**    The failure of the earlier subsidy programs led to refocusing. Requirements for participation in the 1974 revision of Section 235 are designed to exclude many who could have purchased homes under the earlier version. Interest rates are reduced to as low as 4 percent rather than 1 percent, minimum down payments are pegged to the price of the house but are at least 3 percent of the sales price, and minimal annual earnings for participation are much higher. Where the first Section 235 program's emphasis was on including a new segment of the population in the ranks of the prospective homeowners, the post-1974 objective is less ambitious: "The program's focus is on low- and moderate-income families who traditionally have been buyers of new single-family homes but who are priced out of the market."[9] In 1981 families earning up to 130 percent of the median income in the area could qualify for mortgages of up to $40,000. If a participating family's economic condition improves, the size of the subsidy is reduced.

The Brooke-Cranston program, which is available only during recessions in order to stimulate the construction industry, is aimed at more expensive homes. Mortgages for houses costing as much as $60,000 are available at 3 percentage points below the prevailing rate.

Alternatives to the mortgage subsidy program were introduced by the Nixon administration. Section 8 of the 1974 housing legislation provides cash housing supplements not tied to a particular apartment complex. Under this program, families must be approved for participation and then locate an apartment that qualifies for the subsidy. As devised, the program is available to a broader economic range of tenants than is public housing. The 1974 legislation extended eligibility to families earning up to 80 percent of the local median income. Most participants have much lower incomes and Congress has considered lowering eligibility to those earning 50 to 60 percent of the median income.

Participants pay between 15 and 25 percent of their income for rent, depending on family size. While participants can look throughout a metropolitan area for an apartment, there are upper limits on the total cost for rent and utilities. Income eligibility is tied to rent costs; that is, families are ineligible if their earnings are more than four times the amount of the rent plus utilities.

In theory, the rent assistance program allows participants a much wider selection of apartments. In reality, the program as implemented in some cities has unrealistically low limits on the amount of rent which can be paid. In these cities decent units—particularly larger ones—simply are not available for the amount specified by HUD.

Some 40 percent of the units covered by Section 8 have involved rent assistance to families in existing buildings. In new units built under this program, HUD guarantees the developer a subsidized tenant population for 20 years. Because of high construction costs, new units cost almost as much as private single family residences to build.

**Urban homesteading.**    Initially tried by a few cities, an experimental urban homesteading program was authorized by Congress in 1974. In this program abandoned houses are sold for a nominal price—sometimes as little as $1—to purchasers who agree to make whatever repairs are necessary to bring the dwellings into compliance with local housing code requirements. For do-it-yourselfers, urban homesteading provides an opportunity to acquire a house for very little money. The city also benefits to the extent that abandoned property goes back on the tax rolls and neighborhood decay is halted.

**Evaluation of housing programs.**    In 1949 Congress went on record as favoring the idea that all Americans should be able to have a decent home. To achieve this objective, the construction of 810,000 new housing units was authorized. Completion of the task was contingent on Congress's actually appropriating funds for construction, and it was at this point that commitment faltered. Because of the factors noted earlier, which made public housing so unattractive to a large segment of Congress, appropriations were consistently far below levels needed to provide enough housing. During the next decades, only about 80 percent of the new units authorized in 1949 were actually constructed.

The urban riots of the mid-1960s alerted Congress to the unfinished task of providing low-income housing, since inadequate housing may well have been a contributing cause of the riots.[10] In 1968, therefore, Congress reasserted its intention of providing adequate housing. Since urban renewal projects, highway building, and abandonment by landlords had substantially reduced the supply of inexpensive housing, Congress set a goal of six million new low-income units by 1980.

This ambitious goal was not met. As earlier, Congress was less willing to follow through with needed appropriations than it has been to simply set objectives. The president has, at times, been even less interested in meeting housing goals than has Congress. In 1973–1975, President Nixon showed his disapproval for existing programs by refusing to spend money appropriated for new housing projects. Commitments already made were kept, but no new projects were begun. In general, support for low-income housing has been eroded by the Section 235 scandals and the record peacetime federal budget deficits.

Moreover, inflation has caused costs for land and construction to increase, so that each dollar appropriated for housing programs purchases less. Inflation, unemployment, and the acceptance of higher proportions of welfare families has resulted in higher subsidies being needed to operate public housing. In 1980, average annual subsidies were estimated at $4,200 per existing unit and $6,200 per newly constructed unit.[11] By the time the federal obligation is satisfied, a total of $59,000 may have been spent on an existing apartment and a whopping $710,000 on a new unit. The cost of constructing each new unit of Section 8 housing was a hefty $57,000 in 1980.[12]

The price tag attached to public housing causes some to question the efficiency of the approaches currently used. A former deputy assistant secretary of HUD offered this provocative observation: "If [the annual subsidy] amount were provided directly to public housing tenants, it would enable them to rent almost any new apartment now being built privately. . . . If the subsidy were given in cash directly to tenants, it would be enough to lift virtually all of them out of poverty."[13]

Although all options have a sizable price tag, placing the poor in existing units is substantially cheaper than new construction. Greater emphasis is not placed on rehabilitating and leasing existing structures partially because the construction industry—whose lobbying is critical for passage of housing legislation—derives greater profits from building new units. Moreover, apartment vacancy rates have been very low for several years and numerous structures which could be rehabilitated are in undesirable neighborhoods. Consequently housing subsidy programs reach only 5 to 10 percent of those who are eligible. In recent years, a disproportionate share of the new units have been built for the elderly while large, poor families encounter growing difficulties in locating housing. Waiting lists for subsidized housing in some cities contain hundreds of names. Obviously the programs rate poorly in terms of equity.

Despite problems in adopting new legislation and the shortcomings of some recent programs, the use of housing codes in urban areas, urban renewal projects, and federal housing assistance programs have contributed to a general improvement in housing conditions. In 1979, less than 3 percent of the nation's housing lacked some or all plumbing, down from 34 percent in 1950 and 15 percent in 1960. The proportion living in overcrowded conditions (more than 1.5 persons per room) was just under 1 percent in 1977.[14]

**Reagan proposals.**    President Reagan has proposed major changes in the federal approach to helping the poor with their housing needs. These changes would cause rents to rise, eligibility to become more restrictive, and alter the way in which aid is distributed.

In 1981, Congress approved the administration request that families receiving a federal housing subsidy be required to pay 30 rather than 25 percent of their income in rent. Of even greater significance was the president's suggestion that food stamps be counted as income. Since poorer families receive more food stamps, counting the stamps as income would cause the rents charged the very poor to more than double.[15]

President Reagan has also proposed eliminating most of the funds for new construction and using the money for a voucher system. The president explained in his 1983 budget proposal, "The housing construction programs are being terminated because they are very costly, provide too large a subsidy for too few people and do not address the nation's current housing problem."[16] Another reason for discontinuing the construction program is the reduction in the number of substandard housing units. A system of vouchers would give the poor an average of $2,000 per year which they could use to rent privately owned units. Adoption of this change is problematic because of opposition from the building industry.

## Food Stamps

Launched as a limited experiment in 1961, the food stamp program was gradually expanded until by 1973 it became the predominant program for providing nutritional assistance. The food stamp program gives poor people stamps which can be redeemed at stores, for food only. In 1981 the average food stamp participant received a subsidy of about $40 per month.

The history of food stamps resembles that of AFDC, discussed earlier. Both have been marked by rapid growth in recent years and have been tinkered with as Congress has tried to find a balance between reasonable support and spiraling costs. As shown in figure 5-1, participation in the food stamp program increased tenfold during the first five years after passage of the Food Stamp Act of 1964. This growth occurred during a period in which counties had a choice of offering food stamps, surplus food, or no food program at all. By 1974, when food stamps were made available nationwide, participation had risen to almost 13 million. As unemployment soared during the mid-1970s, so did food stamp enrollments. Elimination in 1977 of the requirement that stamps be purchased, resulted in millions of new participants, during another period of high unemployment. (A 1 percentage point increase in unemployment translates into a million more food stamp recipients.)[17] These factors have more than offset reductions caused by stricter definitions of eligibility so that by 1979, 7.5 percent of the nation's families participated in the program. There were millions of others who were eligible but did not receive stamps.

Spreading participation, coupled with provisions which pegged increases in bene-

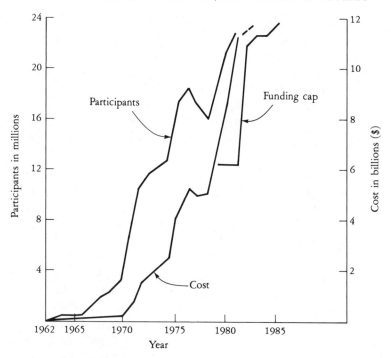

**Figure 5-1** Food Stamp Program participation and costs. (*Source: U.S. Bureau of the Census*, Statistical Abstract of the United States. *Washington, D.C.: U.S. Government Printing Office, annual issues.*)

fits to changes in the consumer price index, have caused program costs to explode. From a minor initial appropriation of $13 million, the costs of the program have doubled repeatedly until the expenses for 1981 stood at close to $11 billion.

Spiraling costs have generated increasingly vocal opposition to the food stamp program which has resulted in tighter eligibility standards and closer monitoring. While acknowledging that many beneficiaries are deserving, program critics complain that under some conditions families earning more than $12,000 a year may qualify for food stamps. It is particularly galling to critics that thousands of voluntary poor—such as students, strikers, and those who have chosen not to work, including at one time the son of a United States senator—have received stamps.

In trying to reduce costs, conservatives in Congress reduced the amount of deductions applicants could claim, made it more difficult for students to qualify, eliminated the eligibility of most strikers, reduced the frequency of cost-of-living adjustments from twice to once a year, and strove to reduce overpayments due to fraud or error. It was estimated that reforms passed in 1981 would eliminate one million recipients.

In addition to manipulating eligibility standards and sizes of benefits, since 1977 Congress has tried to cap expenditures for food stamps. In that year Congress limited appropriations to $6.2 billion per year. In setting appropriations limits, Congress relies on certain assumptions about the rate of inflation and the rate of unemployment for future years. These assumptions have been off-target and Congress, rather than allowing benefits to lapse, has come to the rescue with additional funds. For example, Congress assumed a 5.5 percent rate of inflation and 4.9 percent unemployment for 1980. Thus it was predicted that there would be 15 million food stamp recipients in fiscal year 1981 at a cost of $5.55 billion.[18] In actuality, inflation and unemployment galloped along well above the predicted levels and 23 million people received food stamps, which cost about $11 billion (see figure 5-1). With this kind of track record, it is understandable why one congressman referred to the assumptions as "a matrix of fantasy."[19]

The tightening up of eligibility standards in 1981 did not go as far as conservatives, led by Sen. Jesse Helms (R.-N.C.), had hoped. Should the spending caps imposed for fiscal years 1982 through 1984 (between $11 and $12 billion annually) prove inadequate, conservatives will probably reintroduce some of their proposals which were rejected in the past. These include reducing benefits by an amount equal to what children receive through the school lunch program and reinstating a provision for selling stamps rather than giving them away.[20] Although it would probably have little impact on program cost, Senator Helms would like to see able-bodied recipients participate in public work programs in return for food stamps.

Liberals consider the caps in the 1981 legislation unrealistic. Not simply do they view the 1981 cuts as unjustified, they predict that cutbacks in federal funding for jobs and welfare will force millions more to turn to food stamps. Should this happen, the program costs for fiscal years 1982–1984 could range from $13 to $16 billion.[21] Liberals also cite nutritionists who say that food stamp benefits (currently a maximum of $233 for a family of four) provide only the barest essentials. "For example, one sample menu [devised by the Department of Agriculture] provides one-half pound of hamburger, two-thirds of a pound of liver, a small ham, a chicken, a can of tuna and some bologna as the meat for a family of four for a week."[22]

The biggest ally of the poor in congressional battles over food stamps are food producers and sellers. Enlarging the purchasing power of the poor for groceries generates millions of dollars of additional sales for farmers, processors, and retailers. This linkage is made explicit in the House of Representatives where food stamp legislation is paired with legislation to help farmers. Thus far others who stood to benefit from sales generated by food stamps have been able to protect the program from the more severe cuts which critics would like to impose.

**Reagan proposals.**    The impact of the 1981 budget reconciliation act which cut a million people out of the food stamp program and reduced the value of the stamps given most others was exceeded by the president's recommendations for fiscal year 1983. The president sought to reduce costs by one-fifth by counting a larger share of the earnings of the working poor so that they would qualify for fewer benefits.

Beginning in fiscal year 1984, the president asked that states assume responsibility for the food stamp program, along with AFDC, in return for the federal government taking responsibility for all of Medicaid. Opponents distrust relying on the states to handle food stamps and AFDC. They point out that the federal government launched these programs because states failed to address these needs. Moreover, while federal welfare benefits are pegged to increases in the cost of living, in only two states have welfare payments kept pace with inflation.[23] Also, unless stringent standards are imposed by Congress, there is concern that states would allow the adequacy of food programs to deteriorate or even dispense with them altogether. If responsibility were given to the states with no strings attached, there would certainly be disparity among the states in the level of benefits as there currently are in AFDC and Medicaid, two programs for which states have partial responsibility.

## MEDICAL CARE

Beginning in the 1920s some congressmen urged that federal dollars be used to assure minimal health care for the indigent, and in 1945 President Truman became the first chief executive to lend his influence to this cause. His efforts were unsuccessful, however; and the notion of federally supported health care continued to generate much controversy and little legislation for the next twenty years. Leading the opposition to compulsory health care proposals were the American Medical Association (AMA) and the insurance industry. To rally backers, the AMA tarred the proposals with the "socialized medicine" label. Doctors warned that compulsory health insurance would be the first step toward destroying the existing health care system. Pointing to what happened following nationalization of medical care in Great Britain, the AMA cautioned that Americans were being threatened with loss of the right to select a personal physician, assembly line treatment at clinics, long delays in waiting rooms, and a decline in the quality of medical practices.

The insurance industry, like the medical profession, feared financial loss if the federal government assumed responsibility for guaranteeing health care. Should the government establish a health care insurance program and require all citizens to participate, private insurers would lose substantial revenues.

Conservatives in the House Ways and Means Committee were a powerful ally of the AMA and the insurance industry. For years Republicans and conservative southern Democrats constituted a majority of this committee, which would have to approve any health insurance program. The conservatives' distrust of social welfare programs and unwillingness to use federal authority on behalf of the poor—preferring to leave such matters to individuals or to the states—provided the dominant rationale for blocking health care proposals.

Finally, in 1965 the 89th Congress, boasting the largest liberal membership in a generation, responded to President Johnson's urgings and enacted two health care programs. The Johnson landslide had replaced so many conservative Republicans with liberal Democrats that even traditional foes of health insurance saw the inevitability of what they had dreaded. Wilbur Mills (D.–Ark.), chairman of the Ways and Means Committee, changed his position on federal medical insurance and assumed direction of the legislative effort in the House. Even the AMA, seeing that opposition was futile, proposed a voluntary plan dubbed "eldercare," which would be optional for the states. The forces of change had become too strong, and the AMA's proposal was rejected for a more comprehensive program.

### Medicare

One of the health care programs enacted in 1965 was Medicare.[24] This legislation, which was assigned top priority by President Johnson, provided up to 90 days of hospitalization, 100 days in a nursing home, and 100 posthospital visits by a nurse or therapist. While Medicare benefits cover most of the expenses, the patient must pay part of the cost of extended treatment. Medicare is funded from additional payroll taxes collected along with Social Security taxes. In addition to the hospitalization and related benefits, Congress incorporated one provision from the AMA's "eldercare" alternative and made it possible for the elderly to get federal aid for paying doctors' bills. People over 65 years old can participate in a voluntary program which pays 80 percent of "reasonable" fees for doctors after the patient pays the first $60 each year. Some medical services, such as x-rays and electrocardiograms, were included among the benefits provided by the supplementary plan. Participants in the supplemental program paid $12.20 per month in 1982, an amount which will doubtless increase.

### Medicaid

The second medical program instituted by the 89th Congress provided free care to people receiving categoric aid such as AFDC. Called Medicaid, this is a welfare program in which states can obtain up to 78 percent of the costs of medical treatment for the poor. States are not required to provide this form of assistance, although all but Arizona do participate. States retain control over the program. In fiscal year 1982 the total cost for Medicaid was estimated at more than $33 billlion, with the states paying 45 percent.

**Evaluation of health care programs.**    On the positive side, no one denies that many poor Americans are now receiving health care, which until the mid-1960s they could not afford. Many of the elderly and those receiving welfare, who once had to forgo even critically needed medical attention, now receive treatment, including care from costly specialists. Between 1966 and 1976 hospital admissions among the elderly rose by almost one-third while nursing home usage doubled between 1963 and 1973.[25] Moreover, life expectancy among the elderly rose while infant mortality rates declined. These changes cannot be wholly attributed to Medicare and Medicaid but the presence of these programs doubtless played some role.

Despite the needs being met by Medicare and Medicaid, many policymakers believe that major restructuring of the programs is urgently needed. While a number of shortcomings are pointed out, the underlying cause is rapidly escalating costs. As figure 5–2 shows, the costs of the two programs has doubled repeatedly.

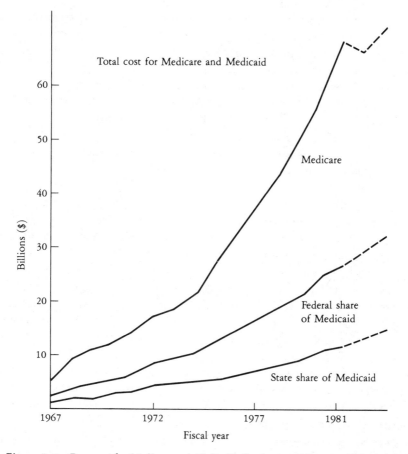

**Figure 5-2**   Expenses for Medicare and Medicaid, fiscal years 1967–1983. Figures for 1980–1983 are estimates. (*Source:* President's Budget Appendices *for appropriate years. Washington, D.C.: U.S. Government Printing Office.*)

By 1982 Medicare cost approximately $35 billion, four times greater than Congress had thought the program would cost in 1990 when it was originally approved.[26] With 28 million elderly signed up for Medicare and another 19 million receiving Medicaid, one-fifth of the nation's population benefits from one of these programs. A number of factors contribute to the cost increases of the health programs.

First, certain inefficiencies are built into Medicare and Medicaid. For example, some expenses will be reimbursed by the federal government only if they are incurred in a hospital. A patient is therefore encouraged to go into the hospital for treatment rather than have the work done on a less expensive out-patient basis, although this is now changing. The program standards also fail to encourage a preventive approach. In addition, since hospitals are reimbursed for all their expenses, there is less incentive to be frugal. Former Secretary of Health, Education and Welfare Caspar Weinberger told the House Ways and Means Subcommittee on Health: "I . . . firmly believe that the faulty design of Medicare and Medicaid is the principal culprit responsible for this super inflation in health care costs. [With the] guaranteed government payment of health care costs in virtually any amount submitted by the provider, and with normal market factors absent in the health care area, inflation was bound to happen, and it did."[27]

Second, expenses for Medicare and Medicaid indicate that the program may be overused. The poor, who in the past would have chosen to spend their limited resources for needs other than health care, are less often forced to make a choice, since the health care is subsidized or in some cases free. A lucrative new industry servicing the health care needs of the poor has developed. One governor has estimated that overuse of the programs costs three times as much as fraud.[28]

Third, the cost of medical care, whether it is for the wealthy or the poor, has risen substantially. The causes of rising costs will be explored in somewhat more detail in the next chapter. Here we will simply provide one illustration. Between 1972 and 1976, Medicaid expenses in Idaho tripled, although there was *no increase* in the number of people enrolled in the program.[29]

Fourth, there has been inadequate monitoring of the operation of Medicare and Medicaid, so that fraud has contributed to rising costs. Critics claim that doctors sometimes submit bills when they have done little more than walk through a ward of Medicare patients. Former Sen. Frank Moss (D.–Utah) has charged that, partly because of poor monitoring and light punishment for those who are caught, Medicare has been defrauded of as much as $1.5 billion annually.[30] In Illinois approximately 20 percent of the payments made for Medicare and Medicaid laboratory services were tainted by fraud.[31] A New York official, who found that nursing home operators were billing Medicaid for mink coats and stereos, testified before a Senate committee: "The conspiracies to defraud the public in the health care field are enormous in scope and complexity and pervasive through every area of our nation."[32]

Inadequate monitoring has also created conditions under which hospitals can "maximize reimbursements."[33] Indeed, the professional organizations for hospitals inform their members how to go about collecting all the money which they legally can from the federal government, which at times runs to more than 100 percent of the cost. Governor George Busbee of Georgia, who chaired the National Governors' Conference task force on Medicaid, asserted that this health program is "the most complex, confusing, duplicative, and administratively wasteful system ever conceived—one that will surely bankrupt the states and the federal Treasury unless substantial reforms are undertaken, both at the state and federal levels."[34]

**Proposed changes.**    Some changes have been instituted and others seem likely. Following disclosures of extensive fraud, Congress created the position of the inspector general in the Department of Health and Human Services. This new office is responsible for catching those who try to cheat on Medicare and Medicaid. Another effort to curb unreasonable expenses involved setting up professional standards review organizations (PSROs) which would determine the standard treatment in a locale. While the federal government has recovered some Medicaid and Medicare money as a result of PSRO reviews, the Congressional Budget Office judges it a losing proposition with each dollar spent on PSROs producing only seventy cents in savings.[35] President Reagan eliminated the PSROs, which were never popular with doctors.

A technique for standardizing hospital charges is prospective reimbursement. Under this system, which is being implemented by the Department of Health and Human Services, the amount that is reasonable for hospitals to charge for treatment or services is determined by reviewing what is generally charged in the vicinity. In time, Medicare and Medicaid patients may come to avoid hospitals whose prices are out of line since the patient will have to pay the amount disallowed by the federal government. Prospective reimbursement may also promote savings since hospitals that have overcharged the government or been inefficient will not be paid all that they request as they have been.

Hospital cost containment is also the objective of proposals to impose standardized reporting requirements. Some federal officials believe that maximizing reimbursements is possible because of the difficulty in comparing the data submitted by hospitals. Hospitals oppose this claiming it would be expensive and that comparability may well be impossible.

Another alternative for reducing costs is to cut services or require that recipients make a larger contribution. Some financially hard-pressed states have already trimmed Medicaid benefits.[36] This approach, however, is the antithesis of what some see as the problem of "medigap," namely, the failure of benefits to cover costs. There are already many instances in which Medicare fails to provide full coverage. Some things, such as dental care or prescription drugs, are not paid for at all. For other services which are covered, patients must pay the difference between what federal authorities determine to be reasonable and what has been charged. About half of all doctors' charges exceed what federal authorities consider to be reasonable costs.[37] Overall it is estimated that Medicare picks up less than half of the medical expenses for the elderly. Approximately half of the Medicare participants have insurance which they believe will cover the gap in Medicare. However, as octogenarian Rep. Claude Pepper (R.–Fla.) has shown, many of these private policies, the cost of which runs to $4 billion annually, are useless. In 1980 Congress established a voluntary program for regulating "medigap" insurance to protect the elderly from shysters but it did nothing to expand benefits to cover the gap.

**Reagan proposals.**    During his first two years in office President Reagan proposed radical changes for Medicaid and Medicare. These reforms were prompted by two central objectives of the 40th president's administration: to reduce the size of the federal budget and to curtail the extent of federal programmatic activities.

In 1981, President Reagan's budget cuts necessitated a scaling back in federal health care funding. Cutbacks resulted in higher charges for the optional insurance to cover Medicare patients, physicians' charges, increased payments by beneficiaries before the federal government picks up the tab, and lower reimbursements for some health care providers.

As federal funds dried up, many states reduced Medicaid coverage. In this jointly funded state-federal program, economizing took different forms from state to state. Some of the changes included:

1. Charging a nominal fee for services which had been free
2. Reducing the rates of reimbursement paid to hospitals, physicians, and pharmacists who cared for Medicaid patients
3. Limiting the number of physicians' visits and the length of hospital coverage for most patients
4. Limiting the rate at which health care providers could raise their charges
5. Limiting the rate at which federal reimbursements given to states will increase, so that if states do not constrain cost increases, they must be prepared to shoulder a larger share of the total cost
6. Threatening to reduce the federal funds given states which do not eliminate all errors in payments

These proposals drew opposition from several quarters. Representatives of beneficiaries objected to charging for what had been free. Some health care providers complained that new limits on reimbursement eliminated profits and therefore they quit serving Medicaid patients. Thus one likely consequence was to reduce the availability of health care, turning the clock back toward pre-1965 conditions. A second potential result was that those who continued to treat people with Medicaid cards would increase what they charged other people in order to make up for expenses which they could not collect from Medicaid.

In 1982 President Reagan unveiled even more extensive plans, especially for Medicaid. In his State of the Union address, the president suggested that the federal government would assume full responsibility for Medicaid, beginning October 1, 1983. Since health care costs have risen more rapidly than have the expenses for other welfare programs, some state leaders were initially attracted to the thought of getting out from under this burden. However, as discussed earlier in this chapter, the strings attached to the proposed trade frightened off many. The proposal was particularly objected to in states that have provided more generous benefits than are given by the minimum federal program. A national takeover of Medicaid would cut benefits in more generous states while increasing them in the less generous ones (especially the South).

In early 1982 President Reagan was toying with the idea of replacing Medicare with a system of vouchers. These vouchers would be used to purchase medical insurance from private companies or to contract for health care from health maintenance organizations (which will be discussed in the next chapter).

For some elderly people, the vouchers would probably not buy coverage sufficient to pay for all of the health care they need, meaning that they would have to pay out of pocket for some expenses. Another concern is that private insurance companies would refuse to enroll people from high risk categories. The elderly, as well as organized labor and insurance companies, have opposed a shift to a voucher system. This opposition might be partially allayed by a guarantee that the value of the voucher would keep pace with inflation.

## CURATIVE PROGRAMS: WAR ON POVERTY

In his 1964 State of the Union message President Johnson announced, "This administration today, here and now, declares unconditional war on poverty in America." A few months later, after the Congress had responded to Johnson's forceful leadership with remarkable speed, the president boasted at the signing of the Economic Opportunity Act: "Today for the first time in the history of the human race, a great nation is able to make and is willing to make a commitment to eradicate poverty among its people."[38] Confidence among poverty warriors was so boundless that some of them predicted that poverty would be eliminated in America by the mid-1970s.

In setting out to eliminate poverty, the Johnson administration was accepting no small challenge. While the poor of the 1960s were far better off than the poor of the Depression had been, there were still some 36 million Americans whose incomes were below the poverty level in 1964. In light of the magnitude of the task, and also the fact that the percentage of the population which was poor had been approximately halved since the Depression, why did President Johnson fix on this as a major goal of his administration? Writers who have tried to explain the motivation behind President Johnson's War on Poverty cite a set of circumstances which coincided to produce the spark needed for a major policy initiative. The first impetus for a new look at poverty predated Johnson's occupancy of the White House. Official concern about the plight of the poor seems to have been spurred by John F. Kennedy's glimpses of the sagging shacks and ravaged bodies in the forgotten hollows of West Virginia during his 1960 primary campaign in that state.

Kennedy's concern became intensified when he read Michael Harrington's book *The Other America*.[39] The president, like many other Americans, was made aware of the extent of poverty in this country, a nation which most middle-class citizens thought of as a land of plenty. Toward the end of his second year, President Kennedy told Walter Heller, chairman of the Council of Economic Advisers: "I want to go beyond the things that have already been accomplished. . . . For example, what about the poverty problem in the United States?"[40] During the remainder of the Kennedy presidency, groundwork proceeded although no new programs with a nationwide scope were launched.

Upon ascending to the presidency, Lyndon B. Johnson turned his considerable legislative skills to getting the Kennedy program enacted.[41] Johnson's attack on poverty, launched in the 1960s, aimed at a quite different target than had the effort of thirty years earlier. In the first place, whereas the Depression-era programs were alleviative, the new ones were supposed to be curative. That is, the War on Poverty was supposed to break the cycle of poverty and to provide escape routes by which millions of people could move into the working class and perhaps ultimately into the middle class. The theme of the War on Poverty was "rehabilitation, not relief."

In sending the War on Poverty legislation to Congress, President Johnson said: "The act does not merely expand old programs or improve what is already being done. It charts a new course. It strikes at the causes, not just the consequences of poverty."[42]

A second difference was that the new program consciously recognized a different clientele. That is, the program designers recognized that the New Deal programs, which had been intended to help middle-class people who found themselves temporarily suffering deprivation, were not adequate for the second- and third-generation poor whom they were now serving.

Third, an important component of the War on Poverty rested on the premise that the poor may be better judges of what needs to be done than are planners, bureaucrats, or legislators. Consequently, unlike other programs, which made funds available for meeting narrowly defined needs, some War on Poverty money was set aside for poor people to use to improve conditions in their communities as *they* saw fit.

To oversee the multifaceted War on Poverty a new agency, the Office of Economic Opportunity (OEO), was created. Sargent Shriver, whose reputation as an administrator was at its peak after a stint as director of the Peace Corps, was tapped to head the OEO. Establishment of a new agency and appointment of a famous and talented director were in keeping with the emphasis placed on the War on Poverty during its early days. Setting up the OEO, rather than parceling out programs to existing offices, was supposed to ensure that the new federal programs moved toward their objective in a coordinated manner. Creation of a new agency would help focus attention on poverty elimination as a goal. Also, giving the programs to a new agency should mean that attainment of objectives would not be subordinated to other organizational goals.

Most portions of the War on Poverty which were intended to be curative were aimed at either young adults or youth. For the former there were programs to improve their employability by giving them basic skills. Youngsters were to be encouraged to stay in school where it was hoped they would be adequately prepared so that they could become self-sufficient adults. The specific programs are discussed in the following sections.

### Educational Programs

In trying to improve educational achievement, designers of the War on Poverty accepted the premise of many educators that by the time a child is old enough to enter public school, he or she may already be past the prime age for learning. Moreover, the child from a culturally deprived background, because of less intellectual stimuli in the environment, may begin public school substantially behind middle-class children who have attended preschool, played with educational toys, and had greater exposure to the books and ideas that are associated with success in school. To offset the disadvantages of growing up in a low-income home, Project Head Start was established to provide poor children with the basic knowledge that most middle-class children have by the time they reach school. In Head Start children were prepared to compete with their more fortunate peers by being taught the alphabet, numbers, colors, and so on. Initially the program operated during the summer and was attended by lower-income children just before they entered school. Because the program became popular with members of Congress, the number of projects was increased and the duration of enrollment broadened, so that younger children could participate and children in school could continue to attend after school, on Saturdays, and during the summer.

Although some early evaluations raised doubts about the effectiveness of Head Start, more recent research indicates that it is a valuable experience. A survey conducted of young people a decade after they were in Head Start found that those who had been through this program differed from those who had not in several ways. Former Head Start students were: (1) less likely to be placed in special education; (2) less likely to fail a grade or drop out; (3) less likely to run afoul of the law; and (4) did better in math courses.[43]

Other programs of the War on Poverty were aimed at encouraging older students to pursue further education. These programs offered opportunities for youngsters from poor families to earn money while staying in school, so that the choice between going to school or to work did not have to be made. The largest of these programs was the Neighborhood Youth Corps (NYC), which provided money for public service employment for young people. In addition to creating jobs, the NYC offered counseling services in an effort to encourage participants currently in school to remain there, and to convince dropouts to go back and earn diplomas.

The Work-Study program sought to facilitate college attendance among the poor. Under Work-Study, federal funds provide 80 percent of the cost of hiring students to work part time on campus or in the community. Since the students can arrange their work around their class schedules, Work-Study has helped a number of low-income students to continue to pursue degrees on a full-time basis.

A program aimed primarily at dropouts is the Job Corps, which is still in effect. Originally modeled on the New Deal's Civilian Conservation Corps, it initially provided work experiences in rural areas. Pressures from people unhappy with camps in their communities, combined with high dropout rates among disoriented urban corps members and the high cost of maintaining each member, led to congressional demands for reform.[44] In response to these demands, the Job Corps has become increasingly urban in its orientation. The rural camps, with their emphasis on conservation, have been replaced by urban training centers, which are meant to prepare enrollees for productive work in the cities.

## Job Programs

The primary emphasis of War on Poverty efforts on behalf of adults was to make welfare recipients self-sufficient. There were several aspects to these efforts, although manpower training received the greatest emphasis. With the call to arms of the War on Poverty, the recent and relatively small manpower efforts of the federal government were increased.

In time a smorgasbord of programs was devised (see table 5–2), so that different types of experiences were available to a wide range of needy. Some of these programs actually provided little structured training, for example the Work Incentive Program (for welfare mothers), and simply placed workers in entry-level, low-paying jobs. These programs rarely included opportunities for participants to get training which would enable them to win promotions. However, providing federal money to state and local governments enabled them to hire people to perform public service work which otherwise would not have been done. Participants in these programs were frequently put to work on conservation projects or as recreation aides, social work aides, or hospital aides.

**TABLE 5–2   Major jobs programs**

| Title | Target | Activity | Present status |
|---|---|---|---|
| Manpower Development and Training Act | Unemployed | Classroom and on-the-job training | Superseded by the 1973 Comprehensive Employment and Training Act; substantially reduced under President Reagan |
| Neighborhood Youth Corps | 16–21-year-old students, and those who might return to school | Public service jobs during summers and after school | |
| Operation Mainstream | Unemployed heads of households | Public service jobs | |
| JOBS | Unemployed | On-the-job training cosponsored by businesses | |
| Work Incentive Program | Welfare mothers | Public service jobs | Elimination proposed in 1983 budget |
| Job Corps | 16–21-year-old school dropouts | Work experience and job training | Still functioning |
| Public Employment Programs | Areas of high unemployment | Public service jobs | Eliminated in 1981 |
| Youth Conservation Corps | Summer jobs for 15–18-year-olds | Federal land improvement projects | Eliminated in 1981 |

A second type of program was intended to provide structured job training. The largest of these was the Manpower Development and Training Act (MDTA). Although not initially designed to help the poor, by 1974 almost two-thirds of the new participants in the classroom component were at the poverty level, as were almost 40 percent of the enrollees in on-the-job training. Even larger numbers of participants, while still above the poverty level, were out of work at the time that they joined MDTA programs.

Another structured training program was JOBS (Job Opportunities in the Business Sector). This program was jointly sponsored by the Department of Labor and the National Association of Business. JOBS was the product of Lyndon Johnson's effort to get the private sector involved in the War on Poverty. Corporations that participated in JOBS were reimbursed for the additional costs entailed in training disadvantaged workers. Thus, if low-income recruits required one more week of training than did nondisadvantaged workers, the federal government would pay for the extra week's training.

As the final column in table 5-2 shows, President Reagan launched a full-scale attack on the existing jobs programs. All of them have experienced cuts in funding if not outright elimination. Opponents charge that these cuts are short-sighted, particularly during a recession, since people who lost these jobs will have to be taken care of with welfare.

### Community Action Programs

The most innovative feature of the War on Poverty was to allow the poor to participate in designing programs and in allocating the funds which were supposed to help them. The program designers felt that the poor would know what their needs were, whereas policymakers with middle-class backgrounds might ignore some of these needs. In addition, some felt that such participation, by giving poor people experience in making decisions and spending money, would help to break the cycle of poverty.[45]

Finally, by building participation of the poor into the poverty programs, some of the policy professionals who created the War on Poverty hoped to redistribute power to the poor. If they were given control over some financial resources, these professionals believed, the poor would become a force to be reckoned with, so that, in time, they might have enough influence to refashion the institutions that serviced them.

To achieve these objectives, two-thirds of the new funds for the first year's poverty effort were given to the Community Action Programs (CAP).[46] These locally run programs, designed to meet local need, were to be carried out with "maximum feasible participation" of the poor. With the federal government contributing 90 percent of the funding for CAPs, a wide range of activities was initiated. Among the more common CAP endeavors were family-planning clinics, legal aid offices, consumer education courses, day-care centers, and recreation centers for the elderly. CAP personnel helped poor people challenge unfair credit practices of local merchants, use rent strikes and other pressures to force landlords to improve living conditions, and organize to seek political concessions from local public decision makers.

This sort of boat rocking was most irritating to local interests confronted by an organization of poor people who were able to use the law as well as electoral muscle in the pursuit of their objectives. Mayors, merchants, and landlords were particularly distressed by the fact that CAP funds came directly from the federal government and therefore were largely independent of the local power structure. Indeed, as some exponents of the CAP concept had hoped, the federal funding enabled some ambitious community organizations to find their way into the chambers of the decision makers.

### Demise of the War on Poverty

The War on Poverty proved to be generally unpopular. There was much interde-partmental infighting and resentment. By 1974 support for OEO had declined so much that Congress abolished it, giving its remaining programs to other depart-ments eager to regain control.

A number of explanations have been offered for the demise of the War on Poverty. As with most important social phenomena, the causes are too numerous and tangled to permit much more than a listing of what appear to be the eight important ones. Undoubtedly a major problem was that the initial goals were un-realistically high. A former OEO administrator has written, "The Johnson War on Poverty was conceived in a mood of political optimism which bordered on naiveté."[47]

In the second place, as the country became more deeply immersed in the quick-sand of war in Vietnam, winning the War on Poverty receded in significance. The dilution of presidential resolve contributed to a third reason for the failure of the War on Poverty, lack of money. Writing in 1967, well before the extent of the ulti-mate collapse of the poverty effort was clear, Donovan observed, "Most of the pro-grams of the Economic Opportunity Act, with the possible exception of the Neigh-borhood Youth Corps and Project Head Start, have never been budgeted at anything more than a pilot-project level."[48] A fourth factor lay in the decision concerning the distribution of poverty programs. In an effort to develop political support by placing programs in a large number of communities, Shriver diminished the likelihood that projects could substantially improve the conditions of any given community's poor. Thus, instead of concentrating the limited funds in a few com-munities and trying to maximize impact, the program's administrators passed out the money in small dollops to hundreds of communities.

Fifth, a number of big-city mayors accused the Community Action Programs of meddling in their cities. They preferred to have the money pass through their hands rather than going directly from Washington to local poverty groups.

Sixth, since Congress had played a small role in the creation of the War on Pov-erty, neither its leaders nor rank-and-file members felt great responsibility for rescu-ing the program when it began to be buffeted by swirling political pressures. The ranks of the program's supporters were ravaged in 1966, when forty Democratic congressmen, most of whom were liberal, lost their seats. The remaining Democrats were generally less committed to OEO's objectives and more responsive to the demands of local political figures that less latitude be allowed in the expenditure of poverty funds.

Seventh, congressional critics leveled charges of mismanagement and misguided objectives by pointing out, for instance, that in Chicago some OEO funds were turned over to the Blackstone Rangers, a street gang; that the costs of training Job Corpsmen were extremely high; and that some Job Corps camps were marked by high dropout rates and antisocial behavior.

Finally, even under the best of conditions, the design of the War on Poverty was such that it could not have eliminated poverty within the time scheduled. Programs emphasizing manpower training had the potential of helping many poor families but offered little immediate help to the millions of poor who were too young, too old, or too infirm to work. The old and the weak could probably not be made self-sufficient by any of OEO's programs. Although the young might be able to use education and job training to escape the centripetal force of the cycle of poverty, even under the best of conditions this would take at least a generation.

## IDENTIFYING THE POOR

When the War on Poverty was declared, administration spokesmen optimistically predicted victory within the foreseeable future. A quick look around us provides sufficient evidence that promises to eliminate poverty have not been fulfilled. Government statistics indicate that in 1980 there were still approximately 29.3 million Americans, or 13 percent of the population, having base incomes below the poverty level of $8,410 for an urban family of four.

Some groups in society are more likely to have low incomes than are others. As table 5–3 shows, people of Hispanic origin are more than twice as likely to have low incomes as whites are. Blacks are the poorest racial group; almost one-third of all blacks are in the low-income set. However, although a larger segment of blacks and people of Spanish origin are poor, two-thirds of all low-income people are white. Other data in table 5–3 show that only 6 percent of all families with a male

TABLE 5-3    Selected characteristics of Americans
below the low-income level

| | Percent of all poor people | | Percent of group | |
|---|---|---|---|---|
| | 1980 | 1974 | 1979 | 1974 |
| White | 67.3 | 67.1 | 10.2 | 8.9 |
| Black | 29.3 | 39.8 | 32.5 | 31.2 |
| Hispanic | 11.9 | 10.7 | 25.7 | 23.2 |
| In families with male head | 48.8 | 56.0 | 6.1 | 6.5 |
| In families with female head | 51.2 | 44.0 | 32.7 | 36.8 |
| Under 18 years of age | 38.8 | 45.1 | 17.9 | 15.8 |
| Over 65 years of age | 13.2 | 13.6 | 15.7 | 15.7 |
| Central cities | 36.3 | 36.3 | 17.2 | 14.4 |
| Suburbs | 25.2 | 23.9 | 8.2 | 7.1 |
| Outside metropolitan areas | 38.4 | 39.9 | 15.4 | 14.4 |
| North and West[a] | 58.1 | 55.6 | 9.7 | 9.5 |
| South[a] | 41.9 | 44.4 | 14.5 | 16.1 |

SOURCE: U.S. Bureau of the Census, Current Population Reports, *Characteristics of the Population below the Poverty Level: 1974*, Series P-60, Nos. 102 and 124 (Washington, D.C.: U.S. Government Printing Office, 1976 and 1980). *Money, Income and Poverty Status of Families and Persons in the United States: 1980*, Series P-60, No. 127 (Washington, D.C.: U.S. Government Printing Office, 1981).

[a]1978 data.

as head of household are poor. In contrast, almost one-third of all Americans in families headed by a female are poor. Age and location also appear to be related to the incidence of poverty. Young people and the elderly are more likely to be poor than is the total population. Poor people are disproportionately represented in rural areas, large cities, and in the South.

While there are 10 million fewer poor Americans now than in 1964, the rate of advance has declined and conditions have worsened in recent years. As figure 5–3 shows, the number of low-income Americans increased since 1973.

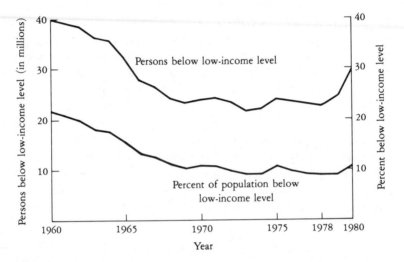

**Figure 5–3**  Numbers and proportions of the population below the poverty level, 1960–1980. (*Sources: U.S. Bureau of the Census, Current Population Reports*, Characteristics of the Population below the Poverty Level: 1978, *Series P-60, No. 124. Washington, D.C.: U.S. Government Printing Office, 1979.* Money, Income and Poverty Status of Families and Persons in the United States: 1980, *Series P-60, No. 127. Washington, D.C.: U.S. Government Printing Office, 1981.*)

There is, however, another perspective from which to view the conditions of the poor. Two economists at the Brookings Institution contend that figures such as those presented in figure 5–3 give an inflated picture of the actual number of poor people.[49] While acknowledging that poverty remains a condition of millions of Americans, they argue that a sizable proportion of the poor (44 percent in 1972) received sufficient amounts of in-kind transfers—for instance, food stamps, housing assistance, or Medicaid—to lift them above the low-income line. A survey by the Bureau of the Census found that more than 27 million households (or almost 35 percent of all American households) received some form of in-kind benefit from the federal government in 1979.[50] President Reagan's chief domestic adviser estimates that if these benefits are added to the recipients' income, then there were only 8 million poor Americans.[51]

A third perspective suggests that even inclusion of transfer payments still overlooks an important consideration: that $8,410 is an unrealistically low figure for the poverty level. The Census Bureau seems to acknowledge the possible inadequacy of

**TABLE 5-4    Selected characteristics of families participating in three welfare programs in 1979**

| | Total population | Food stamps | Subsidized housing | Medicaid |
|---|---|---|---|---|
| Number of families (in thousands) | 79,108 | 5,911 | 2,511 | 7,993 |
| Race: | | | | |
| White | 88% | 63% | 59% | 68% |
| Black | 11 | 35 | 39 | 30 |
| Hispanic | 5 | 10 | 8 | 9 |
| Head of household: | | | | |
| Male | 89% | 58% | 34% | 64% |
| Female | 11 | 42 | 66 | 36 |
| Median income | $16,533 | $5,300 | $6,747 | $5,990 |
| Below poverty level | 12% | 61% | 47% | 48% |
| Households with members: | | | | |
| Over age 65 | 20% | 17% | 34% | 33% |
| Under age 19 | 43 | 66 | NA[a] | 51 |
| Live in central city | 30% | 42% | 55% | 41% |
| Region: | | | | |
| Northeast | 22% | 23% | 32% | 24% |
| North Central | 26 | 21 | 21 | 24 |
| South | 32 | 41 | 32 | 31 |
| West | 19 | 15 | 15 | 21 |

SOURCE: U.S. Bureau of the Census, Current Population Reports, *Characteristics of House-holds and Persons Receiving Noncash Benefits: 1979* (*Preliminary Data from the March 1980 Current Population Survey*), Series P-23, No. 110 (Washington, D.C.: U.S. Government Printing Office, 1981).

[a]Not available.

this figure by also including statistics on the number and characteristics of those earning less than 125 percent of the poverty figure, or over $10,500. If this figure is used, then there would be an additional 10 million poor people in 1979.

Characteristics of participants in three types of federal welfare programs are presented in table 5-4. In all three, beneficiaries are disproportionately minority, below the poverty level and live in central cities.

## PROPOSED REFORMS

Calls for new approaches to welfare stem from the ever-rising cost of the nation's welfare budget and the realization that past programs have left millions of poor people untouched. A review of some of the proposals which have been set forth follows.

### Full Employment

Like the goal of decent housing for all, full employment has been listed among our nation's policy goals for more than a generation. In 1946 Congress passed legislation proclaiming: "All Americans able to work and seeking to work have the right to useful, remunerative, regular, and full-time employment, and it is the policy of the United States to assure the existence at all times of sufficient employment opportunities to enable all Americans to freely exercise this right."

During the recession of the 1970s, when unemployment rates reached a high of 8.9 percent nationwide and stood above 10 percent for months in some areas, the failure of employment policy to live up to the 1946 rhetoric was brought home to many people. In 1971 the federal government took a tiny step toward assuming the role of employer of last resort. The Emergency Employment Act of that year funded a Public Employment Program (PEP), which created more than 200,000 jobs in state and local governments. Under this program and its successors, federal dollars were used to underwrite the bulk of the costs of hiring people to perform public service work for state and local governments.

A second strategy—designed as a countercyclical, short-term measure to reduce unemployment—has been to increase the funding for federal public works projects, such as the construction of sewage treatment plants, thereby creating additional jobs for construction workers.

A third approach would make the federal government the employer of last resort. The Humphrey-Hawkins Act of 1978 reiterated the 1946 pledge of full employment, defined as 3 percent unemployment of the labor force 20 years of age and older. This legislation was the top priority of the AFL-CIO in 1976 and was strongly endorsed by blacks and liberals. The Humphrey-Hawkins Act called for coordinated efforts among the president, Congress, and the Federal Reserve Board to use monetary and fiscal policy to achieve 3 percent adult unemployment within five years. The legislation has been exclusively symbolic, so far, and seems destined to remain so.

Supporters of the Humphrey-Hawkins Act and other legislation intended to curb unemployment argue that such programs are necessary because of the dignity associated with working to pay one's way. The availability of job opportunities, it is contended, will counter the despair that often leads to drug dependency, crime, and family disintegration in areas of high unemployment. They also note that the cost of the program will be offset by reductions in the number of recipients of unemployment compensation and welfare benefits and by increased tax collections. Therefore, according to the Congressional Budget Office, the expenditure of an additional $1 billion on public service employment will actually have a net cost of approximately $615 to $754 million, depending on how many new jobs are created.[52]

Opponents contend that job creation programs are too expensive. They also question whether they are effective. Public works efforts are criticized for being too slow in actually putting people to work, since a planning period is required before unemployed construction workers are given jobs. Public service programs are criticized because they simply allow state or local government units to charge personnel costs, which would otherwise be borne locally, to the federal government and thus fail to create new jobs.[53]

The Reagan administration, while displaying little interest in having the government guarantee jobs for all workers, nonetheless heartily endorses the concept of full employment. The proposals described in chapter 2 which set forth Reagan's economic policy are expected by the administration to reduce unemployment levels. This would be done by stimulating the private sector, not by having the government create jobs.

### Reagan Welfare Proposals

President Reagan has sought to reduce spending for most welfare programs. The president has claimed, however, that the belt-tightening will not harm the truly needy. Instead, Reagan has spoken of a "safety net" which will save the "deserving poor" from want.

To successfully cut the budget without shredding the safety net, there seem to be several assumptions. One is that a sizable share of current expenditures are due to fraud or error. President Reagan has recommended that after 1986, states not be reimbursed for erroneously made welfare payments.

One observer claims that improper payments constitute a negligible share of the cost of food stamps. The observations concerning food stamps may be apropos to other welfare programs.

> [T]he fact is that less than 5 percent of total spending goes to ineligible recipients or is overissued. The rate of fraud is much lower than with income tax returns. Incidentally, the major frauds generally have been perpetrated not by poor recipients, but by crooked caseworkers in collusion with disreputable retailers and hard-core criminals.[54]

This observer goes on to warn that turning programs over to the states is unlikely to reduce erroneous payments: "There is far more corruption, waste and favoritism at the 'grass-roots' level than in the federal establishment."

A second assumption that guides the Reagan administration is that the coverage of welfare programs has become too encompassing. President Reagan disagrees with the efforts of some of his predecessors who sought to extend benefits to the working poor. The idea behind this effort was that by gradually phasing out welfare benefits, there would be a greater incentive for a person to work. In cutting back programs, the Reagan administration and its conservative allies in Congress have opted to reserve the available benefits for the poorest. Thus they have reduced the maximum income at which one can qualify for housing assistance and food stamps. Reducing eligibility standards for federal day-care subsidies has been counterproductive, however, since some mothers have had to stop working and go on welfare in order to care for their children.

A third assumption behind the Reagan approach to welfare is that able-bodied recipients should work for their benefits. The president favors "workfare," a program he instituted while governor of California and may now be tried in other states. As approved by Congress, people on the welfare rolls who are physically able—except for the mothers of small children—can be required to work on public or private jobs at the minimum wage to repay the amount of aid they receive. This idea appeals to those who believe that working enhances one's skill, habits, and self-esteem as well as to those who suspect that some welfare recipients are malingerers. It is attractive also to those who believe that our welfare system provides the wrong kind of incentives. Black columnist William Raspberry writes that the black mainstream probably agrees with the idea behind workfare since "You can work hard on a bad job and try to impress somebody so you get a promotion, or you can go find yourself something else. But welfare just traps you. And the more generous the benefits, the stronger the trap."[55] A similar rationale underlies proposals to see that disability benefits do not exceed what one could earn by working.

Reagan critics claim that workfare had little impact in California. A report released in 1975 by the California Employment Development Department concluded that fewer than 10,000 of the state's 2 million welfare recipients were put to work and that it did not dissuade new welfare applicants.[56]

A number of people who have been active in poverty programs also oppose workfare. They see welfare as an entitlement for which one should not be forced to work on public projects. Others believe that forcing people to work on public projects is demeaning, while some unions fear that minimum wage welfare recipients may be substituted for those who would otherwise be hired.

**Negative income tax.**    The idea of a negative income tax has at times drawn support in Congress and the White House but never enough to secure enactment. A negative income tax would provide cash assistance to people earning less than a specified amount regardless of whether they have children or whether there is an adult male in the household. All people having no earnings would receive money. As incomes rise, the negative income tax benefit would be gradually diminished. To illustrate, if Congress were to decide that each person was entitled to a negative income tax of $1,000 a year, a family of four having no earnings would receive $4,000 from the United States Treasury. Supporters of a negative income tax usually suggest that benefits be reduced by 50 cents for each dollar earned. Thus, a family of four which earned $2,000 would receive $3,000 in negative income tax benefits, while a family earning $4,000 would receive an additional $2,000. Four-person families earning less than $8,000 would get some benefits in this example.

Advocates of a negative income tax point to a number of advantages. First, the program encourages recipients to work. Unlike some programs, such as AFDC, which terminate all benefits once participants' incomes reach a certain level, negative income tax benefits are phased out gradually; therefore, the more a family earns, the greater its total income. Second, administrative expenses for a negative income tax would be much lower than for AFDC. Negative income tax payment could be made on the basis of federal income tax returns, thereby eliminating the need for many of the expenses of investigations and the red tape of need documentation which are found in many current programs. Third, a negative income tax would standardize benefits nationwide and would increase the level of benefits paid in a number of poorer states.

A fourth consideration is that a negative income tax would be a step toward elimination of inequities which sometimes exist between welfare recipients and the working poor. Under current conditions, it has been estimated that a family of four in which the breadwinner earned the minimum wage would end up poorer than would a four-member family in which no one worked but which received Medicaid, AFDC, housing assistance, and a food stamp subsidy.

The mood of the Reagan administration makes it unlikely that a negative income tax will become law during his presidency. However, should such a policy eventually be adopted, two important disputes will have to be resolved. First is the question of the level of benefits. Second is the question of the extent to which the negative income tax should replace current aid programs. Would the negative income tax benefit replace some or all of the current aid programs, or would it provide a layer of benefits above the programs providing food, housing, health care, and money?

## CONCLUDING COMMENTS

Public support for, or at least acceptance of, welfare initiatives is probably keyed to economic conditions. Major expansions in American welfare policy have come during what one might call "the best of times and the worst of times." During the Depression of the 1930s poverty was so widespread that even southern Democrats who have traditionally been opposed to welfare were generally supportive of the relief programs launched by the Roosevelt administration. Then during the optimistic afterglow of the Kennedy years, Congress rubber-stamped Lyndon Johnson's War on Poverty. Under Ronald Reagan, who ran a campaign that questioned the competence of the federal government to resolve the issues of the eighties, it is likely that the federal welfare role will shrink. Unless the rate of inflation falls to levels of a generation ago, the amount spent on welfare will increase, but new programs will not be added and existing ones will be pruned.

Reagan's thumping defeat of Jimmy Carter was one indication that the challenger was in step with most of the electorate. Polls conducted since the election provide evidence that Reagan's approach to welfare is popular. More than 60 percent of a sample of registered voters believed that the Johnson poverty programs either had no effect on the poor or actually made things worse.[57] A bare majority in the same survey showed their suspicions by telling polltakers that they thought that most welfare recipients could get along without these programs. By a margin of almost 3 to 2, Americans were unwilling in June of 1981 to pay more state taxes to make up for cuts in social programs caused by President Reagan's efforts to balance the budget.[58]

These poll results indicate that a majority of the public supports Reagan's efforts to reduce welfare expenditures and apparently believes the president when he says that the cuts will not harm the truly needy. Although Congress may not cut welfare programs as deeply as President Reagan would like, it appears that the public backs his plan to cap Medicaid expenses, remove a million people from food stamp eligibility lists, disqualify hundreds of thousands of AFDC recipients, slow increases in housing assistance programs, and end the emergency employment program. Many have faith that all of this can be done with no trauma being suffered by the poor.

Some economists and many who have worked with poverty programs vehemently disagree. They charge that Reagan's safety net protects the elderly and the middle class but misses many poor people.[59] Moreover, they fear that Reagan budget cuts—particularly of things like public service jobs—will push even more families below the poverty line.

## NOTES

1. Joel Havemann and Linda E. Demkovich, "Making Some Sense out of the Welfare 'Mess,'" *National Journal* 9 (January 8, 1977): 51.
2. *Social Security Bulletin* 45 (January 1982): 51.
3. Gilbert Y. Steiner, *The State of Welfare* (Washington, D.C.: Brookings Institution, 1971), pp. 35–40.
4. Harrison Donnelly, "What Reagan Budget Cuts Would Do to Poor," *Congressional Quarterly Weekly Report* 39 (April 18, 1981): 668.
5. Acting director for policy in the Department of Health and Human Services Office of Family Assistance quoted in Harrison Donnelly, "Millions of Poor Face Losses Oct. 1 as Reconciliation Bill Spending Cuts Go Into Effect," *Congressional Quarterly Weekly Report* 39 (September 26, 1981): 1836.
6. Harrison E. Salisbury, *The Shook-Up Generation* (New York: Harper & Row, 1958), p. 75.
7. Robert E. Forman, "Housing and Racial Segregation," in *Racism and Inequality,* ed. Harrell R. Rodgers, Jr. (San Francisco: Freeman, 1975), p. 55.
8. Chester W. Hartman, *Housing and Social Policy* (Englewood Cliffs, N.J.: Prentice-Hall, 1975), p. 137.
9. President Ford's Secretary for Housing Carla Hill, quoted in Charles Evans, "500,000 Housing Units Will Get U.S. Backing in '77 Budget, Hill Says," *Houston Chronicle,* January 19, 1976, section 1, p. 15.
10. Hartman, *Housing and Social Policy,* p. 3.
11. Laura B. Weiss, "New Middle-Income Housing Plan Passed by Committees," *Congressional Quarterly Weekly Report* 38 (June 7, 1980): 1576.
12. John C. Weicher, *Housing: Federal Policies and Programs* (Washington, D.C.: American Enterprise Institute for Public Policy Research, 1980), p. 55.
13. Ibid., p. 60.
14. Weicher, *Housing,* p. 14.
15. Rochelle L. Stanfield, "Poorest Hit Most by Rent Subsidy Changes, Say Critics," *National Journal* 14 (January 9, 1982): 80.
16. Quoted in *Congressional Quarterly Weekly Report* 40 (February 13, 1982): 277.
17. Estimate of the Congressional Budget Office reported in Linda E. Demkovich, "The Food Stamp Cap Again," *National Journal* 13 (September 21, 1981): 1643.
18. Congressional Budget Office, *The Food Stamp Program: Income or Food Supplementation* (Washington, D.C.: U.S. Government Printing Office, 1977), pp. 61–63.
19. Rep. Thomas Foley (D.-Wash.) quoted in *Congressional Quarterly Weekly Report* 39 (May 16, 1981): 872.
20. Prior to 1977 all but the poorest food stamp program participants had to buy their stamps. The subsidy, which was keyed to income, resources, and family size, was conveyed by providing recipients with stamps having a cash value in excess of what they paid.
21. Harrison Donnelly and Peg O'Hara, "House Panel Makes Cuts in Food Stamp Program, But not All Reagan Wants," *Congressional Quarterly Weekly Report* 39 (May 2, 1981): 771.
22. "What Recipients Eat," *Congressional Quarterly Weekly Report* 39 (February 7, 1981): 278.
23. Jean Mayer, "The Food Stamp Dilemma," *Washington Post,* February 19, 1982, p. E3.
24. In terms of its mode of being financed and the extensiveness of its coverage, Medicare is not a welfare program but instead shares characteristics with Social Security, which is discussed in the next chapter. We have chosen to discuss Medicare in conjunction with Medicaid because evaluations and proposed reforms frequently take the two in tandem and a single agency, the Health Care Financing Administration, has responsibility for both programs.
25. Louise B. Russell, "Medical Care," in *Setting National Priorities: Agenda for the 1980s,* ed. Joseph A. Pechman (Washington, D.C.: Brookings Institution, 1980), p. 179.

26. Linda E. Demkovich, "Reagan Takes on The Elderly Again as He Seeks to Slow Medicare's Growth," *National Journal* 13 (September 12, 1981): 1616.

27. Quoted in John K. Iglehart, "Government Searching for a More Cost-Efficient Way to Pay Hospitals," *National Journal* 3 (December 25, 1976): 1822.

28. Elizabeth Bowman, "Hearings Held on Ways to Cut Soaring Costs of Medicaid, Medicare," *Congressional Quarterly Weekly Report* 34 (August 7, 1976): 2127.

29. John K. Iglehart, "The Rising Costs of Health Care—Something Must Be Done, but What?" *National Journal* 8 (October 16, 1976): 1462.

30. William Hines, "Medicare, Medicaid Said Virtual License to Steal," *Houston Chronicle*, July 29, 1976, section 1, p. 7.

31. "Medicaid Lab Fraud, Kickback Found," *Congressional Quarterly Weekly Report* 34 (February 21, 1976): 454.

32. Quoted in "Medicaid Called 'Greatest Rip-off,'" *Houston Chronicle*, November 18, 1976, section 1, p. 1.

33. This draws on Linda E. Demkovich, "The Touchy Business of Hospital Reporting," *National Journal* 11 (November 17, 1979): 1940–1942.

34. Quoted in Iglehart, "The Rising Costs of Health Care," p. 1462.

35. Russell, "Medical Care," p. 185.

36. *Health Policy: The Legislative Agenda* (Washington, D.C.: Congressional Quarterly, 1980), p. 80.

37. Elizabeth Wehr, "Lobbyists Fight Federal Regulation of 'Medigap' Health Insurance Abuses," *Congressional Quarterly Weekly Report* 38 (February 16, 1980): 403.

38. Quoted in Daniel P. Moynihan, *Maximum Feasible Misunderstanding* (New York: Free Press, 1969), pp. 3–4.

39. Michael Harrington, *The Other America* (Baltimore: Penguin, 1962).

40. Quoted in James L. Sundquist, *Politics and Policy: The Eisenhower, Kennedy, and Johnson Years* (Washington, D.C.: Brookings Institution, 1968), p. 112.

41. For an analysis that disputes the myth that Lyndon Johnson came from an impoverished background (a myth perpetuated by Johnson), see Larry L. King, "Bringing Up Lyndon," *Texas Monthly* 4 (January 1976): 78 *ff.*

42. Quoted in *Congressional Record*, 110, 88th Congress, 2nd Session (1964), 5287.

43. Gil Sewall et al., "A High Grade for Head Start," *Time*, October 8, 1979, p. 102; Spencer Rich, "Lasting Gains Are Found from Preschool Start," *Washington Post*, November 30, 1979, p. 23-A.

44. Edward R. Fried; Alice M. Rivlin; Charles L. Schultze; and Nancy H. Teeters, *Setting National Priorities: The 1974 Budget* (Washington, D.C.: Brookings Institution, 1973), p. 220.

45. John C. Donovan, *The Politics of Poverty*, 2nd ed. (Indianapolis: Pegasus, 1973), pp. 35–43.

46. Moynihan, *Maximum Feasible Misunderstanding*, p. 94.

47. Donovan, *Politics of Poverty*, 2nd ed., p. 113.

48. Donovan, *Politics of Poverty*, 1st ed. (Indianapolis: Pegasus, 1967), p. 122.

49. John L. Palmer and Joseph J. Minarik, "Income Security Policy," in *Setting National Priorities: The Next Ten Years*, eds. Henry Owen and Charles L. Schultze (Washington, D.C.: Brookings Institution, 1976), pp. 519–526.

50. U.S. Bureau of the Census, *Characteristics of Households and Persons Receiving Noncash Benefits: 1979*, Current Population Reports, Series P-23, No. 110 (Washington, D.C.: U.S. Government Printing Office, 1981), p. 8.

51. "Experts Differ on How Many Are Poor," *Congressional Quarterly Weekly Report* 39 (April 18, 1981): 669.

52. Cited in Mary E. Eccles, "Jobs Programs: How Well Do They Work," *Congressional Quarterly Weekly Report* 35 (February 19, 1977): 303.

53. U.S. Department of Labor, *Manpower Report of the President* (Washington, D.C.: U.S. Government Printing Office, 1975), p. 46.

54. Mayer, "The Food Stamp Dilemma," p. E3.

55. William Raspberry, "More Welfare Is Just A Stronger Trap," *Washington Post*, June 1980.

56. "Workfare Failed for Reagan in '70s, Study Says," *Atlanta Journal*, March 30, 1981, p. 6-A; also see Linda E. Demkovich, "Workfare—Punishment for Being Poor or an End to the Welfare Stigma," *National Journal* 13 (July 4, 1981): 1201–1205.

57. CBS News, *New York Times* Poll, released November 15, 1980.
58. CBS News, *New York Times* Poll, released June 30, 1981.
59. See the discussion in Donnelly, "What Reagan Budget Cuts Would Do to Poor," pp. 665–668.

## SUGGESTED READINGS

Donovan, John C. *The Politics of Poverty.* 2nd ed. Indianapolis: Pegasus, 1973.

Harrington, Michael. *The Other America.* Baltimore: Penguin, 1962.

Hartman, Chester W. *Housing and Social Policy.* Englewood Cliffs, N.J.: Prentice-Hall, 1975.

Moynihan, Daniel P. *Maximum Feasible Misunderstanding.* New York: Free Press, 1969.

Rodgers, Harrell R., Jr. *Poverty and Plenty.* Reading, Mass.: Addison-Wesley, 1979.

Sundquist, James L. *Politics and Policy: The Eisenhower, Kennedy, and Johnson Years.* Washington, D.C.: Brookings Institution, 1968.

Weicher, John C. *Housing: Federal Policies and Programs.* Washington, D.C.: American Enterprise Institute, 1980.

# Chapter 6

# Social Programs for the Many

In the previous chapter we discussed a variety of programs designed to provide benefits to the poor or to help them rise out of poverty. Those who succeed in entering the great American middle class will find that in their new economic situation the federal government extends to them a different set of benefits. While the nature of the benefits available to the middle class are unlike those provided to the poor, they are directed at meeting some of the same basic human needs that poverty programs address.

Programs for the middle class have different basic objectives than do those for lower income groups. The latter seek to provide what the majority in society judge to be minimal levels for a spartan existence. Middle-class programs seek either to reduce risk or to relieve financial burdens. These objectives are achieved by having the federal government—and through it society in general—play the roles of insurer or regulator. In Social Security, FHA home loan guarantees, and proposals for national health insurance, financial risks to the middle-class family are minimized by distributing the risks broadly across the population. Tax policy which allows people to deduct payments into retirement accounts, for health insurance, or for interest on home mortgages makes it easier for the middle class to obtain these goods and services. Again, these policies, by reducing tax revenues, have the effect of distributing the cost to society at large. The middle class has sought to reduce risks through passage of a variety of consumer protection statutes. Proposals to regulate the growth in health care costs also have the middle class as their primary benefactors.

The programs discussed in this chapter do not benefit the middle class exclusively. Although there have been proposals to deny Social Security benefits to the affluent, everyone who has paid into the system for a specified amount of time is entitled to benefits. Containing the cost of health care or protecting consumers would also benefit all classes. We treat these topics in this chapter because the middle class is the largest group of beneficiaries, but also because the middle class has relatively few alternatives. The wealthy can, if necessary, get along by relying on their own resources; the poor have various welfare programs which help them meet some of their needs.

The first issue to be considered is federal policy as it affects health care costs. We review proposals for moderating rising health care expenses for people who are not covered by Medicaid and Medicare (discussed in chapter 5). Proposals for national health insurance are also described. A second policy area is housing. Federal initiatives to help the middle class become home owners will be reviewed with a particular emphasis on recent innovations adopted in the face of high interest rates. The third topic is retirement, discussed in terms of the Social Security system. A review of the major aspects of consumer protection legislation is the fourth topic.

## HEALTH CARE

One of the most pervasive fears confronted by the middle class is that the expenses of a serious illness will cause financial devastation. Such fears are far from irrational. Hospital costs rose by 12 to 17 percent a year between 1977 and 1980, doctors' charges have been increasing at only a slightly slower rate, and the number of days of treatment in hospitals or as out-patients, and the number of costly laboratory tests have all been surging ever upward.[1] Because of these trends, the nation's health care budget trebled during the 1960s and it trebled again during the 1970s, reaching about a quarter of a billion dollars in 1980. In the absence of some kind of yet undevised constraints, the rate of increase observed for the last two decades is projected to continue through the 1980s (see table 6-1).

TABLE 6-1   Health care costs for selected years, 1965-1990
(in billions of dollars)

|  | 1965 | 1970 | 1975 | 1978 | 1980 | 1985[a] | 1990[a] |
|---|---|---|---|---|---|---|---|
| Hospital care | 13.9 | 27.8 | 52.1 | 76.0 | 97.3 | 182.8 | 334.6 |
| Physicians' services | 8.5 | 14.3 | 24.9 | 35.3 | 45.0 | 78.2 | 128.8 |
| Dentists' services | 2.8 | 4.8 | 8.2 | 13.3 | 17.9 | 33.9 | 59.4 |
| Nursing homes | 2.1 | 4.7 | 9.9 | 15.8 | 21.6 | 42.0 | 75.6 |

SOURCE: *Health Care Financing Review* (Winter 1980), reprinted in Margaret C. Thompson, ed., *Health Policy: The Legislative Agenda* (Washington, D.C.: *Congressional Quarterly*, 1980), p. 12. Copyright 1980 by Congressional Quarterly, Inc. Reprinted by permission.
[a]Estimates.

While we live in inflationary times, the growth in health care costs has far outstripped the rate of inflation, as shown in figure 6-1. As a consequence the share of the GNP spent on health care has risen from 5.3 percent in 1960 to 9.5 percent in 1980.

The federal government pays more than $70 billion for health care but the great

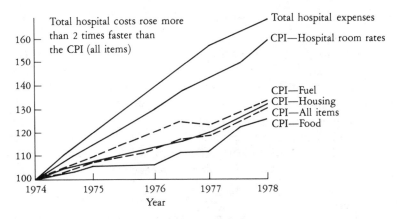

**Figure 6-1**  Relative increases in hospital expenses and several basic needs. To drama-tize his argument for hospital cost control, Health, Education and Welfare (HEW) Secre-tary Joseph A. Califano, Jr., presented this chart during congressional hearings. It showed hospital costs increasing far more rapidly than other elements of the Consumer Price Index (CPI) in the 1974–1978 period. Califano said federal hospital spending alone would exceed $60 billion by 1984, nearly double the 1979 level, if Congress didn't pass the legislation. (*Source: Margaret C. Thompson, ed.,* Health Policy: The Legislative Agenda. *Washington, D.C.: Congressional Quarterly, 1980, p. 22. Copyright 1980 by Congressional Quarterly, Inc. Reprinted by permission.*)

bulk of federal medical aid goes either for Medicaid or Medicare. Middle-class families, particularly those who are in the costly child-rearing years, receive little direct federal assistance in paying medical expenses.

To help with medical costs, an estimated 90 percent of the American public has coverage from some form of health insurance or federal program. The private in-surance programs in which the middle income participate are typically paid for through some combination of contributions by employer and employee. The bene-fits provided vary greatly with some covering virtually everything while others have a short list of basic benefits, and others require the beneficiary to shoulder a share of the cost for the items covered by the policy. To illustrate differences in the ex-tensiveness of coverage for differing kinds of health costs, patients pay for a tenth of all hospital expenses, a third of the bills from physicians, but almost half of the expenses of nursing homes.[2]

During the last decade two major thrusts have characterized policy proposals to change the burden of health care expenses. One is to relieve anxieties by instituting a national, comprehensive health insurance program. The other is to develop tech-niques for retarding the rate of increase in health care costs.

## National Health Insurance

Some consider the lack of national health insurance (NHI) to be a major omis-sion in federal programs to meet basic human needs. From this perspective, some form of national health insurance, the merits of which have been debated since the New Deal, is generations overdue. Even in the aftermath of the swing to the Right in 1980, NHI was favored by a 52 to 37 percent majority of those who had an opinion on the issue.[3]

During the 1970s the most active proponent of NHI was Sen. Edward Kennedy (D.-Mass.). Although the Kennedy plan has varied from year to year, its essential elements have remained the same. He advocates a compulsory program that would cover the entire population. Funding would come from a combination of taxes on employees and employers along with a contribution from the federal treasury. Funding would be sufficient to cover individuals and families lacking a wage-earner. All hospital and medical expenses—with some exceptions for nursing homes, mental health, and dental care—would be provided for. Kennedy's proposals have been the most comprehensive and, obviously, the most expensive of the alternatives considered by Congress.

Proposals less comprehensive than Kennedy's have often provided for voluntary participation and have typically had upper limits on the benefits provided. For example, a proposal endorsed in the mid-1970s by the American Hospital Association would have paid for a maximum of ninety days of hospitalization and nursing home care a year and twelve doctor visits annually. Like the Kennedy proposal, the alternatives called for workers to be covered through their place of employment. Some, but not all, proposals have included provisions for handling the needy. Some plans have called for the federal government to run the programs while others—not surprisingly the one endorsed by a number of insurance companies—would have coverage provided under private insurance policies.

The most limited programs would offer only catastrophic coverage. These have stipulated that benefits would begin only after a family had absorbed a certain level of expense, say $2,500. Participants in a program to provide coverage for catastrophic illnesses could have insurance policies which would help with expenses prior to reaching the threshold for catastrophic coverage.

The rationale behind catastrophic coverage is that since most Americans participate in some program to defray health care expenses, the major need is to protect against the costs few middle-income families are able to save for. At the opposite end of the spectrum, Senator Kennedy sees health care as an entitlement which should be all-encompassing and should not be conditioned by one's bank balance.

## Cost Containment

During the Carter administration a growing number of congressional and administration leaders began to support policy proposals directed toward a far different set of goals than those embraced in previous discussions of national health insurance. Kennedy-style comprehensive health care coverage now seems to have been an idea whose time has come and gone. It was a product of an era when the emphasis of federal programs focused on higher and higher benefits.

The breezes of change felt during the Carter presidency became a stiff gale under President Reagan. Interest in fuller benefits was supplanted by a concern for limiting the rise in the cost of health care. Two basic avenues for achieving this objective have been suggested. One, which initially enjoyed greater popularity, was the regulatory approach. Its antithesis, which David Stockman (Reagan's Director of the Office of Management and Budget) sponsored while a member of Congress, would encourage freer competition among health care providers.

**Regulatory approach.**    Two early, limited attempts to restrain health care cost inflation sought to eliminate needless duplication of facilities and to prevent unnecessary treatment. This effort at planning was adopted by Congress in 1974, terminating the Hill-Burton Act, which had encouraged new hospital construction. Congress endorsed planning when it became apparent that there were at least one hundred thousand surplus hospital beds, which cost a total of between $1–2 million dollars annually to maintain.[4] Not only was it hoped that planning by federally subsidized state and local agencies would prevent further unneeded hospital expansion, it was also intended to discourage nearby hospitals from acquiring costly new technology when the demand is low enough that physicians in the area could share a single unit. The local health services agencies which were responsible for overseeing the development of local plans have not been popular, can document little in the way of savings, and have been slated for extinction by the Reagan administration.

Attempts at cost containment by having local physicians review the quality and necessity of procedures (PSROs, discussed in chapter 5) have also drawn criticism. Moreover it has been estimated that they saved only seventy cents for every dollar it cost to operate them.[5] With such a dismal record as a money saver it was not surprising when funds for this program were cut from the Reagan budget.

More drastic steps for cost containment have been proposed but not adopted. President Carter suggested that a lid be placed on the annual rate at which hospital expenses would be allowed to rise. With hospital charges increasing by 15 percent a year, the American Hospital Association violently opposed the idea that it should be restricted to a 9 or 10 percent increase. The association pointed out that in the absence of across-the-board price controls like those imposed by President Nixon, it would be unfair to single hospitals out. Hospitals, unlike many industries, are both labor and technology intensive, meaning that they must cope with costly new equipment as well as rising salary demands.

Congress rejected President Carter's approach to capping health care costs. The Reagan administration, whose leading members are far more attracted to the concept of a free-market economy, has shown more interest in enhancing competition rather than regulating costs.

**Competition approach.**    Ronald Reagan ran for president saying, "What ails American medicine is government meddling and the straitjacket of federal programs."[6] The Reagan approach is most likely to stress competition and to turn more toward private insurers than to federal agencies for protection against excessive health care costs. It may also seek to have individuals bear a larger share of the costs, turning away from the efforts of liberals to provide maximum services.

One type of participant in the more competitive arena would probably be the health maintenance organization (HMO). HMOs have played a role in providing health care on the West Coast since World War II, when the Kaiser-Permanente program was created to meet the health needs of workers in the Kaiser shipyards. The assumptions underlying HMOs are quite distinct from—indeed one might say the polar opposite of—those behind traditional health care. As its name implies, an HMO takes a preventive approach and seeks to maintain the good health of its participants. In contrast, most doctors, hospitals, and clinics are oriented primarily to curing the ill.

The financial arrangements create a situation in which the physicians affiliated with an HMO have an incentive to keep their patients well. Members of HMOs pay an annual fee which entitles them to treatment by the staff of the organization's physicians at no additional cost, much like student health services arrangements on many campuses. The staff of an HMO includes both those who concentrate on family practice as well as a number of specialists. If a patient's illness requires consultation with one or more specialists, it usually involves nothing more than seeing additional doctors at the same facility, often with no need for a separate appointment. This is in contrast with the procedure in most doctors' offices where the patient pays separately for each visit. If one's physician feels that the services of a specialist are needed then the patient is referred to another doctor, in another office, at another time, for which another fee will be charged. Each visit and each test produce additional revenues for the provider.

An HMO director commenting on the differences between HMOs and the traditional fee-for-service arrangement said: "It has always been a paradox that doctors and hospitals are dedicated to keeping people well and healthy, yet generally derive most of their income from sickness. By contrast, when prepayment is made directly to providers of care, both the hospitals and doctors are better off if the patient remains well."[7] Moreover since the annual fee is set, there is no incentive for doctors to prescribe unnecessary tests or treatments or for hospitals to place patients in more expensive surroundings (such as intensive care units) than they need.

By 1979 it was estimated that 7.5 million Americans were enrolled in 217 HMOs. Many of these were on the West Coast where approximately 10 percent of the California population receives health care from an HMO. The number of HMO participants rose by 74 percent between 1973 and 1979, even though federal programs have not been as supportive as HMO advocates would like.[8] There have been relatively few federal dollars appropriated to help HMOs get started or to expand.

While federal assistance has been welcomed, the initial 1973 legislation came wrapped in so much red tape that HMOs complained that it was often impossible to provide services for less than the traditional fee for service physicians. Subsequent amendments have relaxed the range of services which HMOs were initially required to provide to be eligible for federal assistance, allowing them to charge extra for services such as preventive dental care for children. Charges for these services should make HMOs more competitive.

The federal health planning procedures discussed earlier have been another obstacle to HMOs. In a situation in which the left hand seemed to be unaware of the right hand's activities, planning requirements sometimes thwarted development of an HMO alternative in areas where current capacity was judged to be sufficient. These judgments were made by people closely attached to the traditional health care structure who do not encourage HMOs, since they would offer a cheaper alternative. Because of these obstacles HMO participation has grown slowly.

Nonetheless Stanford economist Alain Enthoven, a major proponent of the concept of increased competition, has developed a proposal which relies heavily on a network of HMOs. Under Enthoven's proposal, each family would receive a voucher with which to purchase health care. Workers would get theirs through their jobs, the elderly could receive theirs from Medicare, while vouchers for the poor could be issued through the Medicaid apparatus. These vouchers, which would be uniform per capita, would be used to prepay for health care. HMOs and other providers would compete for consumers' vouchers. Once a year people would be allowed to switch providers. Providers would have to offer a basic set of benefits so that consumers could easily compare across competing programs. The competitive situation, Enthoven predicts, would bring down costs. Doctors, insurance companies, and, to a lesser degree, hospitals, have shown little enthusiasm for increasing competition.[9]

Another proposal for reducing costs by promoting competition, which could be operated in conjunction with HMOs, would be to make patients more aware of health care costs. Since the vast majority of Americans receive some assistance in paying for health care, particularly for hospital treatment, two consequences emerge, both of which contribute to higher costs. First, since consumers do not pay directly for treatment—instead third party payment is made by the insurer or the government—they have less incentive to try to minimize costs. Second, since the insurer may pay for treatment administered in a hospital but not on an out-patient basis, there is an inducement to go to the hospital even though such treatment is more costly.

To make the public more aware of costs, some have recommended that the extent of third party payments be reduced. If people had to pay a share of the bill themselves, they might shop around for more economical care. If reimbursement were at a fixed level for a procedure, then there would be an inducement to select the cheaper out-patient option.

Another technique to make the costs of health care more visible is to alter the tax laws that allow employer and employee to deduct expenditures for health insurance. Current tax laws which allow these deductions encourage employees to bargain for more generous health coverage since it provides a tax-free benefit. Since this policy reduces federal revenue, in the fall of 1982 the Reagan administration was considering limiting the size of the deductions, anticipating that this would raise billions of dollars toward the goal of a balanced budget. Organized labor opposes changes of this nature.

**Evaluating the alternatives.**    Although backers of all of the proposals discussed here argue that these innovations will at least slow the rate at which costs increase, if not actually pushing costs down, change remains problematic. There are three major sources of obstacles to the adoption and implementation of proposals for promoting competition. First, the network of HMOs needed to promote competition does not exist; ten states have no HMOs at all.

The second obstacle to competition and a reason that the requisite programs have not been adopted is that it is not clear that there is strong public support for these innovations. For example, in one situation in which a set of federal employees could opt for different levels of coverage, each with a commensurate price tag, most of the young families opted for a high level of coverage even though they had to pay a part of the premium themselves.[10]

This lack of interest may be due, in part, to the fact that many Americans do not feel competent when it comes to behaving as rational consumers of health care. In this field more than most, few people have expertise and therefore depend heavily on the recommendations of their doctors in deciding what treatment to get. Compounding the problem, even if Americans can shop intelligently for health care, many live in areas which are too poor or too sparsely populated to support competing health care providers.

Another cause for lack of enthusiasm for competition is the great fear of being presented with a huge medical bill. Therefore, if employers were required to offer alternative levels of health care, each having a distinct price tag, some observers believe that many people would opt for the top of the line model even if it required them to pick up a share of the tab.

Further undermining support for HMOs is the warning by critics that these will lead to assembly line treatment and that one may have to wait weeks for routine checkups. Since an HMO's profit margin is reduced if additional treatment is provided, there is some fear that HMO doctors will not give expensive but needed care.

All of this helps explain why Americans have not adopted a cost-benefit approach to health care as some economists would have us do. The premise behind NHI, Medicare and Medicaid, and a major component of cost increases has been the belief that one's income should not determine the availability or quality of health care. New equipment, such as neonatal or cardiac units or CAT (computerized axial tomography) scanners, is terribly expensive. Dialysis for victims of kidney failure is a costly procedure. Furthermore, doctors and hospitals have learned, as a result of million-dollar malpractice suits, that it is risky not to prescribe the full range of diagnostic and treatment procedures, irrespective of cost. In recent years Americans have rejected the idea that health care is a scarce commodity, the distribution of which will be determined by family resources.

The third major obstacle is that proposals to promote competition face powerful political opponents. Insurance companies and many doctors and hospitals oppose proposals that would alter their current relationships with customers and patients. Since these groups are generous contributors to the campaign coffers of congressional candidates, they are able to get a hearing for their position on the matter. Indeed, their campaign work has won them well positioned allies in Congress.

If we are to continue and perhaps expand the availability of third party payment of health care, the trends noted at the beginning of this section seem destined to persist. If payment for a larger share of the cost of health care is made a public responsibility, then it is likely that reallocation will occur within the federal budget as additional resources for health are taken from other programs.

Alternatively, if the burden of paying this growing tab is judged to be too great, some form of rationing will emerge. If people are left to their own resources, then the type of treatment received will once again depend on one's financial resources. If public authorities, perhaps in consultation with doctors, make the determination of who gets extraordinarily expensive treatment, then some form of triage may be instituted. This might operate so that extraordinary procedures are reserved for those who show the greatest promise of recovery, or for the young, or for those whose skills are most valuable to society. Other possibilities for distributing scarce treatment would be through use of a waiting list (as is done with public housing) or through random selection (as was done with kidney dialysis). About all that can be safely predicted for the 1980s is that some shifts in responsibility for payment for health care seem inevitable.

## HOUSING

One dream of middle-class youth is that one day they will own their own home, complete with shade trees, two-car garage, and central air conditioning. Since the New Deal, federal programs have turned this dream into reality for millions. But is the dream viable for a new generation? The inflation of the 1970s, which relentlessly pushed prices and interest rates to unheard of heights, has so changed the world of home financing that observers see home ownership as slipping beyond the grasp of a growing share of the young middle class. While groups that purport to speak for home owners see this as a serious problem, some economists believe that a redirection of financial resources from homes to industry is desirable for the nation's economic well-being.

In this section are reviewed federal policies that have facilitated the purchase of homes. We will then describe recent changes in home financing, and conclude with a discussion of the consequences for prospective purchasers and for sellers.

### Making Home Ownership Easier

During the 1930s the federal government initiated programs which brought the purchase of a home within the reach of the middle class. As with so many New Deal programs, these home-financing initiatives were intended to stimulate the economy by increasing demand through the creation of a new set of consumers.

Prior to the creation of the Federal Housing Administration (FHA) in 1934, the purchase of a home required a substantial down payment, frequently as much as half the purchase price. The terms of the loan would call for repayment within five to ten years. Each year the borrower would pay the interest which had accrued on the note and then at the end of the period the entire principal would be due. If the borrower could not make the "balloon" payment (that is, the repayment of the principal in one installment) or get the lender to renew the loan, then the bank could foreclose.

The FHA induced banks and savings and loan associations to make loans for longer periods (twenty to forty years) to people who made smaller down payments (as little as 5 percent). Repayment came in a series of equal monthly installments with an increasing share being applied to the principal and a declining share being for interest. The interest rate was fixed for the duration of the loan, regardless of subsequent fluctuations in the money market. Lending institutions accepted these terms because FHA absorbed the risk. FHA guaranteed the loan so that if the buyer defaulted, FHA repaid the principal, took title to the house, and sustained any loss. To maintain a supply of mortgage money, the Federal National Mortgage Association would buy mortgages from lending institutions, thereby providing funds to be lent to new home buyers.

After World War II, FHA activities were augmented by an aspect of the GI bill. The Veterans' Administration (VA) guarantees the home loans of former service men and women under even more advantageous terms than are offered by FHA. VA loans require no down payment.

Of course both VA and FHA require that an applicant have an income sufficient to indicate a strong likelihood of repayment. So although not everyone qualified for a loan, the opportunity to spread the cost over a generation or more greatly enlarged the pool of potential purchasers. The success of the federally backed programs led thrift institutions and mortgage companies to offer similar terms on loans which were not secured by a government promise of repayment. Thanks to the availability of mortgage money the proportion of homeowners in the country grew from 40 percent in 1940 to 65 percent in 1980.[11]

### Changes in Financing Arrangements

For many years mortgages based on the terms introduced by FHA worked well. Homes were affordable for an ever-growing number of families. This demand kept a major component of the economy, the housing industry, healthy. Savings and loan institutions and other lenders made profits as they could charge a few percentage points more in interest than they paid to their depositors. This set of happy arrangements was spoiled by inflation that produced unprecedented interest rates in the 1970s.

Until the 1970s the upper limit for interest charges was prescribed by state usury laws. During that inflation-riddled decade, however, investors refused to make money available for mortgages if they could obtain higher returns on other investments. As mortgage money dried up, builders, realtors, and savings and loan banks prevailed on state legislatures to raise usury ceilings. Once the lid had been removed, the rates for housing loans rose and (occasionally) fell, keeping pace with the costs for borrowing money for other pursuits.

With the trend in interest rates being primarily upward, savings and loan institutions found themselves holding portfolios full of mortgages paying less than 10 percent interest. Many mortgages made a few years ago paid the lenders lower rates of interest than they were having to pay out to today's investors. Lenders became reluctant to commit money for a fixed return for thirty years. In order to attract depositors it became necessary to pay substantially higher rates, thus severely cutting into the earnings of lending institutions, forcing some toward bankruptcy.

To compete for investors' dollars, mortgage institutions have asked for and been granted flexibility in adjusting the interest rates charged for home loans. An early deviation from the fixed rate mortgage was the graduated payment mortgage, which allowed the lender to increase the rate by an amount agreed upon by the lender and the borrower at the time that the loan was made. The timing of the increases was also set out in the mortgage contract. Interest on these loans was initially below the rate for fixed loans but would rise above the fixed loan rate during the life of the mortgage.

The graduated payment mortgage helped buyers purchase homes which otherwise they would be unable to afford until their earnings increased. Because the graduated payment loan established an upper limit for interest charges, however, it has failed to keep up with the amounts investors could earn in other spheres.

Greater flexibility is allowed the lender by renegotiable rate and variable rate mortgages (VRM). The first of these provides a loan on which the interest rate may fluctuate by a half point a year but only for a few years—too few to pay off the principal. At the end of the period (usually three to five years), the loan is renegotiated for another five years or less. Over the course of thirty years, the interest rate may go up by no more than 5 percentage points. A VRM is made for the full life of the loan. The interest rate can vary by half a percent a year with a maximum increase of 2.5 points. Maximum increases of 2.5 or 5 points, while preferable from the lenders' standpoint to fixed rate loans, have not allowed enough of an increase to keep up with interest rates.

In 1981 the Federal Home Loan Bank Board took yet another step toward flexibility, approving the adjustable rate mortgage (ARM). Interest rates on ARMs can be adjusted monthly and, unlike with other flexible rate loans, there are no limits on the maximum increase. Rates are pegged to an established index, such as the yield on Treasury bills, or what savings and loan institutions pay for funds, or the national average for interest rates on houses that are resold. Although lenders could adjust rates monthly, most alter rates less frequently.

The ARMs clearly go further than other available options in reducing the lenders' risk that they will have their funds committed to a portfolio paying less than could be earned by other investments. Not surprisingly, lenders like the ARM, while borrowers approach it hesitantly. As can be calculated from table 6–2, an increase of a few percentage points in the interest rate can result in significantly higher monthly payments. For example, on a loan of $50,000, if the interest rate increases from 12 to 15 percent, the monthly payments go from $514 to $632. Although an ARM, like a VRM or renegotiable rate, will drop if interest rates fall, few declines have been experienced recently. If rates go up, an ARM will not simply produce a number of unpleasant surprises as payments creep skyward, it may actually force those whose incomes grow at a slower rate to default. This has led a critic to complain that "the American people are being robbed of the opportunity to own their own homes and the opportunity to a future of stable housing and stable communities."[12]

**TABLE 6-2**  Monthly payments for principal and interest depending on amount borrowed and interest rate (principal repaid over 30 years)

| Interest rate | Amount borrowed | | | | | |
|---|---|---|---|---|---|---|
| | *$40,000* | *$50,000* | *$60,000* | *$70,000* | *$80,000* | *$90,000* |
| 12% | $411.45 | $514.31 | $ 617.17 | $ 720.03 | $ 822.89 | $ 925.75 |
| 13 | 442.48 | 553.10 | 663.72 | 774.34 | 884.96 | 995.58 |
| 14 | 473.95 | 592.44 | 710.92 | 829.41 | 947.90 | 1,066.38 |
| 15 | 505.78 | 632.22 | 758.67 | 885.11 | 1,011.56 | 1,138.00 |
| 16 | 537.90 | 672.38 | 806.85 | 941.33 | 1,075.81 | 1,210.28 |
| 17 | 570.27 | 712.84 | 855.41 | 997.97 | 1,140.54 | 1,283.11 |
| 18 | 602.83 | 753.54 | 904.25 | 1,054.96 | 1,205.67 | 1,356.38 |
| 19 | 635.56 | 794.45 | 953.34 | 1,112.22 | 1,271.11 | 1,430.00 |
| 20 | 668.41 | 835.51 | 1,002.61 | 1,169.71 | 1,336.81 | 1,503.92 |

SOURCE: Calculated by Jeffrey Howard.

Another way to look at the figures in table 6–2 is to see how much one can purchase for a given monthly payment. For example, if a family's budget calls for $720 a month for principal and interest, they can afford a $70,000 mortgage at 12 percent interest. If interest rates go to 14 percent they lose about $10,000 in purchasing power and can afford only a bit over a $60,000 mortgage. At 17 percent interest, $720 a month will be adequate for a mortgage of about $50,000 while at 22 percent (not shown) this family could not even afford a $40,000 mortgage. At the bottom end of the scale, a family that could afford $411.45 for a mortgage of $40,000 at 12 percent would be able to borrow only $28,959 at 17 percent interest and have the same monthly payment.

## Tax Incentives

Allowing home owners to deduct their interest and property taxes when computing their income tax liability is a major incentive to buy rather than rent. Since during the initial years of a mortgage, the bulk of each monthly payment goes for interest charges, home buyers are charging off a sizable share of their housing costs to the federal government. The progressive nature of the federal income tax means that the size of the benefit a family receives through tax deductions increases with its income. For most middle-income families, the largest deduction is for interest paid on their homes. Home owners' interest deductions in 1981 totaled an estimated $39 billion and might reach $82 billion by 1986.[13]

The tax laws also help home owners when they sell their residences. No capital gains taxes are collected if the profit on the sale is reinvested within eighteen months in a residence costing as much or more. If, after age 55, a home owner decides to move to a less expensive dwelling, no taxes are levied on as much as $100,000 in capital gains realized from the sale of a home.

### Consequences of Federal Policies

The encouragement federal policy has provided for home ownership has been a major factor in shaping America's urban landscape. Tax policy has made it more advantageous economically for the middle class to be owners rather than renters.[14] It has also encouraged the ownership of large homes. Until the high interest rates of the late 1970s, federal policy succeeded in making it relatively easy to buy homes.

These conditions, coupled with the demand for new homes by returning World War II GIs, touched off the suburbanization of America. Among the consequences of this phenomenon were the decline of most central city shopping districts, a drop in quality of many city school systems, a smaller population in most central cities, and a decline in their political influence. Urban sprawl has necessitated the development of vast new road networks. Indeed, the population is so farflung in cities such as Houston and Los Angeles that there is no satisfactory alternative to the automobile for most residents. The spatial distribution also contributes to energy shortages and pollution.

Some economists have pointed out some other consequences of federal support for home ownership. Encouraging millions of families and thousands of lending institutions to tie their funds up in residences deprives the economy of capital which could be used to refurbish the nation's aging factories, make them better able to compete in the world market, and create jobs. One critic said, "Housing does not beget more jobs. If you build a factory, it will produce something and employ people, but that isn't true of a house."[15] Housing specialists Steinlieb and Hughes write that "reindustrialization versus housing, the current version of 'guns and butter,' is the major unfolding issue" of the 1980s.[16]

There is nothing to suggest that the tax advantages which accrue to home owners will be eliminated in the near future. The pressures from home owners, realtors, and builders are sufficient to block any such proposal. It appears more likely that a maximum annual amount of interest to be deducted—perhaps $5,000 to $10,000—might be set.

Instead of flowing from new policy directions, the changes occurring in housing are due to broader changes in the economy. Interest rates of 15 percent or higher, coupled with the 146 percent increase in the cost of the median-priced home during the 1970s, make it impossible for a growing number of families to buy the traditional single-family, detached home. To illustrate, "In 1978, according to the National Association of Realtors, the monthly payments on a median-priced home exclusive of taxes averaged $383, or 22.8 percent of average family income. At today's interest rates, the monthly payment on the median home has risen to $810, or about 37 percent of estimated average family income."[17] In order to buy a home today, purchasers must forego a greater range of other goods and services in order to divert more than one-third of their income for shelter.

As adjustable rate mortgages become the norm, prospective buyers will need to have some uncommitted income in order to meet higher interest rates which may come. This will produce several results. First, some share of the population will no longer be able to purchase homes. In 1981, it was estimated that only 3 percent of the population earned enough to buy an average-priced home, which cost $88,400.[18] Second, another segment of the population will have to settle for small homes, row houses instead of detached dwellings, or condominiums. Third, some people who bought their homes when interest rates were relatively low will be unwilling to move. Even a sizable salary increase will not offset the increased house payments caused by higher interest rates nor will it relieve the anxieties caused by an adjustable mortgage.

Fourth, because high interest rates force people to lower their housing aspirations, the pool of purchasers for any but inexpensive dwellings is reduced. This makes it harder for a person to sell a home. To make a sale the owner may have to reduce the price and/or participate in what realtors call "creative financing." This means that the seller has to give the buyer a second mortgage which will be paid over a few years rather than getting the full equity at the time of sale. The seller, consequently, will have less for a down payment when buying new shelter. Fifth, the future demand for housing may be reduced. Steinlieb and Hughes go so far as to speculate that "the largest single reservoir of housing for the 1980s, therefore, may well be secured through the partitioning of extant one-family units."[19] A further consequence would be to make earning a living more difficult for millions of construction workers. It could also mean that young people may need to reside longer with their parents and, perhaps, put off marrying.

Since the changes in the financing and selling of homes have serious consequences for so many, it would be surprising if those who are being hurt do not turn to the federal government for relief. If restraining budget deficits and reducing federal involvement in the economy remain high priority items with our national leaders, pleas for assistance may fall on deaf ears. Developing a subsidy program to keep interest rates low would be very expensive. Returning to the "good old days" of home financing is unlikely. On the other hand, the pressures for relief may be too great to be ignored.

A proposal, which has drawn little support so far but which might be embraced by families desperate to buy a home, would give lenders a share of the equity. If consumer opposition could be overcome, the Federal Home Loan Bank Board might authorize loans in which the lender would be entitled to a share of the increase in the value of the property. Thus if one bought a residence for $75,000 and sold it five years later for $100,000, the lender would receive not only the balance of the principal but also a predetermined percentage of the $25,000 increase in value. If lenders knew they would get some of the appreciation in the property's value, they would probably lend funds at a lower rate.

This idea may seem farfetched today, but today's interest rates and adjustable mortgages seemed improbable just a few years ago. The housing market and federal policy have undergone cataclysmic changes. Continued change should characterize the 1980s.

## SOCIAL SECURITY

There are probably very few readers of this book for whom retirement is a major concern. Even though retirement may be decades away, federal policy in this sphere has some very immediate consequences. The funding available for the retirement sometime during the next century of today's college student will be determined in part by decisions made in the next few years. If plans are not made now to finance the retirements of those who are part of the post–World War II baby boom, millions of people who were middle class during their working years will live out their old age in poverty. In addition, the magnitude of the Social Security benefits paid to earlier generations of retirees depends upon the willingness of today's workers to tax themselves.

The Social Security system, established in 1935, has become the largest and fastest growing federal program. Approximately 115 million workers pay into the system and more than $150 billion is paid out to 36 million beneficiaries. Expenditures may almost double by the mid-1980s.

Social Security, or more formally, Old Age, Survivors, and Disability Insurance (OASDI), provides benefits to the retired and their dependents and, under some conditions, to survivors of deceased contributors. OASDI benefits are available to retirees until they die. For dependents of deceased contributors, eligibility depends on age; children cease to receive benefits once they mature.

Social Security is seemingly a well-established component of our domestic public policy. Its greatest supporters are the people who receive monthly social security checks. Payments are pegged to the level of earnings the recipient enjoyed while working with the maximum benefit being $789 per month in 1982.

Although few political leaders seriously suggest dismantling Social Security, the program has its critics. One charge is that the program is not actuarially sound. With our population aging and the number of people receiving benefits increasing, while the ratio of workers to beneficiaries is decreasing, money is being paid out at a faster rate than new revenue is being collected. After peaking at $48 billion in fiscal year 1975, the Social Security trust fund declined precipitiously until it was projected that the portion designated to pay retirement benefits would be exhausted during 1982. More frightening yet was the projection that the fund might come up $100 billion short during the first half of the 1980s. Since it is inconceivable that Social Security administrators would simply close their offices and declare bankruptcy, substantial reforms are required.

In fashioning a response to the funding crisis, Congress and the president must resolve conflicting demands. Retirees—who are the largest set of beneficiaries— have become a potent political force as their numbers have grown. More than one-tenth of the population is now over age 65 and, thanks to early retirement inducements, the number of retirees and their spouses is even greater. Retirees have a valuable ally in organized labor. The elderly and their labor allies not only oppose any talk of reducing or delaying benefits, they want to see benefits increased.

In the past, Congress has responded to the pleas of beneficiaries that they are unable to survive on what Social Security pays. There have been periodic increases in benefits which, since 1973, have been adjusted annually to keep pace with the Department of Labor's consumer price index. By one measure it appears that Social Security benefits have outpaced inflation. In 1973 the average benefit equaled 39

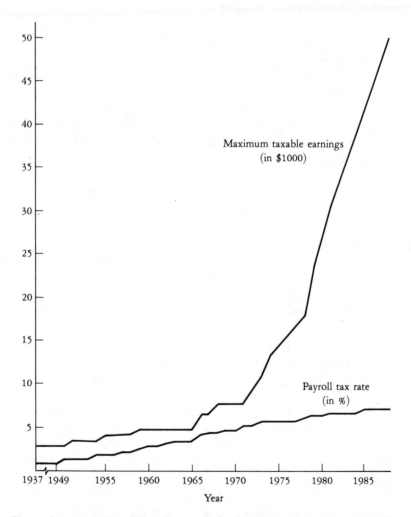

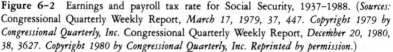

**Figure 6-2**  Earnings and payroll tax rate for Social Security, 1937–1988. (*Sources:* Congressional Quarterly Weekly Report, *March 17, 1979, 37, 447. Copyright 1979 by Congressional Quarterly, Inc.* Congressional Quarterly Weekly Report, *December 20, 1980, 38, 3627. Copyright 1980 by Congressional Quarterly, Inc. Reprinted by permission.*)

percent of what the typical retiree had been earning when working. Eight years later the replacement figure stood at 55 percent.[20]

Opposing demands for a more liberally funded Social Security are contributors to the system. Current contributors' opposition is, at least in part, traceable to their uncertainty over whether they will benefit from the program and, in part, to the growing unwillingness of Americans to pay additional taxes.

OASDI is funded by payroll taxes levied on earnings. In 1983 both employee and employer paid a tax of 6.7 percent on all earnings up to $35,000. Since the upper wage limit on which Social Security is collected now rises as incomes rise, data for the last years in figure 6–2 are estimates. Some have projected that by 1990, a tax rate of 7.65 percent may be levied on as much as $66,000 in earnings. Or, to put it in another perspective, "The maximum Social Security tax paid by an individual, $374.30 in 1970 was $1,403.77 [in 1980] and [was] $1,975.05 [in 1981]. It is likely to exceed $3,000 in 1985 and could top $10,000 in 1990."[21]

Even though the size of the Social Security tax bite and the amount on which it is levied are projected to increase, analysts predict that an additional 1 to 1.5 percent tax rate will be needed to pay benefits to today's young workers, if the system is not changed. In part this is because as our population ages, there are fewer workers contributing to pay for each beneficiary. In 1982 there were about 3.3 workers per beneficiary, down from a ratio of 16.5 workers per beneficiary in 1950. By the year 2050 the ratio may be as low as 1.4 to one.[22] If demographic trends, Social Security tax rates, and payments continue along the paths they now follow, OASDI could be $1.5 trillion short between now and the middle of the next century.[23]

These gloomy projections stand in sharp contrast with the buoyancy that accompanied the adoption of the 1977 tax program to fund Social Security. At the time, the largest peacetime tax increase in our history was supposed to insure the system's fiscal integrity into the next century. However, high rates of unemployment reduced contributions, while high inflation resulted in higher payouts.

The Reagan administration has joined workers in opposing an expanded Social Security system. In his efforts to reduce the magnitude of the budget deficit, President Reagan has proposed cutting some benefits and eliminating others. The president's cuts, if approved, might reduce Social Security outlays by as much as $80 billion between fiscal years 1982 and 1986.

### Proposed Reforms

As is often the case, the easiest solutions are politically unacceptable. Pressures from the elderly are sufficient to block major reductions in current benefits while workers are unwilling to assume a larger burden in order to keep the system afloat at its present level of expenditures.

One technique strongly favored by organized labor as a means of avoiding the horns of the dilemma would be to make up the shortfall by dipping into general revenues. It is argued that the payroll tax is regressive since it is applied to all of a low-income worker's wages but only to a fraction of the earnings of a wealthy person. Thus the use of money raised through the income tax would be more equitable. Those who favor reliance on general revenue also claim that the employers' current payments, since they are passed on to consumers, contribute to inflation.

The switch away from the payroll tax is opposed for several reasons. The idea that Social Security is, at least partially, a social insurance scheme and that forcing contributions to keep pace with benefits keeps a lid on the program would be undermined according to some. Since Congress enjoys passing out benefits but only reluctantly raises taxes, linking benefits to taxes helps enforce a degree of discipline.

Another proposal provides that when one of the three Social Security trust funds (there are separate funds for retirees, disability, and Medicare) is low on money, a loan could be arranged from a still solvent fund or from general revenues. But, unless there were stringent repayment requirements, interfund borrowing would bankrupt all of them in the not too distant future. As a stopgap measure, Congress in 1981 allowed the retirement fund to borrow from the other two during 1982, hoping that by the end of that year a more permanent solution would be achieved. In the early 1980s, Republicans in Congress have been reluctant to approve interfund borrowing, while Democrats are more willing to use the method.

As an alternative to changing the method of funding, President Reagan has suggested changing benefits for future retirees. One proposal, which immediately set off howls of protest, would raise the eligibility age. Receipt of full benefits would be moved back from age 65 to 68 and receipt of partial benefits would be delayed from age 62 to 65. These delays are justified, according to their proponents, since the average life expectancy is ten years longer now than when Social Security was instituted. To discourage early retirements, it has been suggested that the level of benefits for those retiring before age 65 be cut from 80 percent of what currently is paid to a person at age 65 to only 55 percent. When President Reagan suggested that these changes be implemented immediately the Senate objected unanimously. The president retreated and proposed gradually phasing in the changes. In table 6-3 the impact of the Reagan proposal is compared with current benefits for three income levels.

The president has also urged a more conservative approach to calculating initial benefits. Under the president's proposal, beginning in 1985, the extent to which Social Security replaces what a retiree had earned would be diminished. These reductions would accelerate the trend initiated by Congress in 1977. For a person of average income, the replacement value would drop from its 1981 peak of 55 percent to 39 percent in 2000 under the Reagan proposal.[24] This is just 2.6 percentage points below what is called for by the 1977 legislation. In the long run this would save hundreds of billions of dollars.

Other aspects of President Reagan's Social Security reform would affect the computation of annual increments in benefits. Postponing the annual adjustment from July to the beginning of the new fiscal year in October would save between

**TABLE 6-3** Retirement benefits compared

| Earnings category[a] | Existing law | Reagan proposal[b] |
|---|---|---|
| **Retire at age 62 in January 1987:** | | |
| Low | $384.40 | $225.20 |
| Average | 580.70 | 348.30 |
| Maximum | 755.60 | 430.00 |
| | | |
| **Retire at age 65 in January 1987:** | | |
| Low | $477.10 | $447.40 |
| Average | 719.00 | 691.90 |
| Maximum | 942.80 | 860.30 |

SOURCE: *Congressional Quarterly Weekly Report*, May 16, 1981, 39, 842. Copyright 1981 by Congressional Quarterly, Inc. Reprinted by permission.

NOTE: Figures assume that worker entered covered employment in 1956 and worked steadily thereafter. Future earnings (for retirement in 1987) follow trend under intermediate assumptions in 1980 Trustees Report.

[a]"Low earnings" are defined as the federal minimum wage in each past year and the 1981 minimum increased by the change in average wages in future years. "Average earnings" are defined as the average wage for indexing purposes in each year. "Maximum earnings" denote the contribution and benefit base in each year.

[b]Proposed benefits include effect of: (1) 55 percent benefit rate (instead of 80 percent) for retirement at age 62; (2) age-65 computation point (instead of age 62) for all ages at retirement; and (3) 50 percent reduction in wage index used in primary benefit formula for 1982–1987. Benefit amounts are for workers only. Worker is assumed to reach exact age shown in January.

$6.3 and $27.8 billion over five years.[25] Of greater consequence is the possible substitution of the wage index in place of the consumer price index. Using whichever of the two rose more slowly would save the federal government billions of dollars.

In 1981 Congress approved some relatively minor changes proposed by President Reagan. Social Security benefits to students now cease once they reach age 16—previously those who attended college or technical schools remained eligible. Also eliminated was the $255 death benefit if the deceased left neither a widow nor children. The minimum monthly payment of $122 for retirees who made only modest contributions to the program was eliminated for those who retired after January 1982. It was claimed that most of the people affected were retirees from the federal government (who contribute to their own system in lieu of Social Security) who worked in jobs covered by Social Security for a few years. (Needy retirees receive benefits through the Supplemental Security Income program, discussed in chapter 5.)

### The Politics of Social Security

The vigor of the opposition to President Reagan's proposal to immediately raise the age for receipt of full benefits and to expeditiously institute other cost-cutting measures gives a preview of what may be a major conflict in American politics of the future. Many elderly subscribe wholeheartedly to the notion that Social Security is a social insurance program which should provide for *all* their basic needs. But that objective, while certainly desirable for retirees, bears little similarity to the initial goals of the program. It was never intended that Social Security do more than augment other resources such as savings, annuities, private pensions, or support from one's family. The insurance analogy is another misconception. Unlike an insurance policy, Social Security does not guarantee a precise return upon the occurrence of a specified event. If one dies but does not leave a widow or minor children, his/her heirs are not entitled to the amount the deceased paid into Social Security. On the other hand, the benefits a retiree can draw are not limited to the amount the individual paid into the system. The maximum a person could have paid into Social Security from its inception through 1980 was $12,791. Many retirees receive this amount back in benefits within three years. Ironically, only 15 percent of a 1981 national sample thought they would get back more than they had contributed.[26]

Obviously today's worker pays for yesterday's worker's retirement while looking to the contributions of the next generation to secure his/her own retirement. And there is the heart of the problem. Today's worker would rather keep as discretionary income the money taken from his/her paycheck to pay for someone else's retirement. This is, of course, partially due to the fact that most people now doubt that the Social Security fund will have money in it by the time they retire. Among workers age 18 to 29, 73 percent question whether there will be funds available. Younger workers contend that their retirements would be more secure if they could invest the money they and their employers pay to Social Security. While this may be accurate, one wonders how many people would prepare adequately for their retirement if not compelled to pay into Social Security. Those who failed to create a nest egg would ultimately have to be supported by taxpayers.

Hints of what may become an intergenerational battle are already visible in responses to a CBS News-*New York Times* Poll. For example, the idea that participation in the Social Security system be voluntary is approved by more than 60 percent of those under age 44 but by only a third of those over 64 years. Similarly, President Reagan's proposal to cut the benefits of those retiring before age 65 is most strongly supported by young adults while most opposed by those nearing retirement age. A majority of those under age 44 opt for limiting benefits to restore the financial well-being of the system. Less than 40 percent of those over 55 years prefer that option.

The strongest supporters of President Reagan's approach to balancing the Social Security budget are the young, while the elderly are most opposed. Although out-numbered now, the elderly are better organized, more politically active, and perceive a more critical self-interest. Unless reducing the cost of Social Security becomes a far more salient concern to millions of young Americans, it is likely that "gray power" will prevail in Congress.[27]

Congress has been unwilling to face the ire of beneficiaries denied what they consider to be a birthright and has therefore not acted to substantially reduce the benefits to current recipients. Its strategy has been to try to patch the system together and keep it limping along. To the extent that plans to cut benefits are approved, the effect is to close off benefits to future retirees who, since they are not losing something that they now enjoy, will not be too outraged. Thoughtful legislators do not believe that minor tinkering can save the system. Jake Pickle, who chairs the House subcommittee responsible for overseeing Social Security, points up the critical issue facing Congress as it looks into the yawning pit of projected deficits. "I don't know if Congress has the will to make the tough decisions. I hope we do the right thing, but I know I have to recognize the world of realities."[28]

## CONSUMER PROTECTION

Individual consumers in the United States are responsible for two-thirds of the spending in our economy, and most of it is done by the middle class. In spite of the tremendous potential power available to consumers (since all of us are consumers), until the 1960s consumer issues were not news items. The word *consumerism* was not in Webster's dictionary until 1971, and there were no well-known consumer crusaders. Yet today consumer issues are featured in news stories, presidents appoint consumer advisers, and many local television stations have popular consumer advocates. What gave rise to the consumer movement, and what legislation and policies have been fostered by the movement?

The American economy is so diverse and complex that protecting consumers in the marketplace is a dynamic issue with no simple answer. For example, federal regulation of the drug industry by requiring stringent tests for safety appears to be a valued end. However, a number of critics point out that unjustifiably rigorous tests have prevented life-saving drugs from being available in the United States. How do we ensure that worthwhile new drugs make it into the marketplace while harmful drugs are kept out? What research techniques are to be used? What is the "right" time period for such tests? Should the federal government do the testing or monitor the test results of the drug companies? In short, the question is: Given the range of products produced in the United States, to what extent can the consumer be protected?

### The Consumer Movement

Among the principal objectives of the consumer movement are the following:

1. Safe products and services
2. Quality products and services at the lowest reasonable prices

3. Objective information about products, services, and the workings of the market-place to facilitate sound value comparisons in making buying decisions
4. Effective channels to make complaints and suggestions and to obtain timely response
5. Clearly stated warranties and guarantees which are honored
6. Elimination of fraud and deception in the marketplace
7. Honest advertising relevant to products and services
8. Sales and service personnel who are knowledgeable about products and services and are responsive to customer requests for information

All of these goals at face value seem reasonable and, more important, attainable. After all, the consumer movement was generated by such malpractices as unsafe products; deceptive labeling, packaging, and advertising; misleading pricing; unsatisfactory products; unreliable and costly services; hidden credit charges; and unsanitary food products. If the goals listed above were achieved, then we could write a simple chapter on how government policy has dealt with each of these issues. Unfortunately, it is not that simple.

Consumerism has not achieved all its goals for a number of reasons. In the first place, the consumer interest is unorganized, largely because most of us are basically much more interested in our jobs as producers, and therefore the consumer interest is difficult to articulate and represent. Most of us at one time or another have been stuck with a "lemon" and have attempted to right the wrong involved. However, almost none of us has ever tried to organize a sustained plan of action to ensure that others stuck with a similar lemon do not meet our fate. We go about our business, at worst bearing the loss, and do not reorder our lives around long-range consumer issues. Because most Americans do go about their business (participation in the production of goods or services), the consumer interest remains fragmented and unorganized, and unorganized interests are very difficult to articulate and represent in an efficient manner. On the other hand, producer interests, which are comparatively narrow in focus, are more easily organized, articulated, and represented; thus, public policy responds to these interests more forcefully. In short, consumerism suffers from diffusion and from a lack of intensity, since our awareness of ourselves as consumers is much lower than our awareness of ourselves as workers, parents, or students.[29]

As a result of these factors, the consumer interest is difficult to define. Everyone can uphold the notion of consumer protection, although people often differ in their notions of what is required to protect consumer interests. Ronald Reagan can say he is for consumer protection by accepting the National Association of Manufacturers' contention that a list of its members' products may be used by consumers seeking to purchase good-quality products. Certainly Ralph Nader's view of the consumer interest is very different from Reagan's; yet both claim to be consumer advocates because they define the problem differently. Moreover, under these conditions it is ultimately the government that defines the consumer interest, through the adoption of consumer protection policies. Long-range consumer protection depends on whether the president adequately defines consumer interests—a chancy business at best—in his capacity as a policy agenda setter.

A further problem has to do with the question, Who benefits? Some policies benefit all consumers approximately equally, while other policies affect some consumers more than others. Another way to make this distinction is to use Nadel's terms *collective benefits* and *differential benefits*.[30] By a collective benefit he means any consumer policy that affects all citizens equally, regardless of income level. If meat is not properly processed and inspected, both rich and poor alike suffer if they eat it. A differential benefit is any benefit that favors one income group over another. For example, the decision not to charge for information phone calls (411 calls) and to pass the costs off to all telephone users confers differential benefits. Since middle- to upper-income telephone users (salesmen, realtors, and so on) account for 90 percent of all information calls, any policy that makes all phone users pay equally is unfair to the poor. On the other hand, the poor are far more likely to be victims of fraud in advertising and lending than are the middle classes. Most of the consumer legislation passed during the 1960s is of the collective type, for example, providing information to consumers regarding effective interest rates, or labeling and marketing food products fairly.

## MODERN CONSUMERISM: THE 1960s

In the early 1960s consumer issues began to achieve a standing on the policy agenda of the government. The surge of consumerism came with the publication of Ralph Nader's *Unsafe at Any Speed,* and legislation on consumer issues peaked during the 1960–1970 period.[31] Modern consumerism differs from the consumerism of the pre-1960s in a number of ways. The politics of the old consumerism were characterized by a lack of consumer organizations and were usually precipitated by a perceived crisis. In contrast, the consumer politics of the 1960s were generated by public interest groups and sustained by consumer-oriented congressional advocates. Moreover, unlike the pre-1960 period, modern consumer politics are not contingent on or a part of some broader movement. In short, modern consumerism became a movement in its own right and as such has sustaining support from both special interest groups and relevant government officials.

In this section we analyze the groups and individuals outside the federal government who are consumer advocates and then turn to federal officials (both bureaucrats and congressmen) who are involved in consumerism. Finally, we list and briefly discuss the legislative achievements of the new consumerism.

### Private Consumer Groups

The consumer groups outside the federal government are concerned with representing and articulating consumer interests to the federal government. They press to bring issues to the fore and help manage them through the legislative maze to a satisfactory conclusion. There are essentially two types of consumer advocates. The first consists of large organizations whose techniques of exerting pressure are similar to organized interests in other policy areas. Second are those groups and individuals who employ techniques novel to current consumer politics.[32]

Interest groups have two primary functions. One is to articulate the views of the group or groups that they represent; the other is to increase the size of the group they represent. Consumer interest groups are often called public interest groups because they seek collective or widely shared benefits. The oldest such consumer interest group in the United States, the National Consumers League, was organized in 1899 to use consumer pressure to obtain better conditions for workers, and it supported minimum wages and social insurance. Over time its purposes changed, and the group moved to support such issues as pure food and drug legislation.

The Consumer Federation of America came into being in 1967 and serves as an umbrella organization for about 200 consumer groups, such as the Consumers Union, the Connecticut and Illinois consumer organizations, a number of labor unions, and several consumer cooperatives. (The National Consumers League recently became a member.) The federation was established, primarily by the labor unions, to serve as a centralized unit for the consumer movement, which was already gaining ground in 1967. Another group worth mentioning is the Consumers Union, primarily because it publishes the magazine *Consumer Reports*, which has over one million subscribers. However, most of its resources are spent in product testing (reported in *Consumer Reports*); it did not become a direct advocate of consumer legislation until 1969, when it opened an office in Washington, D.C.

Interest groups direct their lobbying activities toward both Congress and the administration. Consumers' groups communicate with Congress mainly through their testimony at congressional hearings. In addition, consumer groups closely follow the progress of consumer bills—what are the controversial points, who is opposed, what compromise is necessary—and, on the basis of such information, determine when and where to apply pressure. In each of these activities the consumer groups have been heavily aided by labor unions. In fact, without union help the consumer groups would be much less successful than they have been. Because of this support, consumers' groups have been quiet on low tariff legislation, which would benefit consumers but which would also hurt unions.

While consumer groups have been relatively successful at lobbying Congress, they have not been so successful with administrative lobbying.[33] Administrative lobbying involves working for the appointment of administrators favorable to a certain point of view, and using congressional influence to gain privileged position in the bureaucracy. In these areas consumers' groups have been weak. For example, although consumer groups testify frequently at congressional hearings, they hardly ever testify at administrative agency hearings. Agencies, we should note, often issue rules and regulations of much importance for consumers.

Another activity of these interest groups is public relations. Here the groups try to create an attitude of basic public support for their activities—support for consumerism in general and for specific legislation. Public relations campaigns are directed to alert consumer group members to the matter at hand, and then to use the media to attempt to build broad public support. For example, in the cyclamate case, consumer groups kept members informed, released statements to local and national media, and urged their members to contact relevant government officials. Strategies to ensure that appropriate legislation is enacted vary somewhat from issue to issue.

### Ralph Nader and the New Consumers

Unlike most of us, Ralph Nader has reordered his life around the consumer issue. As Patrick Anderson put it, "Nader is genuinely and deeply outraged at what he considers to be the abuses and irresponsibility on the part of giant corporations. ... [He] is driven by a keen sense of personal responsibility and the public interest."[34]

After graduating from Harvard Law School in 1958, Nader practiced law in Hartford, Connecticut. While in Hartford he tried without much success to interest the Massachusetts and Connecticut legislatures in automobile safety. In 1964 he moved to Washington, D.C., and was invited by then Undersecretary of Labor Daniel Patrick Moynihan to work within the Labor Department to influence auto safety from within the government. By 1965 Nader felt that the internal strategy was not working, and in November 1965 he published *Unsafe at Any Speed*. However, it was not until 1966 that the book and Nader achieved star status. Early in 1966 Nader learned that General Motors had been investigating his personal life in an attempt to discredit him and his book. Within months Nader was a household name, and auto safety legislation was on its way to passage. Within two years Nader broadened his consumer efforts and was enshrined as "consumer crusader," a title he has kept to this day.

Nader's consumer philosophy has two basic elements. First of all, he believes that big business and big government abuse consumers by inflicting violence on them—via automobile accidents, mining disasters, food poisoning, air and water pollution, and the like. Nader believes that such practices occur because corporation executives are not held responsible for safety lapses; even if people do not care about safety as an issue, he contends, they have a right to be protected. Second, Nader holds that corporations and big government abuse consumers by depriving them of income; that is, government and business are often in league with each other to charge more for a product than the market would bear if there were no such collusion. Federal subsidies to airlines, which keep consumer prices high, and foreign investment tax credits to multinational oil companies are examples of ways in which government and business work together to take consumers' incomes. Nader's goal is very simply to right these wrongs, and he works hard to do so.[35]

As a result of his dedication, Nader is no longer a person but an institution—a climate of opinion. Thus, when we speak of Nader, we more likely mean "Nader's Raiders" and organizations such as the Center for the Study of Responsive Law, the Center for Auto Safety, the Project for Corporate Responsibility, and the Public Interest Research Groups—organizations manned by idealistic young professionals who work for much less than they could earn elsewhere.

The combination of old consumer groups, the new activists, and a rising public consciousness on consumerism proved fertile ground for the explosion of consumer legislation passed in the 1960s. However, none of these forces can on their own account for consumer legislation. Although the new conditions and new activists were responsible for articulating consumer demands, the congressional response to those demands must also be considered.

### Congressional Support for Consumerism

Beginning with John Kennedy in 1962 and continuing through at least Richard Nixon's first term as president, the chief executive took an active position on consumer issues. Lyndon Johnson was most deeply concerned with the issue and pushed it hardest. It is not surprising, therefore, that the majority of new consumer legislation was passed during Johnson's administration. Lyndon Johnson's consumer policies were formed by Democratic consumer activists who controlled the relevant congressional committees. For example, the Senate subcommittee looking into prescription drugs worked very closely with the Food and Drug Administration (FDA). In short, the input for Johnson's consumer policy formulation came from consumer advocates working through their Democratic supporters in Congress. Who were the major supporters of consumerism in Congress, and how did they get the legislation through the congressional maze?

**Committees dealing with consumerism.**    Since most legislation in Congress comes from committees, and since committees have much impact on the final content of legislation, it is important to list the major committees dealing with consumerism.[36] In both the House and the Senate the major consumer committees are the commerce committees (the Commerce, Science, and Transportation Committee in the Senate; the Interstate and Foreign Commerce Committee in the House). Over 60 percent of the consumer legislation of the 1965–1970 period was reported out of these two committees. The Agriculture Committees in both houses reported out significant consumer legislation, as did the Banking and Currency Committees. Of course, the whole committee usually did not deal with each piece of consumer legislation; rather, different subcommittees were responsible. Of the two legislative bodies the Senate was the more active in publicizing consumer issues and in developing legislation.

Both in the relevant committees and in the fight for passage of consumer legislation, liberal northern Democrats were most supportive. Nadel's analysis of who supported consumer legislation in the 1965–1970 boom period clearly demonstrates that both northern and southern Democrats were far more consumer-oriented than the Republicans.[37] In the Senate, members like the late Philip Hart (D.–Mich.), Warren Magnuson (D.–Wash.), and Gaylord Nelson (D.–Wis.) led the fight. On the House side Richard Ottinger (D.–N.Y.), Neal Smith (D.–Ia.), and Leonor Sullivan (D.–Mo.) were strong and active supporters of consumerism. The major pieces of consumer legislation passed during this era were supported almost unanimously by northern liberal Democrats, and on any given issue about half of the southern Democrats voted with their northern counterparts. Thus, in an era dominated by a strong liberal president buttressed (particularly in the 89th Congress) by a large number of Democrats, consumerism in the form of legislation achieved its apogee.

**Major consumer legislation.**    The conditions outlined above resulted in a virtual outpouring of consumer legislation too voluminous to analyze piece by piece. Rather, the following list itemizes the topics of the major consumer legislation passed during the 1960–1970 period:

1. Auto safety
2. Credit bureau regulation
3. Drug safety and efficacy
4. Flammable fabrics
5. Interstate land sales
6. Natural gas pipeline safety
7. Postal fraud
8. Poultry inspection
9. Product safety
10. Toy safety
11. Truth in lending
12. Truth in packaging
13. Wholesome meat

These policies obviously cover a wide range of consumer issues. Roughly, they can be divided into policies that seek to give consumers accurate information about the product being purchased, and legislation to protect consumers from unhealthy and unsafe practices and products. The information policies seek to inform buyers not only about the content and quality of the product but also about where it can be repaired and by whom and at what price. The truth-in-lending provisions and the Fair Packaging and Labeling Act of 1966 are examples of this type of legislation. Both acts seek to assure that those borrowing money and purchasing products are given accurate, readily understandable information. Manufacturers are required to give accurate information about their products, so that the consumer can rationally choose between competing products in the marketplace. For example, the statement warning prospective cigarette buyers that smoking is hazardous to their health is a piece of information that can aid the consumer in determining whether or not to buy the product. It was also proposed that cigarette manufacturers print on each package of cigarettes the amount of tar and nicotine present in their product. Such legislation seeks to protect the buyer by providing relevant information about the particular product.

Protecting consumers' health and safety is the second major area of concern. Here the purpose is to protect the buyer from unsafe industry practices and products that may endanger physical safety. Thus, children's clothes must meet a minimum standard before they can be sold; automobile manufacturers are required to provide as standard equipment certain features such as seat belts; and certain pesticides have been banned.

In discussing what the federal government has done to protect consumers, we should also ask: What *hasn't* the government done? The answer depends on the answer to a prior question—namely, How do we protect consumers? Here differences exist because of what is called the Mortimer Snerd problem. (Mortimer Snerd was, of course, the ventriloquist Edgar Bergen's dummy—literally and figuratively.) If one assumes that even the most stupid and irrational must be protected against their gullibility, then the government ought to legislate many more restrictions and prohibitions on manufacturers. If, however, one assumes that consumers are by and large rational, then policies which give the buyer accurate information concerning products are adequate for consumer protection. Depending upon which of these alternatives is assumed, choices about public policy concerning consumers differ greatly. Thus, analyzing what the government hasn't done that should be done depends on different perspectives.

## Policy Implementation

The combination of electoral results, Naderism, and a sympathetic president resulted in an outpouring of consumer legislation during 1965–1970. How were the policies applied or implemented by the federal government? As shown in chapter 1, the way a policy is implemented often affects the policy itself. Covering every one of the consumer policies passed during this era is not feasible; therefore, our purpose here is to use the Federal Trade Commission as an example of how bureaucracy acts to implement policy decisions.

**The Federal Trade Commission.**   The early consumer protection activities of the FTC[38] were based on the Wheeler-Lea Act of 1938, which specifically authorized the commission to engage in consumer protection by enlarging its jurisdiction to include "unfair or deceptive acts or practices" and the false advertisement of foods, drugs, cosmetics, and curative devices. An advertisement is defined as false if it is "misleading in a material respect." Other consumer protection legislation under the control of the FTC deals with the labeling of fur, wool, and textile products; grocery product packaging; truth-in-lending requirements; fair credit reporting; and product warranties. In enforcing these laws, the commission can employ various enforcement techniques; fines and jail sentences also can be sought for the false advertisement of foods, drugs, cosmetics, and curative devices, although this has not often been done.

Over the years, the FTC has devoted much of its enforcement efforts to the prevention of deceptive practices, especially false or misleading advertisements. Examples of deceptive practices stopped by FTC action include a claim by the makers of J-O Rat Paste that it would not only kill rats but that the rats would leave the premises to die; a claim that Dry-Tabs, a drug preparation, would correct the bed-wetting habit; claims by the Murray Space Shoe Corporation that its shoes would correct, prevent, or relieve arthritis, high blood pressure, indigestion, and stomach ulcers; and a Rapid Shave television commercial which purported to show that its use would permit effective shaving of sandpaper (and by implication, really tough beards), when in reality what was being shaved was loose sand on plexiglass. One of the most famous FTC cases involves a sixteen-year effort to compel the maker of Carter's Little Liver Pills to delete "liver" from the product's name. Carter's pills are laxatives which have no therapeutic effect on the liver (however much motion they may create elsewhere in one's innards). Carter's was also directed to desist from claiming that the pills would prevent one from feeling "blue," "down in the dumps," "fagged out," "grouchy," "all in," and the like. The Carter's case is often cited by critics as an illustration of the commission's tendency to deal with trivial matters.

Given the huge volume of advertising messages generated in our society through electronic, newsprint, mail, billboard, and other modes of advertising, the FTC can monitor only a small portion of them. As a consequence, its enforcement priorities and actions are substantially shaped by complaints received from competitors and others; that is, by the mail bag. Complaints transmitted to the agency by members of Congress are especially likely to be acted on. Once the commission moves against an advertiser, the burden of proof rests on it, not the advertiser. A successfully completed case applies only to the advertiser and advertising claims involved. Recognizing the limitations in the case approach, the FTC in recent years has put more emphasis on rule making to control advertising.

Some of the new responsibilities assigned to the FTC are illustrated by the Consumer Credit Protection Act of 1968 and the Fair Credit Reporting Act of 1970. The Consumer Credit Protection Act, better known as the truth-in-lending law, is intended to ensure that consumers receive accurate information on costs of purchasing on credit. They must be informed on both the total charges and the rate of interest, expressed as the actual annual rate on the unpaid balance, for purchases on credit. This law is enforced by the commission over finance companies, retail stores, nonfederal credit unions, and other creditors.

The Fair Credit Reporting Act applies to credit bureaus, credit-reporting companies, detective and collection agencies, lenders, and computerized credit information companies. The commission is responsible for ensuring that credit-reporting activities are conducted in a fair and equitable manner. The individual borrower's right to privacy is considered as important as the informational demands of creditors. The commission is authorized to make sure that customers (borrowers) have access to information contained in their credit files and the right to correct erroneous information. The act also prohibited the distribution of unsolicited credit cards and placed a personal liability limit of $50 on lost or stolen credit cards.

How effective these two statutes have been in the protection of consumers' credit relationships is open to conjecture. Clearly, though, they represent an effort to deal with some of the problems arising in an economic system in which credit outweighs cash in the purchasing of goods and services.

In carrying out its responsibilities, the FTC has fluctuated between periods of activity and quiescence. Thus, during the 1940s and 1950s the commission was regarded as rather stultified by its critics. One observer declared that the only way to correct its "utter bankruptcy was to wipe out the FTC completely and start afresh."[39] A reform effort in the early 1960s stimulated the FTC to become more vigorous, to focus especially on antimonopoly activity, and in 1963 to issue an all-time high of 454 cease and desist orders. However, by the end of the decade the commission had again become rather quiescent, at least as measured by formal case activity.

Criticism of the FTC's activities has been a persistent feature of the agency's history. Thus, examinations of the commission by Henderson (1924), the Hoover Commission (1949), Landis (1960), Nader's Raiders (1969), and the American Bar Association (1969) have all taken the agency to task.[40] Nader's Raiders, for example, found the FTC guilty of such sins as cronyism and political favoritism in staffing, incompetent personnel, and insufficient concern for consumer protection. The American Bar Association (ABA), which studied the commission at the request of President Nixon, also found many failures on the part of the agency: overreliance on complaints from the public, excessive reliance on voluntary procedures, delay in action, inadequate planning in the use of resources, and some incompetent personnel.

The Nader and ABA reports helped create the setting for a "revitalization" of the FTC during the Nixon administration. Prior to these reports the FTC's response to the new consumerism of the 1960s had been minimal at best. Until 1968 the commission held public hearings on consumerism and established a program to handle consumer complaints in Washington, D.C. When the ABA and Nader studies were released in the late 1960s, the FTC was inundated with complaints. The agency responded with bigger budget requests, internal reorganization, more competent personnel, and relatively effective leadership by three different chairmen (Caspar Weinberger, Miles Kirkpatrick, and Louis Engman). In addition, the FTC established a legal council to propose improvements in FTC procedures which had contributed to commission delays. The result of these actions was a more bold and innovative agency. Business spokesmen soon began to criticize the agency as being hostile to business, overzealous, and acting in excess of its legal authority.

In the area of consumer protection the FTC moved beyond simply stopping unfair or deceptive practices to initiating action to undo or correct their effects. Thus, some companies were required to engage in "corrective" advertising; that is, they must admit that prior claims for their products may have misled the public, or they must provide accurate information on the products. In 1976 the manufacturer of Listerine mouthwash was directed to expend $10 million over a two-year period on advertising to correct consumers' misimpressions concerning the effectiveness of Listerine in the treatment of colds and sore throats. Under the Advertising Substantiation Program, companies are required to file information with the FTC to support their advertising claims. Restitution to injured parties has been required—as, for instance, in some cases involving excessive credit charges.

By the mid-1970s the Federal Trade Commission shed most of its image as the "little old lady of Pennsylvania Avenue." However, the commission under Carter—a proconsumer president—continued to be criticized by the business community. Business interests are a crucial part of the commission's constituency, because they are directly affected by its actions. Consumers generally are unaware of the agency in the absence of some major problem or crisis. Businessmen are more likely to make actionable complaints about adverse action by their competitors; consumers, on the other hand, often may not know that they are being deceived or defrauded, or that they have recourse to the FTC. Agencies are more likely to respond to their attentive constituents, whereas consumers tend to be inattentive. Whoever keeps the strongest pressure on the FTC is likely to have the greatest impact on its policy actions.

## CONSUMER POLICY IN THE 1970s

During the heyday of consumerism Presidents Kennedy and Johnson, working with liberal consumer groups and supported by a Democratic Congress, were responsible for passing much consumer legislation. When Richard Nixon became president in 1969, the pattern of friendly relations with consumer groups, which had characterized the Johnson presidency, disappeared. The Nixon administration, the consumer groups, and the Democratic Congress often disagreed over consumer policy. Furthermore, the president's congressional contacts on consumer issues were with Republicans, not Democrats. Now that the president was a Republican, Democratic congressmen and liberal consumer groups could and did begin to attack federal agencies responsible for safeguarding and administering the consumer interest. Thus, the Nixon-Ford period was characterized by partisan differences over "consumerism." In scope, intensity, and quantity the consumer legislation enacted during this period was less than during the Johnson years. The major piece of consumer legislation passed during the Nixon years was the 1972 act which created the Consumer Product Safety Commission. The most controversial consumer issue of the 1970s involved the creation of a federal consumer advocacy agency with real powers to protect consumers. This had been before Congress continually since 1969 and constituted the major battlefield of consumerism. In this section we briefly sketch the role and function of the Consumer Product Safety Commission and discuss at greater length the consumer agency controversy.

### Consumer Product Safety Commission

The 1972 Consumer Product Safety Act created the Consumer Product Safety Commission (CPSC), a five-person commission with wide jurisdiction. It inherited enforcement of the Hazardous Substances Act, the Child Protection and Toy Safety

Amendments to that act, the Poison Prevention Packaging Act, the Flammable Fabrics Act, and the Refrigerator Safety Act.

The major goal of the commission is "to reduce the unreasonable risk of injury to consumers from consumer products." The CPSC has authority to establish mandatory product safety standards, to ban hazardous products, to conduct research on product safety, to engage in educational and informative programs, and to establish an Injury Information Clearinghouse. Any citizen or group may petition the commission for the issuance, amendment, or revocation of a consumer product safety rule.

The CPSC's first year was widely acclaimed to be successful. The commission fought the White House for the right to appoint the agency's top staff, forced affected industries to withdraw or recall thousands of items which might have been hazardous, promoted guidelines for standard writing, and encouraged consumers to become involved in its work.[41] This pattern of initial activity follows Bernstein's theory that newly created regulatory bodies begin with a bang.[42]

A part of the commission's problem was that there are over 400 private standard-setting agencies, usually controlled by business, which carry a good deal of weight with the commission. For example, in mid-1975 the commission stalled over standards for architectural glass. The Consumer Safety Glazing Committee (a glass industry organization) chose to omit standards for window glass, despite the fact that breaking glass causes many human lacerations. The commission could not decide what standard, if any, to apply and therefore did not act to establish any standards. Similarly, the commission attempted to ban aerosol sprays propelled by vinyl chloride but *forgot* to include an environmental impact statement and thus was held unable to ban such sprays at that time. Another problem is that the commission tried to take on impossible issues such as banning handgun ammunition as a hazardous substance. (Congress later removed ammunition from the commission's jurisdiction.) Generally, the commission has received many thousands of product complaints but it has lacked priorities for separating the wheat from the chaff, which has reduced its effectiveness.

## Proposals for a Consumer Protection Agency

The most controversial consumer issue of the Nixon-Ford and Carter years had to do with the creation of a consumer protection agency with cabinet-level status. The history of this issue is a study of organizational response to consumerism by the office of the president. In the early 1960s John F. Kennedy appointed a Consumer Advisory Council (CAC) to advise the president on consumer matters, make proposals on consumer affairs, and contribute to making economic policy. In 1964 Lyndon Johnson reorganized the CAC as the President's Committee for Consumer Interest (PCCI) and appointed (with cabinet status) a special assistant for consumer affairs. Shortly thereafter, and again in response to the consumer movement, Johnson created another Consumer Advisory Committee, composed of twelve private citizens. Under the leadership of Betty Furness, the PCCI became the main force in consumer matters. However, in the Nixon-Ford era the PCCI was transferred out of the president's office to the Department of Health, Education and Welfare. Thus, the most powerful "in-house" voice for consumers was taken out of the inner circle and subordinated to HEW.

The idea for a cabinet-level consumer agency had been proposed as early as 1934 by Frederick Schlink, a consumer activist, and again in 1961 by Senator Estes Kefauver. The first proposal for such an agency during the modern consumer era was made in 1968. Congressman Benjamin Rosenthal of New York introduced a bill in the House to create such a department. The department would take over a number of functions from existing agencies; it would, for instance, take over the function of food grading and marketing from the Department of Agriculture and the function of supervising packaging and labeling from the Department of Health, Education and Welfare. More important, the agency would have the power to represent the consumer in court and before regulatory agencies. The agency would also handle consumer complaints, establish an Office of Consumer Information, and conduct economic surveys. Variations in this bill were before Congress continually after 1969, although the notion that the new agency should have cabinet-level status was dropped. In the 93rd Congress (1973–1974) the House passed the measure, but it was filibustered to death in the Senate. In the 94th Congress the Senate passed a bill to create a consumer agency by a vote of 61 to 28, and the House passed a similar bill 208 to 199. The conference bill, which was a compromise of the two (House-Senate) bills, was vetoed by President Ford, and a two-thirds majority could not be obtained in the House to override the veto.

Supporters of the measure believed that such an agency was necessary because, in Ralph Nader's words, "Unlike corporations, which have the money and power to control or influence federal agencies, individual consumers have none of these assets."[43] Particularly important to the agency's backers was the power of the agency to represent consumers in court and before federal government agencies. Supporters argued that without such powers the agency would be ineffective. With such powers the agency could truly represent and articulate the consumer interest. Supporters of the bill included *all* national and state consumers' groups, the National Governors' Conference, Common Cause, the U.S. Conference of Mayors, the AFL-CIO, the Senior Citizens' Council, the National Farmers Union, Mobil Oil, Gulf and Western Industries, and Polaroid. Opponents of the measure included the Chamber of Commerce of the United States, the National Association of Manufacturers, the Gas Appliance Manufacturers' Association, Gulf Oil, and General Motors.

The Ford administration's response to the proposals for a consumer agency was to propose the creation of consumer representatives within the various departments and agencies. Thus, the Department of Agriculture would have one or two consumer advocates within its ranks and so on for each governmental organization. Critics argued that the agencies and departments often worked with industry against consumer interests and that such a plan buried the consumer viewpoint. Such a proposal, they claimed, was symbolic politics designed to give the appearance of concern without really dealing with the issues. On the other hand, proponents of Ford's plan said that it was better to have a few consumer representatives within existing agencies than to create a new inefficient federal bureaucracy, saying that the bill for the consumer agency "would create one more costly agency, hamstring other agencies, and bring the American businessman under even more red tape."[44] Thus, the Democratic Congress and the Republican president arrived at a stalemate.

With the election of Jimmy Carter, the prospects for a consumer protection agency improved. In the summer of 1977 Carter announced his support for an Agency for Consumer Advocacy with broad powers to represent consumer interests before other federal agencies. This endorsement, plus the large Democratic majorities in the House and Senate, seemed to guarantee the creation of the consumer protection agency. The Democratic Congress, however, did not enact a consumer protection act. Strong business lobbying caused the House to reject the creation of the agency by a narrow margin. The failure of Congress to establish the consumer agency and the growing strains on the economy, then acted to push consumer affairs off the government agenda. There were subsequently no serious efforts on the part of the Carter administration to revive the issue. Consumer advocates were left to work through the regular channels of the FTC and the FDA. In some cases agency heads pushed consumer issues such as the proposed requirement of air bags in automobiles. Overall, however, consumer issues were not at the forefront of the Carter political agenda.

### Consumerism under Reagan

The election of Ronald Reagan to the presidency did more than continue to keep a consumer agency and consumer affairs off center stage. Reagan's victory was viewed as a decided setback for Ralph Nader and consumer advocates, since they do not have ready access to influential people in his administration, and the more conservative nature of Congress reduces the possibility of legislative successes. In his initial budget address in 1981 President Reagan proposed a one-third reduction of funds for the CPSC. The head of the commission and consumer advocates fought the proposed reduction both within the administration and in the media. They were, however, singularly unsuccessful. In another message a few months later, Reagan proposed the elimination of the CPSC. However, Congress did not act on this proposal before it adjourned at the end of 1982.

It is clear that consumerism of the Nader variety will have little chance for success during the Reagan years. What we can expect is that policies passed in the 1960s which were collective in nature and provided information to consumers about products will continue to be enforced. Regulatory agencies such as the FTC will spend less time on consumer issues, and fewer legal actions against producers will be forthcoming. In early November of 1981, the new chair of the FTC, James C. Miller, stated the new policy direction of the commission. Miller asserted that the FTC had overregulated business and overprotected consumers and that caveat emptor was not a bad form of consumerism.

Business interests have adjusted to the legislation of the 1960s, and most did not find it detrimental to good business practices and profitable operations. In fact, many companies have supported consumer legislation which requires accurate descriptions of goods and services. However, consumer issues will not be on the administration's agenda, and consumer advocates will not be placed in important positions. A policy of benign neglect will dominate consumerism in the Reagan years and administrative agencies will not be as consumer-oriented as they were under Carter.

## CONCLUDING COMMENTS

The middle class is concerned about financial security and a lessened economic burden. In essence, middle-class citizens want a better lifestyle and fear that in the absence of federal assistance and protection they will lose what they have accrued and slip down the economic ladder. In recent years the grip on the ladder has become precarious for some middle-class families. The hopes of those new to the labor force as well as those who have retired, or are about to do so, have been dashed. Young adults see their dream homes receding before them like a mirage. The elderly discover that what they had thought would provide a comfortable retirement is inadequate.

Young and old may be expected to clash increasingly over the issue of Social Security. Retirees want larger benefits and oppose any postponement of their receipt. Young workers doubt that the system will be functioning when they retire and, faced with escalating housing costs, higher fuel bills, and across-the-board inflation, they want to minimize their contribution to Social Security.

Despite age-related disagreements on Social Security, age will probably not divide the middle class on issues such as health care cost containment and home financing. The costs of a serious, protracted illness can ruin the budget of anyone of any age, although it is more likely to hit the elderly. High-priced or unavailable mortgage money hurts people of all ages by making it difficult for buyer and seller to consummate a transaction desired by both parties.

The climate of the Reagan administration is not encouraging for middle-class policy goals. With President Reagan and his congressional followers reducing the federal budget by tens of billions of dollars, it is unlikely that funds will be earmarked for bailing out the Social Security system or for national health insurance. Moreover, the Reagan penchant for reducing federal regulations and relying more upon the states to administer social programs leads one to doubt that attempts will be made to restore low interest rates or cap hospital costs through government fiat. Instead, at least in the short run, the middle class will be increasingly dependent on the outcomes of competition to determine the prices it pays for health care and home loans. It may also be increasingly left to its own devices to prepare for an adequate retirement income through pensions and annuities.

The conclusion for consumer issues is somewhat different. The middle-class consumer never strongly favored legislation that conferred differential benefits on the poor. However, they have favored legislation that helped consumers generally, such as by giving them an opportunity to evaluate the quality or safety of products on a fair basis. Thus Reagan's consumer policies will not be met by strong opposition from a middle class more concerned with other issues.

## NOTES

1. Margaret C. Thompson, ed., *Health Policy: The Legislative Agenda* (Washington, D.C.: Congressional Quarterly, 1980), pp. 19–23.
2. Louise B. Russell, "Medical Care" in *Setting National Priorities: Agenda for the 1980s*, ed. Joseph A. Peckman (Washington, D.C.: Brookings Institution, 1980), p. 178.
3. CBS News-*New York Times* Poll, May 2, 1981.
4. Thompson, *Health Policy*, p. 22.
5. Russell, "Medical Care," p. 185.
6. Linda E. Demkovich, "Reagan's Cure for Health Care Ills—Keep the Government's Hands Off," *National Journal* 12 (December 13, 1980): 2124.
7. Quoted in Thompson, *Health Policy*, p. 68.
8. Ibid., p. 67.
9. Linda E. Demkovich, "No Regulation Here," *National Journal* 13 (August 1, 1981): 1389.
10. Elizabeth Wehr, "Competition in Health Care: Would It Bring Costs Down," *Congressional Quarterly Weekly Report* 37 (August 4, 1979): 1590.
11. Robert J. Samuelson, "Shelter Squeeze," *National Journal* 13 (September 5, 1981): 1595.
12. Rochelle M. Stanfield, "High Interest Rates Are Sparking a Revolution in Home Financing," *National Journal* 13 (January 31, 1981): 172.
13. "Home Tax Breaks Up Prices, Study Says," *Atlanta Journal-Constitution*, October 10, 1981, p. 3A.
14. John C. Weicher, *Housing: Federal Policies and Programs* (Washington, D.C.: American Enterprise Institute for Public Policy Research, 1980), pp. 138–143.
15. The staff director of the Senate Banking, Housing, and Urban Affairs Committee quoted in Timothy B. Clark, "The American Housing Industry—From 'Sacred Cow' to 'Sacrificial Lamb,'" *National Journal* 13 (December 5, 1981): 2157.
16. George Steinlieb and James W. Hughes, "Housing: Past and Futures," in *Housing Finance in the Eighties: Issues and Options* (Washington, D.C.: Federal National Mortgage Association, 1981), p. 23. Also see Amitai Etzioni, "Housing: An Early Reagan Reindustrialization Test," *National Journal* 12 (December 20, 1980): 2196–2197.
17. Samuelson, "Shelter Squeeze," p. 1595.
18. Colleen Teasley, "Latest Figures Price 97% of Nation Out of Market to Buy a New Home," *Atlanta Journal*, October 6, 1981, p. 8D. Of course, these estimates do not take into account that one may already own a home. A large equity from an existing home that could provide a large down payment would allow a family to purchase a home for which their monthly income would not qualify them. Also, remember that these figures are based on the average national cost of a home. Larger proportions of the public can afford less expensive dwellings.
19. Steinlieb and Hughes, "Housing," p. 35.
20. Timothy B. Clark, "Saving Social Security—Reagan and Congress Face Some Unpleasant Choices," *National Journal* 13 (June 13, 1981): 1054.
21. Ibid., p. 1052.
22. "Social Security Crisis: Demographics Tell the Tale," *National Journal* 13 (July 11, 1981): 1262.
23. Pamela Fessler, "Threat of Bankruptcy Spurs Action on Social Security Bill; Long-term Changes Studied," *Congressional Quarterly Weekly Reports* 39 (September 19, 1981): 1776.
24. Clark, "Saving Social Security," p. 1056.
25. Timothy B. Clark, "Social Security Spending Cuts Will Allow Tax Cuts, Reagan Tells Congress," *National Journal* 13 (May 16, 1981): 895.
26. CBS News-*New York Times* Poll, July 16, 1981.
27. Figures in these paragraphs are from ibid.

28. Fessler, "Threat of Bankruptcy Spurs Action on Social Security Bill; Long-term Changes Studied," p. 1777.

29. Mark V. Nadel, *The Politics of Consumer Protection* (Indianapolis: Bobbs, Merrill, 1971), pp. 235–247.

30. Ibid., chap. 6.

31. Ralph Nader, *Unsafe at Any Speed* (New York: Grossman, 1965).

32. This discussion is based on Nadel, *Politics of Consumer Protection*, chap. 5.

33. Ibid., pp. 170–172.

34. Patrick Anderson, "Ralph Nader, Crusader: Or, the Rise of a Self-Appointed Lobbyist," *New York Times Magazine*, October 29, 1967, p. 25.

35. Nadel, *Politics of Consumer Protection*, pp. 178–180.

36. On the importance of committees see Richard Fenno, *Congressmen in Committees* (Boston: Little, Brown, 1974).

37. Nadel, *Politics of Consumer Protection*, chap. 4; see also *Congressional Quarterly Almanac*, 1965 through 1970, for specific votes.

38. See the *U.S. Government Manual* for a complete description of its duties and powers.

39. Quoted in George W. Stocking and Myron Watson, *Monopoly and Free Enterprise* (New York: Twentieth Century Fund, 1951), p. 548.

40. Gerard C. Henderson, *The Federal Trade Commission* (New Haven, Conn.: Yale University Press, 1924); *U.S. Commission on the Organization of the Executive Branch of the Government* (Washington, D.C.: U.S. Government Printing Office, 1949); James M. Landis, *Report on Regulatory Commissions to the President-Elect* (committee print), Senate Committee on the Judiciary, 86th Congress, 2nd Session, 1960; Edward F. Cox, Robert C. Sell, and John E. Schulz, *The Nader Report on the Federal Trade Commission* (New York: Baron, 1969); *Report of the ABA Commission to Study the Federal Trade Commission* (Chicago: American Bar Association, 1969).

41. Jonathan Spivak, "A Risky Business," *Wall Street Journal*, July 11, 1973, p. 28.

42. Marver Bernstein, *Regulating Business by Independent Regulatory Commission* (Princeton, N.J.: Princeton University Press, 1955).

43. Nader's testimony before the U.S. Senate Committee of Government Operations, 91st Congress, 1st Session, 1969.

44. Sen. James Buckley, "Controversy over Proposals to Establish a U.S. Consumer Protection Agency," *Congressional Digest* 53 (November 1974): 277.

## SUGGESTED READINGS

*Housing Finance in the Eighties: Issues and Options.* Washington, D.C.: Federal National Mortgage Association, 1981.

Nadel, Mark V. *The Politics of Consumer Protection.* Indianapolis: Bobbs, Merrill, 1971.

Thompson, Margaret C., ed. *Health Policy: The Legislative Agenda.* Washington, D.C.: Congressional Quarterly, 1980.

Weicher, John C. *Housing: Federal Policies and Programs.* Washington, D.C.: American Enterprise Institute for Public Policy Research, 1980.

# Some Final Considerations

There are two aspects of the policy process deserving more explicit treatment than they received in earlier chapters. These are the characteristics of policy change and the impact of policy. This chapter concludes with some commentary on what we can expect from the Reagan administration in the way of policy action.

## POLICY CHANGE

By policy change we mean both the adoption of new policies and the modification or repeal of existing policies. In this section we will contend that policy change may take three forms: (1) incremental changes in existing policies, (2) the enactment of basic statutes in particular policy areas, and (3) major shifts in public policy as a consequence of realigning elections.

### Incrementalism

Most policy change in the American political system takes the form of limited or marginal changes in or additions to existing public policies.[1] However, some statutes, for example, go beyond marginal changes and make basic or fundamental changes in policy. Whether a particular policy change is incremental or basic in nature is open to argument, especially in close cases. It is a little like determining whether a particular animal is a large pony or a small horse. (The Interstate Commerce Commission, incidentally, once put itself in the position of possibly having to make such a decision by providing different truck rates for the transportation of horses and ponies.) To some, every or almost every policy is incremental, but such a view makes the concept meaningless, because then it neither describes nor explains any particular category of things. For example, if all people are tall, the concept of tallness has no real meaning, since it distinguishes no one.

The distinction we are making can be illustrated by the Fair Labor Standards Act of 1938 and subsequent amendments. The 1938 law marks a basic change in public policy, since for the first time the national government became involved in the general regulation of wages and hours of work. Where previously there had been no regulation, a substantial portion of the labor force was now covered by federal labor standards. One can find a few antecedents, such as the Adamson Act of 1916, which provided an eight-hour day for railroad workers; but in no meaningful sense can the Fair Labor Standards Act be regarded as merely a limited or marginal addition to existing national policy. Since 1938 many incremental changes have been made in the law—increasing or sometimes decreasing its coverage, hiking the minimum wage, and the like. Over the years the minimum wage has been increased from the initial requirement of 25 cents an hour to the 1982 standard of $3.35 an hour. These, in the best sense of the word, represent policy increments.

Why is incremental change the most common kind of policy change in the American political system? In our discussion of the reasons, we again make use of our sequential policy model of chapter 1.

In the first place, at any given time there are numerous public problems on the policy agenda, many of them quite technical or complex. Policymakers have neither the time, the information, nor the ability to fashion complete "once-and-for-all" solutions to these problems. Also, uncertainty exists as to what should be done and as to the likely consequences of particular alternatives. Thus, a limited or piecemeal approach may seem the safest way to proceed in alleviating or partially resolving many problems.

Second, power is fragmented and dispersed along many points in the American political system—national, state, and local governments; legislative, executive, and judicial branches; upper and lower legislative houses; a variety of administrative departments, agencies, and commissions; organized lobbies; and a multitude of political interest groups. Majority building, or otherwise winning the approval necessary for securing the adoption of policy alternatives, is a major task and concern confronting those involved in formulating and adopting policy. Negotiation, bargaining, and compromise become necessary to win the support or reduce the opposition of those who could block adoption. On its way to enactment, therefore, a statute may be reduced in scope, shorn of some of its provisions, and otherwise modified in strength and impact.

Third, political expedience can contribute to incremental policy change. It is easier to secure agreement on limited policy changes than on those of a sweeping or drastic nature. An incremental policy may well satisfy the need or demand for action, the notion that "we have got to have a bill," which often motivates policymakers to act. The search for a policy alternative often ends when any plan is found that will work, even though that plan is not the ideal solution.

Fourth, the beneficiaries of existing programs, the agencies and officials who administer them, and those who regard them as wise or proper public policy can be counted on to resist sweeping changes, or perhaps any changes, in them. Comprehensive deregulation of business is unlikely to result because of the interests of the regulated and those who regulate them. Both have a stake in the status quo. Limited or piecemeal deregulation is more likely to win approval because it will create less opposition. For example, the Nixon administration's proposal for a guaranteed annual income, which would have constituted a basic change in welfare policy, failed partly because many persons would receive higher benefits from the existing welfare programs than they would have received under the administration's proposal.

Finally, governmental bodies and officials are often reluctant to take action or, once moved to action, are not inclined to act in a radical fashion. Action, or change, may be unsettling, disruptive of established routines, productive of conflict. Subtle or incremental change is less disturbing and thus preferred over something more jarring or far-reaching.

## Basic Policy Change

Basic policy change in particular policy areas is not a well-studied phenomenon, and thus generalizations are hard to come by. Therefore, we will begin by giving some examples of basic change and comment briefly on them.

One example of basic policy change is the Atomic Energy Act of 1946. Until World War II atomic energy was only a theoretical possibility. After Enrico Fermi, Albert Einstein, and others in the Manhattan Project had successfully split the atom, and President Truman had ordered the use of atomic bombs on the Japanese, theory became reality. In the Cold War atmosphere after 1945, it became necessary to develop an explicit policy on atomic energy. Who was to be in control? What form should control take? The Atomic Energy Act made nuclear energy a government monopoly and vested control in the Atomic Energy Commission, a civilian agency. In Congress, the Joint Committee on Atomic Energy was given jurisdiction over such legislation. In 1946 a basic, nonincremental policy change was necessitated by a technological innovation and national security considerations.

Another striking example of basic policy change is federal air pollution policy under the 1970 amendments to the 1963 Clean Air Act.[2] The example is especially notable because until 1970 changes in this policy area were essentially incremental. In 1955 a subcommittee of the Public Works Committee devoted less than a day's hearing to air pollution. In 1963 growing interest in the problem of pollution caused the Senate to form a Subcommittee on Air and Water Pollution, chaired by Sen. Edmund Muskie (D.–Maine). Consideration of the Clean Air Act in that year focused on the question of "whether or not" the government should set standards for air quality. The Air Quality Act of 1967 demanded that state and local air pollution programs be established. Yet, by the time of the 1970 legislation there was no federal agency with either the expertise or the resources to oversee such state and regional programs. With regard to moving sources of air pollution (autos, trucks, etc.), the picture for the 1955–1970 period is much the same. Both the Air Pollution Control Act of 1955 and the Schenck Act of 1960 emphasized research and problem definition. The Clean Air Act of 1963 and the Motor Vehicles Air Pollution Control Act of 1965 set weak federal emission standards. The politics of air pollution during this period are described as showing "a reasonably close fit" to incrementalism.[3] In sum, from 1955 to 1970 pollution control policy was characterized by multidimensional complexity and many special interest groups seeking to shape action; the result was incremental public policy produced by the need to build congressional majorities for legislation.

What occurred in 1970 to change air pollution policy from incremental to innovative? The answer lies essentially in the magnitude of public response in 1969–1970. Public opinion about the environment was intense, and the public outcry seemed to be clearly in support of clean air and clear water. Congress and the president responded quickly and dramatically. The National Environmental Protection Act was passed, the Environmental Protection Agency was created to enforce federal standards, and the 1970 amendments to the Clean Air Act established stringent federal emission standards. For example, by 1975 automobiles were to have reduced pollutant emissions by 90 percent from the 1970 emission levels. This was done even though the federal government lacked knowledge of the tradeoffs between the economy and the environment, and the expertise to reduce automobile emissions to the specified standard was not present. Instead of the normal incremental policy process, where majority support has to be built for a policy, "in 1970 air pollution policymakers had to find a policy for [the] coalition."[4] In sum, public pressure had created a mandate for clean air and water, and the political system responded with a nonincremental policy.

It would be foolish to try to generalize about basic policy change in particular areas from these examples. We can see, however, that different types of conditions can give rise to basic policy developments. In the case of atomic energy, policy was nonincremental and decisive because of the nonexistence of atomic energy before World War II. Technological innovation and national security considerations led to the Atomic Energy Act. The 1970 amendments to the Clean Air Act were a consequence of intense public pressure for strong action to protect the environment. A real or perceived crisis, or dissatisfaction with state action and strong pressure from an interest group can also lead to major policy changes.

**Realigning elections.**    Although the configuration of interests and institutions in the United States is such that limited adjustments in public policy are often all that are possible, during certain periods in American history major policy shifts have occurred. In 1876 policies were adopted which helped institutionalize industrialism, and in 1896 the Populist threats to industry were deflected.[5] In 1933 the federal government's role in regard to the economy shifted dramatically. The New Deal of Franklin Roosevelt went far in converting the United States into a modern welfare state. Thus, during certain periods policy is innovative rather than incremental. In this section we describe the conditions under which major policy "revolutions" can take place.

Over time, in any given society, social crises will arise.[6] These crises may be the results of fundamental imbalances in the social order; and if the government cannot solve the problems, either a new regime or a new type of government results. Such crises are timeless: when in the fifteenth and sixteenth centuries the middle class in England grew in economic strength and in numbers, the old feudal order gave way to a stronger monarchy and ultimately to parliamentary government. In the nineteenth and twentieth centuries, as the laboring classes grew in number, governments shifted to welfare policies and away from laissez faire. Every industrial society has experienced a crisis of the old order, when the economy shifted further from an agricultural toward an industrial economy. During such periods of crisis the various issues involved are translated into a major pressing issue, and the government must resolve the crisis by dealing satisfactorily with the issue or suffer defeat at the polls.

In the last eighty years the United States has experienced at least two such crises. The first was the threat to the industrial order from agricultural interests during the 1890s; the second was the crisis created by the Great Depression in the 1930s. In both cases there was an overriding question. In the first, What future was in store for America—industrial or agricultural? In the second, What should government do to combat the effects of the Depression? In the American political system such questions are resolved in critical elections which bring to power a new set of party leaders who are believed able to act across a number of policy areas to combat the crisis. Perhaps the best way to illustrate how critical elections bring about major changes is to briefly describe how the critical elections of 1932 and 1936 resulted in major policy changes.

In the early twentieth century business and business values reigned supreme in the United States. Government actors were firm believers in this American way of life; President Calvin Coolidge once put it, "The business of America is business." As a result, social welfare was largely a private concern, and government intervention in the economy was minimal. The market economy was in its heyday. There were, of course, some protests from groups such as farmers, who were especially subject to the ups and downs of the marketplace. Nevertheless, it is accurate to say that the role of government in everyday life was negligible. The consensus which had formed around these business values was shaken when the stock market crashed in 1929. The effects of the Great Depression steadily worsened, and by 1932 in any given three-month period over half of the American people suffered some unemployment. In one day in Mississippi one-quarter of the farmland in the state was up for sheriffs' auctions; and in Davenport, Iowa, irate farmers took over the town to prevent tax sales of their land. In short, the American dream of unlimited progress and prosperity seemed to be turning into a nightmare.

The great question of the era became: What should the government do to combat the effects of the Depression? On one side were those who argued that the national government must actively pursue policies that would alleviate the effects of the Depression—policies such as loans to farmers and businessmen; programs to guarantee that banks would not collapse and leave depositors without money; provisions for feeding and clothing people until they could go back to work; and improved distribution of economic goods and services. The other side took the traditional position of "hands off." President Hoover, for instance, contended that "economic depression cannot be cured by legislative action or executive pronouncement. Economic wounds must be healed by . . . the producers and consumers themselves." In this great debate the two major political parties took opposite positions. The Republicans, who were in power, took the position that the government could not and should not enact programs to combat the effects of the Depression. The Democrats by 1932 had formulated activist programs such as a $900 million federal works program, a billion-dollar Reconstruction Finance Corporation loan fund, and a $100 million mercy money fund. The Democratic platform in 1932 differed markedly from the Republican platform on issues regarding the aggregation of wealth, control of the distribution of wealth, and the exercise of governmental power. In sum, the parties differed fundamentally over the government's role in curing the Depression.

The election of 1932 became a referendum over this question. The election results gave Franklin Roosevelt and the Democrats an overwhelming victory. Democratic candidates swept to power in unprecedented numbers in both the House and the Senate. The newly elected president and Congress believed that they had a mandate to act, and act they did. In the first four years of the Roosevelt era, more social welfare and economic regulatory legislation was passed than in the previous 140 years. Social Security, labor legislation, public works, and economic stimulation programs abounded. American public policy shifted sharply from laissez faire to welfare statism. The result of the electoral realignment of the 1930s was to create the basis for the government we know today. And if the reader thinks about previous chapters in this book, it is clear that these policy changes occurred across all policy areas and not just in isolated areas. From consumerism to social welfare, the New Deal groundswell changed the face of American government and public policy.

The elections of 1932 and 1936 provided the basis of support for these policy changes. Northern urban ethnics and blacks, who had traditionally voted Republican, changed parties and became Democrats. Those voters who had been hard hit by the Depression favored the Democratic programs to combat the Depression. Attempts by Republicans and others to eliminate the government management and social welfare programs of the New Deal were turned back because those favoring the policies could and did continue to elect majorities to Congress who supported the New Deal. It was not until the Republicans accepted the main outlines of New Deal policies that they elected a president—Dwight Eisenhower in 1952.

The crisis of the Depression, then, produced a policy question that was comprehensible to the average voter. The major parties adopted profoundly different policy stands on the central question of the role of government in the economy. The Republicans defended the old order while the Democratic platform advocated an activist government. The election results in both 1932 and 1936 affirmed and reaffirmed the people's preference for an activist government. The newly elected (1932) president and Congress formulated and adopted sweeping policy changes. In addition, they created a bureaucracy capable of implementing the new welfare policies. In sum, the crisis resulted in the election of a new majority, which enacted nonincremental, fundamental changes. The crucial elements in such realigning elections are the nature of the questions generated by the crisis and the fact that the election results in a massive turnover of elected officials. The newly elected officials, chosen on the basis of their stand on the critical question, enact policy changes consistent with their party's stand.

In this century, only the New Deal period clearly involves a realigning election with the attendant major policy changes. However, both Woodrow Wilson's and Lyndon Johnson's elections were characterized by high electoral turnover of members of Congress and special circumstances surrounding the election. (The question of the Reagan election is considered in a later section.) Wilson's election was partially the result of Theodore Roosevelt's break with the party over Progressive policy. In one sense, then, the 1912 election can be interpreted as a mandate for Progressivism. Johnson's landslide victory in 1964 followed the death of John Kennedy and the subsequent nomination of a very conservative Republican for president. In both the 1912 and 1964 elections a large number of new representatives were elected, and they were strong supporters of the new policies associated with Wilson and Johnson. Under such electoral conditions the adoption of policies which are nonincremental is far easier than in "normal" times. In sum, major policy changes are much more likely to occur during periods of rapid electoral turnover associated with crisis periods.

In terms of our sequential policy model, the social or economic crisis generates policy demands for a solution to the problem. The policy formulation stage becomes dominated by the need to resolve the crisis. Under these conditions policy formulation and the political agenda merge. That is, during crisis the government must formulate policies to deal with the socioeconomic problems on everyone's mind; thus, the problem becomes the agenda. The party in control of the government and the opposition have normally formulated alternative policies to deal with the crisis, and the realigning election determines which party will control policy-making. In the newly elected Congress the majority party and its president readily adopt the policies and formulate new ones to deal with problems. This is in distinct contrast to normal elections, in which representatives, senators, and the president run on different issues, and policy adopted in these Congresses is a matter of compromise. In short, policy adoption in Congress is normally a bargaining process where many interests must be accommodated—thus watering down the policy (incrementalism). The politics of policy adoption in true election realignments is different because the legislators and the president were elected specifically to deal with the problems causing the realignment.

The newly enacted policies are normally implemented by the bureaucracy. Meier and Kraemer argue that during realignments (especially in 1932) there is high turnover of personnel in established agencies as well as the creation of new agencies and bureaus to implement the new policies.[7] Moreover, the newly created agencies and bureaus are, initially at least, very serious and motivated about their jobs. While we do not know much about implementation during realignments, it seems plausible that the combination of new agencies and new personnel is sufficient to see that the new policies are implemented, at least more effectively than if they were handled by old-line agencies with their commitments to older policies. In conclusion, at each stage of the policy sequence policymaking during realignments differs from what it is at other times.


## THE IMPACT OF POLICY

What impact does public policy have? Does policy really solve anything? People often express concern that while government action persists and expands, so do public problems; hence, nothing ever seems finally resolved. Why, people ask, cannot government solve "problem X" once and for all and be done with it?

Part of the answer lies in the very nature of public problems. They involve on-going conditions or situations and therefore require continuing governmental action. Such problems as the prevention of monopolistic business conditions, the deception of consumers, pollution of the environment, the provision of social security, adequate transportation services, or full employment do not admit easy, once-and-for-all solutions. Unemployment cannot, for example, be wiped out by an inoculation program as was done with smallpox. And even in the case of smallpox continued vigilance is necessary lest it recur.

Part of the answer also lies in differing perspectives on public policies. From one perspective, policies obviously do make a difference—roads are built, welfare benefits paid, price-fixing agreements broken up, sewage treatment plants constructed, and so on. We can point to many public policies and programs that have been successful, which have greatly lessened or ameliorated the conditions at which they were directed. Social Security, labor union rights, public school desegregation, rural electrification, conservation of forest resources, and the elimination of child labor are cases in point. On the other hand, of course, one can also point to some public policies and programs which have had less success. Examples might include some facets of the War on Poverty, urban renewal, coal mine safety, and the Nixon administration's wage and price controls. An example of an abortive public policy was the swine flu vaccination program launched in 1976 by the Ford administration. Although the predicted swine flu epidemic did not occur in the winter of 1976–1977, the vaccination program can be given little credit. Chalk up the failure to either environmental conditions or incorrect prediction.

From another viewpoint, however, public policies solve few problems totally, because few if any public policies satisfy everyone. Thus, while some would say that policy was successful if most air pollution was eliminated, others would deny its success as long as *any* air pollution existed. Most policies, moreover, are the products of bargaining and compromise and thus satisfy no one fully. If they indeed accomplished all that they were intended to accomplish, some people still would contend that more needed to be done about the matters at hand. We could totally eliminate environmental pollution (or any other problem) if we could reach complete agreement on the nature of the problem, what sort of future environmental conditions we wanted to exist, and what sort of actions were necessary to bring them into existence, and if we were willing to pay whatever costs were necessary to achieve these goals. Given a lack of consensus on such matters, controversy will continue—with some claiming that policy is ineffective while others contend that it seeks to do too much.

### Reasons for Policy Failure

Leaving such broad questions aside, we now turn our attention to a more specific question: Do public policies achieve their stated goals or have their apparently intended impact? That is, even though they are not designed to do all that some persons want, do they achieve what was intended? In recent years numerous public agencies and private scholars have engaged in the evaluation of public policies. A major conclusion emerging from their research is that policy often fails to have its intended effect, to accomplish its stated goals. A variety of factors are discussed below that may contribute to this result.[8]

Inadequate resources may be provided for the implementation of a policy. For example, the War on Poverty started by the Johnson administration was not wholly successful because only limited resources were provided for its various programs. Some say that antitrust policy would be much more effective in eliminating monopolistic activity if more dollars and personnel were devoted to its enforcement. Opposition to these two policies continued after their adoption, and critics have been able to restrict their impact by limiting the resources devoted to them and otherwise impeding their administration.

New problems and policies may distract attention from older problems and policies. To take the policies cited in the previous paragraph, the war in Vietnam shifted attention from the War on Poverty, and it was argued (especially by opponents of the War on Poverty) that we "couldn't have both guns and butter." During the 1930s opponents of vigorous antitrust action contended that it would interfere with economic recovery; during the 1940s they said that it would impede the war effort; and now, in the age of the energy crisis, they say that it will hamper the development of energy supplies. Those who favor competition, in contrast, have a rather weak lobby, however popular the notion of competition might be in economic theory.

Policies may be inadequately administered. This has been the case, for example, with equal employment opportunity programs. The Office of Federal Contract Compliance has been reluctant to crack down hard on discrimination by government contractors. The Equal Employment Opportunity Commission has been hampered by internal strife and desultory enforcement processes. Again, the Bureau of Mines never displayed much enthusiasm for the enforcement of mine safety legislation.

People affected by policies may react to them in such a manner as to lessen or nullify their impact. Much discretion usually remains with those subject to given policies. Thus, farmers confronted with crop control programs took their poorest acres out of production and used increased amounts of fertilizer on the remaining acres. The consequence was greater production from fewer acres and more surpluses for the government. Until 1978 price controls on natural gas sold in interstate commerce were partly avoided by increased sales by producers in the unregulated intrastate market, with the result that less gas was available in the interstate market. There was nothing illegal in such actions, unlike the "black market" that developed during World War II to evade price and rationing controls.

Policies adopted at different times in response to different problems and pressures may conflict with one another. Thus, while some units within the Department of Agriculture in the 1950s and 1960s were trying to control farm production, other units, through research and conservation programs, were working to expand production. Again, the government has acted to discourage smoking at the same time it has supported prices for tobacco farmers. Fiscal and monetary policies have sometimes been used in contradictory fashion to control inflation or recession, as was seen in chapter 2.

Public problems are often very complex, being caused by a number of factors or conditions. Such is the case with poverty. A policy that focuses on only one cause of poverty—say job training to eliminate the lack of job skills—will have only limited impact on the total poverty problem. Moreover, uncertainty may exist as to the causes of a particular problem, such as inflation or juvenile delinquency; as a result, the policies formulated to deal with the problem will necessarily be tentative, modest, or restricted in scope and strength. They may even miss the target.

The solutions for some problems may involve greater costs than the society, or important segments thereof, finds acceptable. Thus, it is estimated that hundreds of billions of dollars would be required to totally eliminate environmental pollution. Moreover, such extensive pollution control activity may substantially increase energy usage at a time when there is growing concern with energy scarcity. Improved mass transit systems would do much to reduce traffic congestion in many metropolitan areas, but the great cost involved is a barrier to their installation. Consequently, minor palliatives like one-way streets, bus lanes on freeways, and car-sharing plans are resorted to, and traffic congestion continues.

Some problems simply may not be soluble, at least not totally. Many jobs will continue to be dull, tedious, or intellectually unsatisfying unless as a society we eliminate such tasks as garbage collection, housework, retailing, and meat packing, which seems unlikely. No matter what we do, some children are probably not going to learn much in school. And crime has been with us since Cain slew Abel.

Finally, the adoption of policies only marks the end of one phase of the policy process and the struggle over policy. Many groups and individuals will do their dead-level best to ensure that a statute enacted by Congress will have the least possible impact. Judicial challenges, efforts to limit administration, procrastination, noncompliance, attempts to secure amendments or repeal, and other means may be resorted to. This tactic is illustrated by the "massive resistance" to school desegregation in the South after 1954. Another example is the railroad industry's attack on the Interstate Commerce Act of 1887, in the courts and elsewhere, which greatly weakened it by the end of the century.[9]

The foregoing discussion should not be taken as a counsel of despair, or as an argument that policy is mostly ineffective. As policy analysts we need to be concerned about factors that may limit the impact of policy along with other facets of the policy process. As policy advocates, knowledge of such factors can make advocacy more realistic and likely of somewhat greater success if we act accordingly.

## THE REAGAN PRESIDENCY

Ronald Reagan has initiated major changes in American public policy. The largest tax cuts in U.S. history have been enacted, the largest deficit in U.S. history has been projected, the domestic budget has been sharply cut, and the defense budget has risen above $250 billion. Most recently, the largest-ever tax hike was enacted. Reagan has proposed other major policy changes, such as the return of scores of federal programs to the states. There is a new skeptical attitude toward environmental protection and consumer protection. Newspaper stories and television commentators speak frequently of the "Reagan Revolution" in American politics.

Many maintain that this portends changes in public policy significant enough to be labeled a realigning change. Only the Roosevelt era (1932–1938) and the Great Society of Lyndon Johnson changed so much so rapidly. Was the 1980 election a realigning election? The policy changes associated with the New Deal were permanent. American society and government differed greatly pre-New Deal to post-New Deal. Roosevelt's policy innovations were permanent because there was a majority constituency that favored the change toward more activist government. Each time the Republicans ran presidential candidates who wanted to dismantle parts of the New Deal, they were defeated. As stated earlier, it was only when the Republican Party accepted the broad outlines of the New Deal that they were able to win presidential elections. Moreover, from 1932 to 1980 the Democrats controlled both Houses of Congress for all but four years. If the Reagan revolution is to succeed, there will have to be a shift in the electorate similar to that enjoyed by Franklin D. Roosevelt and the Democrats in 1932. There will also have to be a new majority constituency, which will continue to elect officials committed to Reagan's policy changes.

There is some evidence that 1980 was a realigning election. The Republicans won control of the Senate for the first time since 1952, and they gained over thirty seats in the House of Representatives. In addition, the new Republican members of the Congress voted almost across the board for the Reagan budget and tax cuts. The Republicans in Congress in 1981 acted as though the 1980 election was in fact a mandate for significant policy changes. In the Senate the Republicans were unified, while in the House a combination of Republicans and conservative Southern Democrats (called the Conservative Coalition) voted together to pass Reagan's major policy changes. Thus in terms of electoral success and the partisan voting associated with realigning elections, 1980 initially seemed to be something of a realigning election.

On the other hand, a good deal of evidence exists to suggest that 1980 was not a realigning election. First and foremost, in every other American realignment the new majority party completely controlled the House, the Senate, and the presidency. Moreover, in every realignment since 1860 the new party majority controlled all three parts of the government for fourteen consecutive years. Obviously the Republicans did not achieve this in 1980. And without such single-party control of the government it is difficult to sustain policy initiatives. Such was the case for Lyndon Johnson and the Democrats in the mid-1960s. Johnson won a landslide victory in the 1964 presidential election, and in a very short time period he was able to pass the 1965 Voting Rights Act, the War on Poverty, and the Elementary and Secondary Education Act, among other important pieces of domestic legislation. Yet by 1966 the president was in trouble. Deeply mired in an unpopular war in Vietnam and faced with recalcitrant congressmen, the Democrats lost seats in both the House and Senate in the 1966 elections. The war continued and opposition to Johnson within his own party forced him to retire from the race for the Democratic nomination in 1968. The result was that with the exception of civil rights much of the Johnson program has been abandoned.

Was the Reagan-Republican victory in 1980 to be like the Johnson-Democratic win in 1964—short lived—or was it like the Roosevelt-Democratic victory in 1932—permanent? If Reagan's victory was like Roosevelt's, then there would have been a majority constituency in the country for continuing to elect Representatives and Senators who favored a diminished economic and social role for the federal government. But if the 1980 victory was like that of 1964, then the policy changes generated would not be long lasting and policy would revert to incremental change. Thus the future of Reagan's policy changes depended on the outcome of the 1982 congressional elections. Given that the Republicans lost seats in 1982 in the House, one can safely assume that 1980 was not in fact a realigning election. One certain result of the 1982 elections is that President Reagan's programs will have a difficult time passing in the House of Representatives.

The president's record in 1982 stood in sharp contrast to his success in 1981. (A major factor hurting Reagan was the predicted budget deficit of considerably over $100 billion for fiscal 1983. The supply-side economists predicted an upsurge in business activity after the budget and tax cuts; however, in the fall of 1982 no upsurge was evident.) High interest rates, decreased federal revenues, and general business apprehension over the state of the economy kept the economy slack and unemployment high, although there was a decline in inflation. Under these economic conditions many Republicans in Congress moved to disassociate themselves from Reaganomics and, in addition, the Democrats in Congress began to feel confident about the 1982 election. This, in combination with Reagan's declining popularity as measured by various opinion polls, made Reagan's legislative leadership suspect. The second session of the 97th Congress was characterized by legislative deadlock, not legislative success. The fact that quite a few members of the president's party voted against him on budget deficits, cuts in military spending, and other matters made the 1980 elections look more like 1964 than 1932.

The Democratic win in the 1982 elections meant an end to Reagan's policy initiatives and issued in an era of compromise between a Republican president and a House controlled by Democrats. However, the Republican-controlled Senate (54 R., 46 D.) will keep the Democrats from pushing liberal programs—in short, drift rather than mastery. Clearly the 1982 elections were far more significant than normal off-year elections. Since the results were not like those of 1934, when the president's party gained seats, the Reagan revolution will be quieted, and future policy innovations will have to await the results of the 1984 presidential election. Thus, the future of American public policy lies in the hands of the voters—which is where democratic nations ought to resolve differences.

## NOTES

1. See Charles E. Lindblom, *The Intelligence of Democracy* (New York: Free Press, 1965).
2. The following discussion is based on Charles O. Jones, "Speculative Augmentation in Federal Air Pollution Policy-Making," *Journal of Politics* 36 (May 1974): 438–464.
3. Ibid., pp. 439–440.
4. Ibid., p. 453.
5. Benjamin Ginsberg, "Elections and Public Policy," *American Political Science Review* 70 (1976): 65.
6. The best interpretations of such crises can be found in V. O. Key, Jr., "A Theory of Critical Elections," *Journal of Politics* 17 (1955): 3–18; V. O. Key, Jr., "Secular Realignment and the Party System," *Journal of Politics* 21 (1959): 198–210; Walter D. Burnham, *Critical Elections and the Mainsprings of American Politics* (New York: Norton, 1970); and James R. Sundquist, *Dynamics of the Party System: Alignment and Realignment of Political Parties in the United States* (Washington, D.C.: Brookings Institution, 1972).
7. Kenneth Meier and Kenneth Kraemer, "The Effects of Realigning Elections on Bureaucratic Politics" (unpublished paper, Rice University, 1976).
8. This discussion draws on James E. Anderson, *Public Policy-Making*, 2nd ed. (New York: Holt, Rinehart and Winston, 1979), pp. 171–173.
9. Ari Hoogenboom and Olive Hoogenboom, *A History of the ICC* (New York: Norton, 1976), chap. 1.

# Index